Understanding and Controlling

STROBE LIGHTING

A Guide for Digital Photographers

JOHN SISKIN

Amherst Media, Inc. ■ Buffalo, NY

For Susan:
Sine qua non.

All photographs by the author unless otherwise noted.

Published by:
Amherst Media®
P.O. Box 586
Buffalo, N.Y. 14226
Fax: 716-874-4508
www.AmherstMedia.com

Publisher: Craig Alesse
Senior Editor/Production Manager: Michelle Perkins
Assistant Editor: Barbara A. Lynch-Johnt
Editorial Assistance by Sally Jarzab, John S. Loder, and Carey Miller.

ISBN-13: 978-1-60895-242-7
Library of Congress Control Number: 2010904517
Printed in Korea.
10 9 8 7 6 5 4 3 2 1

CONTENTS

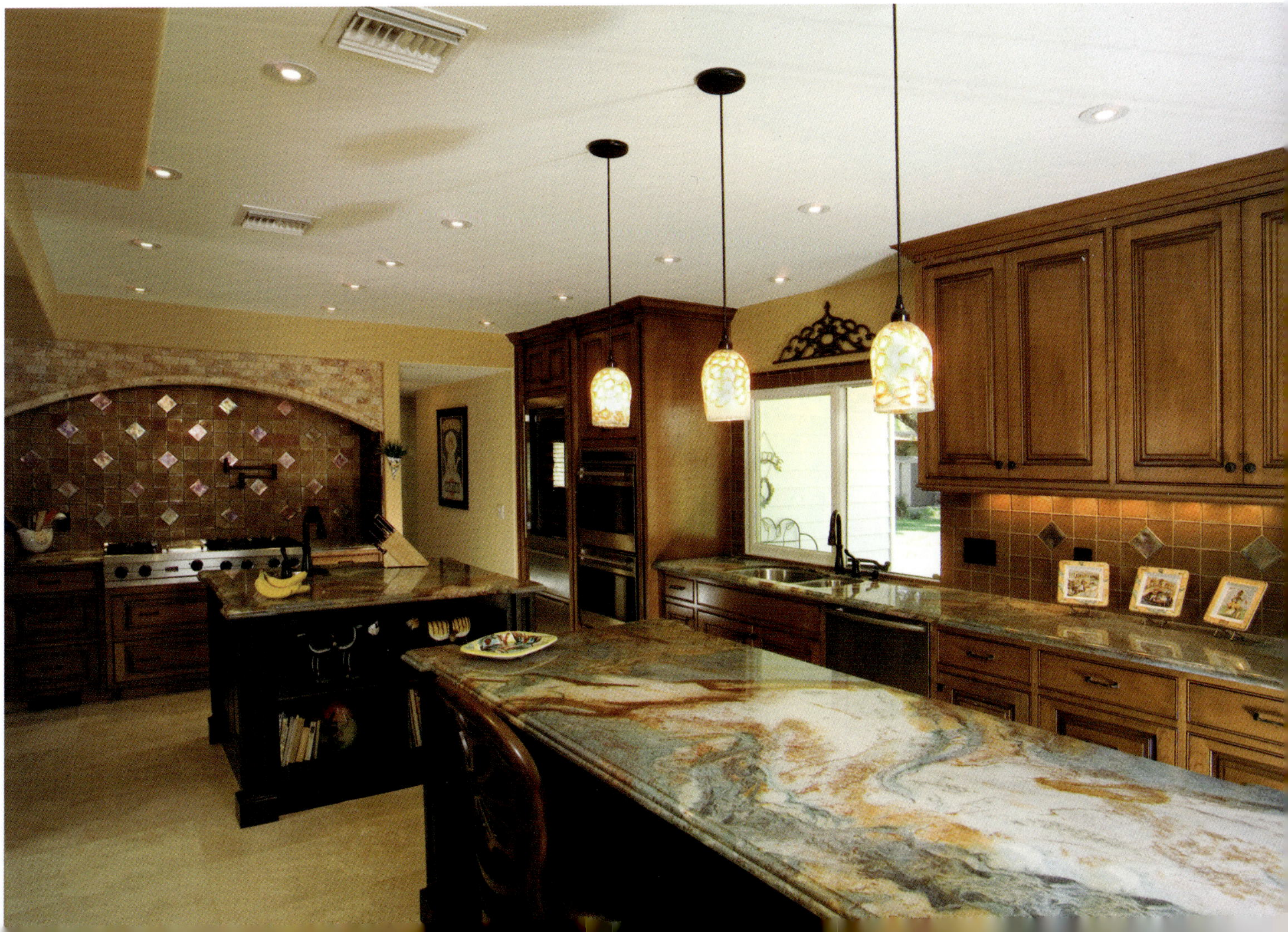

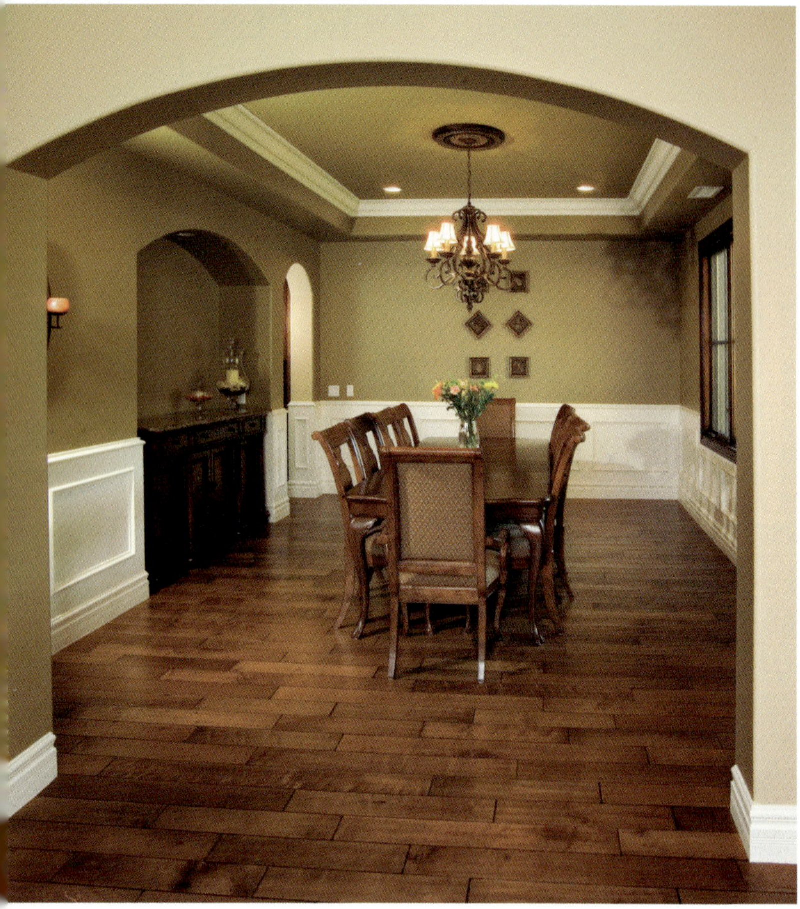

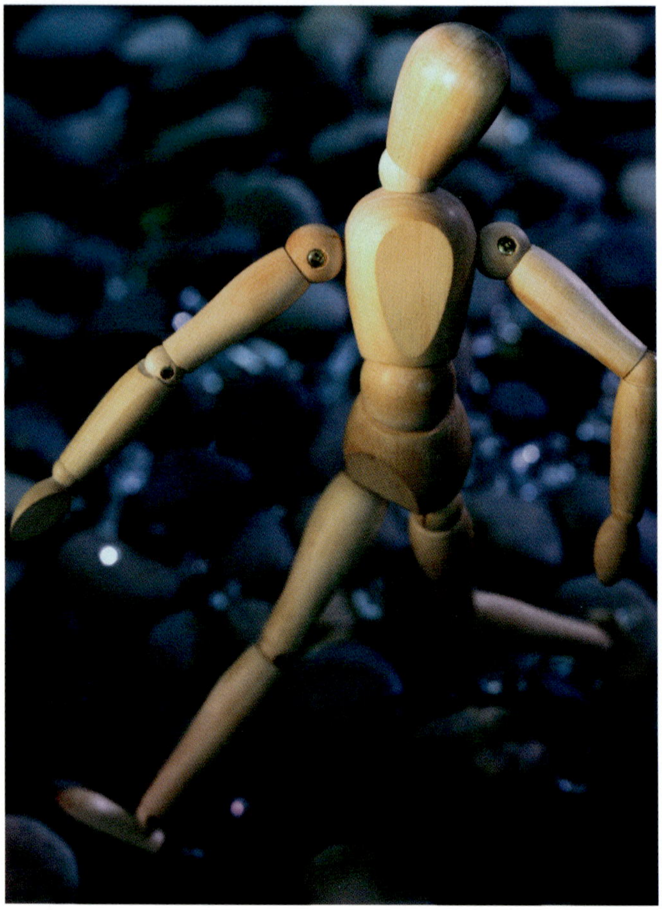

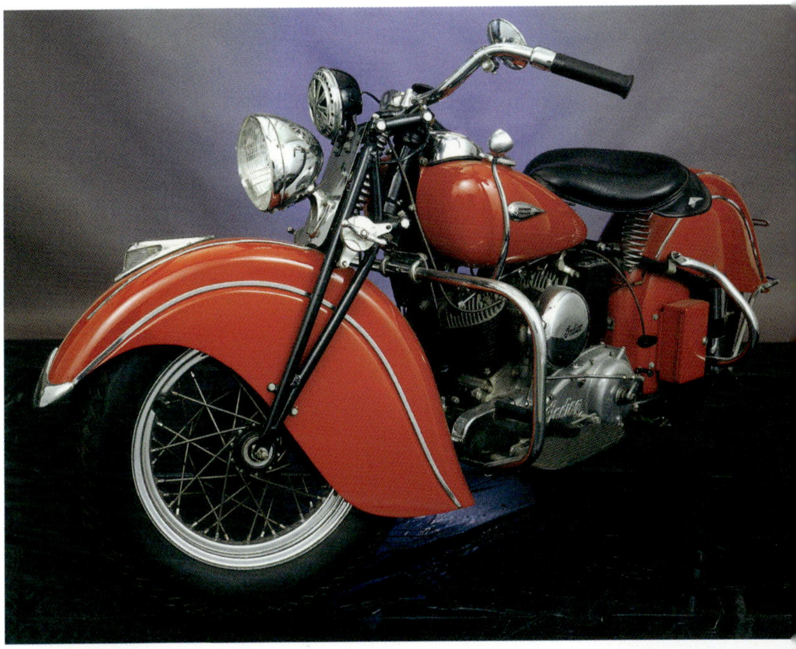

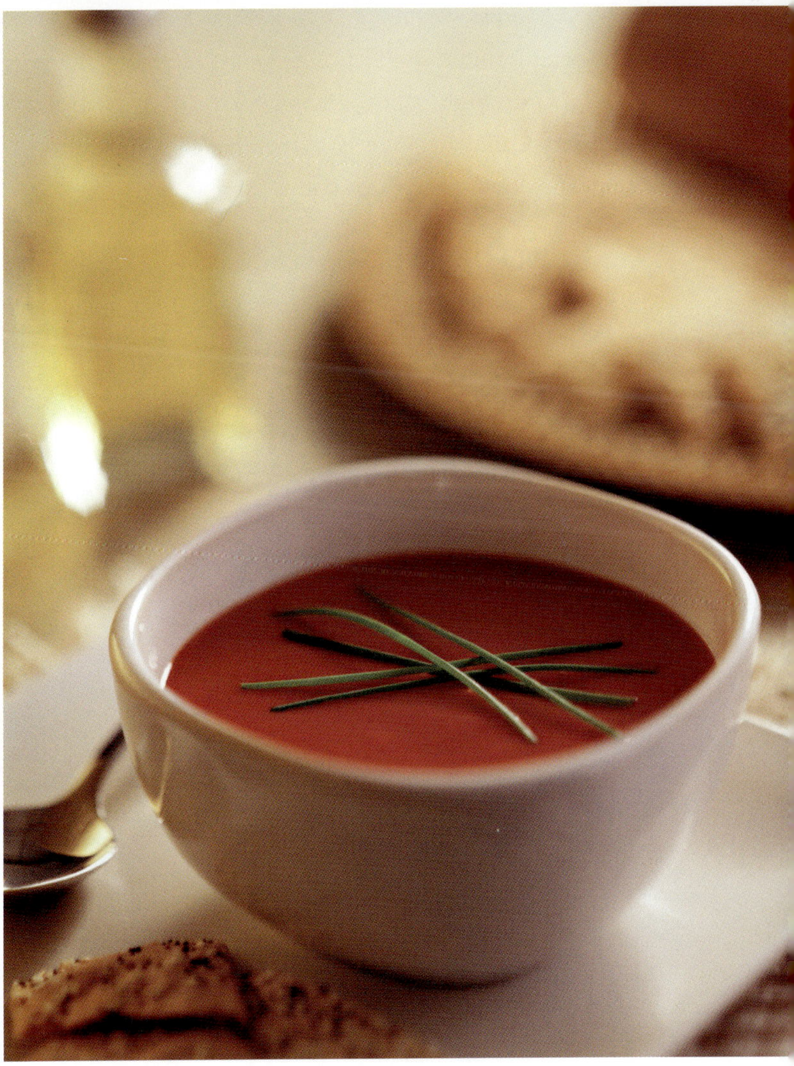

ABOUT THE AUTHOR

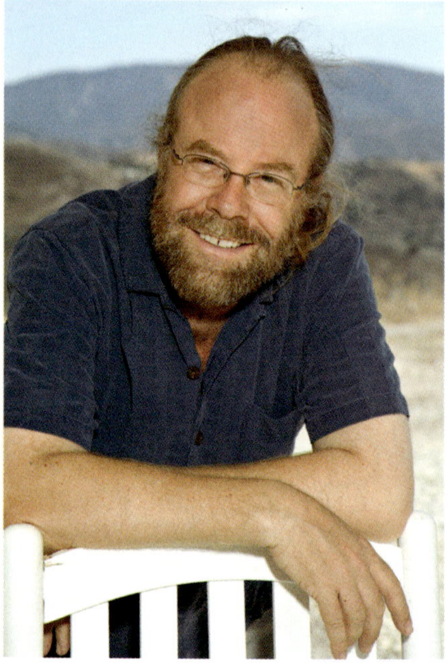
Author photo by Lance Craig.

John Siskin is a fine art and commercial photographer who often works with landscape and architectural images. His work has been part of many exhibits at the Brand Library, 2nd City Art Gallery, Harold's Gallery, Farmani Gallery, and The Atelier. He has been a regular participant in the Valley Studio Tour.

His work has been published in a number of magazines, including *View Camera, Photo Technique,* and *Shutterbug*. You can view some of his magazine articles and more of his work on his web site at www.siskinphoto.com.

He has done a large number of commercial jobs including projects for General Motors, Disney, and AidsWalk. His portraits for AidsWalk have been displayed on the streets of Los Angeles, Atlanta, San Francisco, and New York.

John has taught photography for more than twenty years at colleges in Southern California. He is currently teaching lighting and portrait classes online at www.betterphoto.com.

ACKNOWLEDGMENTS

In life, there are many people who should be acknowledged, but there are just a few who can be mentioned in this book. First, I have to thank:

- Tom Ferguson, who went over this book as it came into being. I really couldn't have finished this without you.
- My wife, Susan Siskin, who knows as much about photography as I do, but in different areas. It is a great blessing to have a wife who understands what you do. Without her encouragement, this book wouldn't be finished.
- Lance Craig, for assisting and for taking photos of me.
- Jennifer Halsworth, who modeled for me several times as this book was coming together. Great job running with sparklers, Jen!

There are a few people I have to thank more generally. When you first begin to learn photography, it seems more magic than science. Arnold Rubinoff and Steve Berman are the wizards who started me on my photographic journey. Thanks to Chuck Grossman, Harlan Goldberg, Dr. David Walker, Rico Mandel, and everyone involved with www.betterphoto.com. Many thanks, too, to my parents, Sheldon and Cynthia Siskin.

INTRODUCTION

This book is for any photographer who wants to take control of the light in a picture. Some will find the task of lighting daunting—it involves an investment of time and money—but the reward is real control over your images. I spent years learning about light and trying to harness it. This book contains what I've learned in a straightforward presentation.

In this book, I will explain some simple concepts that can give you the power to create good—even great—light in all your photographs. One thing you'll need is a willingness to experiment. After all, you are going to learn to write with light!

I will explain how to use light to make better portraits and product shots, and even how to light architecture. This book will also enable you to make informed choices about buying equipment and how to grow as a photographer.

So, please join me!

Thanks,
John Siskin

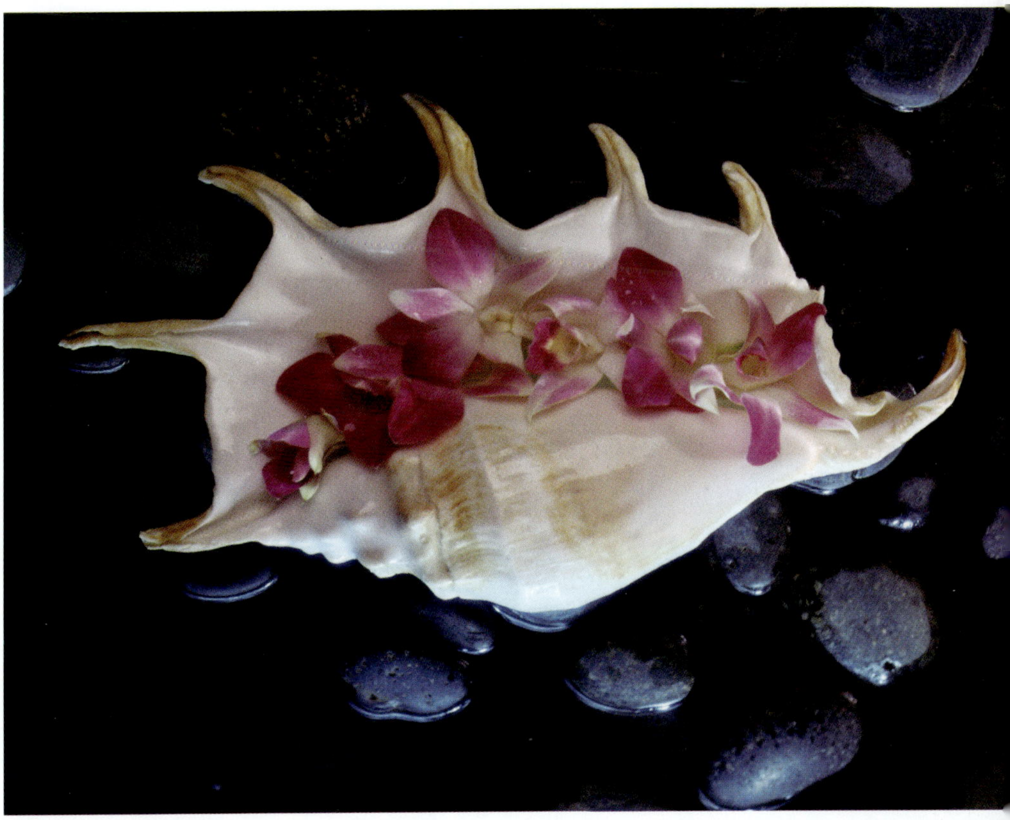

All of the light used for this shot comes from a single source. I placed an umbrella with a light panel at the bottom of the shot. The panel was on its side so I could direct light over it. I used a large reflector at the other side of the shot to bounce light back into the scene, directly from the umbrella. This setup created soft light with a very subtle gradation.

1. HOW LIGHT WORKS

WRITING WITH LIGHT

"Photography" means "writing with light" in Greek. And, while photography is the world's most popular hobby, very few people write with light. Most see a subject that is compelling and press the button. They take a picture. A few people make pictures; that is, they take control of an image, making it into something more than just the record of that moment. There are many artistic considerations that go into making a picture. For instance, you can take a shot from an angle other than eye level, swap out your normal lens for a fish-eye lens, or bring the image into Photoshop for a little postproduction enhancement. However, one of the most important ways you can make an image is to take control of the light—to literally write with light.

CONTROLLING YOUR SOURCES

The Color of Light. Color is a critical characteristic of light. If you shoot with a red light, everything will be shown as a different density of red. Things that reflect more red (e.g., white or red subjects) will be brighter than things that absorb red (e.g., blue items).

There is a more important aspect of color: various sources produce a color cast in your scene. For instance, one light may be somewhat red or blue in

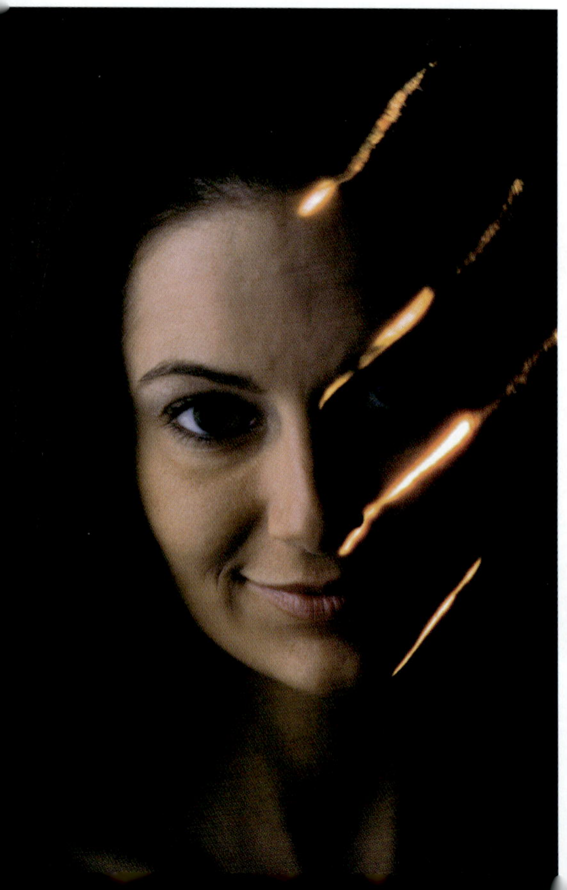

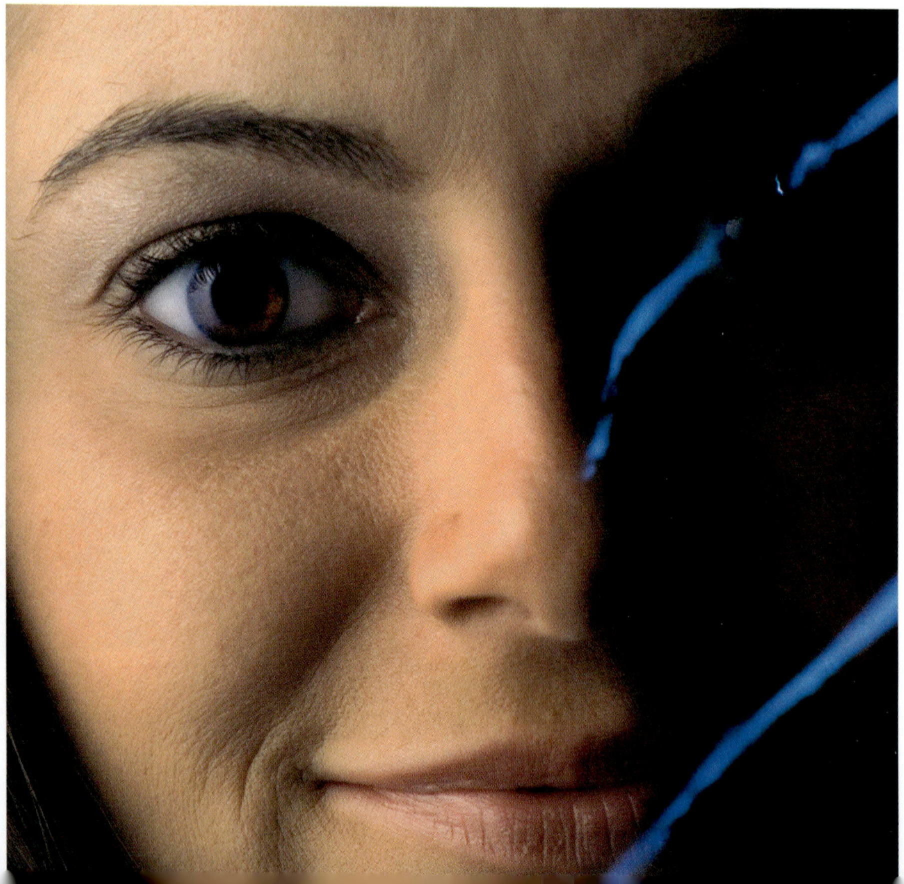

Left—In this shot, I used the light from a strobe and a slide projector to create a light that defines the subject in a dramatic way. **Right**—One of the great advantages to working with light is that you have control over color and density. You can make great images that start in your mind's eye.

nature, and the variation in color will show up in your picture. If you use a 100-watt lightbulb (a more red/warm light source) with daylight (a more blue/cool source), then part of your picture may be too blue or too red, depending on how the camera chooses to balance the shot.

Color is described using a Kelvin temperature rating. The idea is that an object heated to a specific temperature will glow with a specific color balance. Objects go from red hot to yellow hot to blue hot, so blue is the higher temperature. A 100-watt bulb is about 2900°K and average daylight is around 5500°K, while an overcast day is about 7000°K.

IN MANY SCENES, THERE ARE NUMEROUS LIGHT UNITS THAT THROW LIGHT OF VARYING COLOR TEMPERATURES.

There is a great deal of difference in the color of light that we see as white. When we are indoors and photographing under household light sources, for instance, the light in the scene has a yellow cast. The eye compensates for this. Most digital cameras feature white balancing software that will allow you to correct for this problem. In many scenes, there are numerous light units that throw light of varying color temperatures. In mixed lighting situations, the digital camera won't be able to balance the color.

There is another problem: many lights do not create a continuous color spectrum, so they don't balance like daylight. Photographers commonly use tungsten lights, which have a color temperature of 3200°K, and strobes, which have a color temperature of 5500°K, the same color as daylight. There are fluorescent lights designed for photography, and these are designed to be close in color to daylight, but as they don't have a continuous spectrum, they can produce bad results in some situations.

Although you cannot rely on your camera's white balance feature to bring multiple light sources into balance, you can use filters to modify the color or the sources. A tungsten light can be made to match daylight when a Full CTB filter (from Rosco) is used on the light, and a strobe can be made to match tungsten when the light is fitted with a Full CTO filter. There are also filters that can change your light to any color to add color to your shot.

The Size of the Source. Another important quality in lighting is the size of the light source (or, more accurately, the size of the light source relative to the size of the subject, which depends on the distance between the light source and the subject). For instance, the sun is quite large, but it occupies a small part of the sky on a sunny day. Therefore, on a sunny day, you will see detailed shadows and small, bright reflections. The transition from light to shadow is very quick, too, which is one reason why the shadows are so detailed. This is referred to as hard light. On an overcast day, the clouds diffuse the light coming from above us. There are no hard shadows, and the light is diffuse and even. This is not some magical property of clouds, it is what happens when you spread light over a large area. This quality of light is referred to as soft light.

When we are working with studio lighting, the same rules apply. When a bare-bulb strobe is used to light a subject from several feet away, the light is hard. When the light is moved closer to the subject, the light it produces is softer. When that light is set inside of a softbox, the diffusion panel renders the light softer. It doesn't really matter what the shape of a light source is—you can use a softbox or an umbrella, for example—but the size is critical.

In this series of shots of the wig head, I moved the light source, a small softbox, farther from the subject. You can see how the light becomes more contrasty and the transitions from light to dark are faster as the light-to-subject distance increases.

The Position of the Light. The light source you are working with will act larger or softer depending on its position. When the sun is directly overhead, it acts like a small source relative to your subject and can produce harsh shadows (as will a small artificial light source placed far from your subject and at the wrong angle). In contrast, when the sky is overcast, the sun's light will be much softer.

THE LIGHT SOURCE YOU ARE WORKING WITH WILL ACT LARGER OR SOFTER DEPENDING ON ITS POSITION.

Note: If you must shoot on a day when the sky is clear, you may want to wait until the "golden hour," when the sun is near the horizon, as the shadows that are formed will fall across the subject rather than from above. During golden hour, the color of the sun's light also changes as well, and the effect can be very pleasing.

Changing the position of the light relative to your subject can also help you achieve the effect you are after. There is a caveat, though: if you have a large light source, moving it a couple of feet won't make much difference, but for a small light source, you'll find that the effect of moving the light can be huge.

CHOOSING THE RIGHT LIGHTS

Not every light and quality of light can be used to produce the kind of image you're after. Before buying your lights, you'll want to consider these points:

Quality. The quality of light refers to the color of light. Some types of light do not have a continuous spectrum—in other words, there are bright and dark lines in the color spectrum produced by these lights. Sunlight has a continuous spectrum in the visible range, so it gives us accurate color. Sunlight is the standard for accurate color.

Quantity. The quantity of light describes how much light a type of light can provide. If the only light sources in the shot are your lights, then your only concern is whether you have enough light to work at a given combination of aperture, shutter speed, and ISO. If you are working with sunlight or another source, you need to have enough light to give you control over the ambient lighting. For instance, I have taken half-hour exposures in the studio where my lights are the only light, but if I were outdoors, sunlight would ruin that shot. I often need enough light to make the sunlight the secondary light

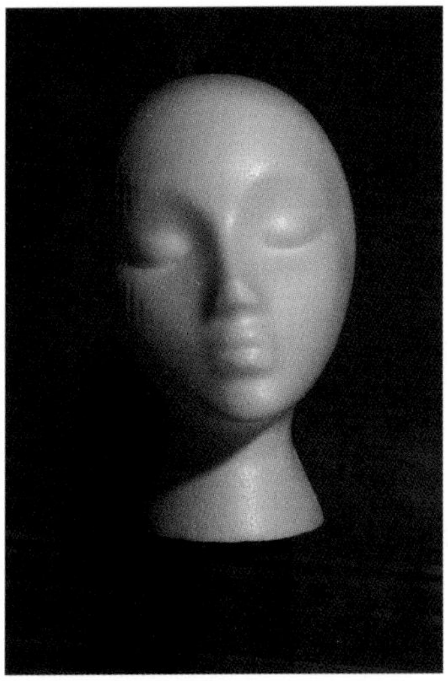

Strobe tube and a clip-on reflector.

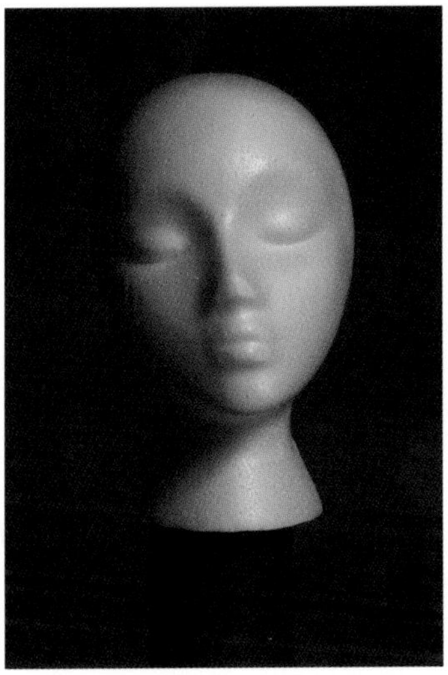

A 30-inch umbrella. The transitions are already softer.

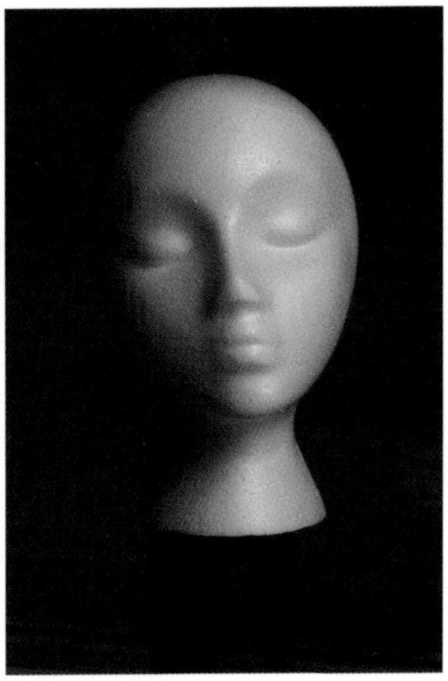

A 60-inch umbrella.

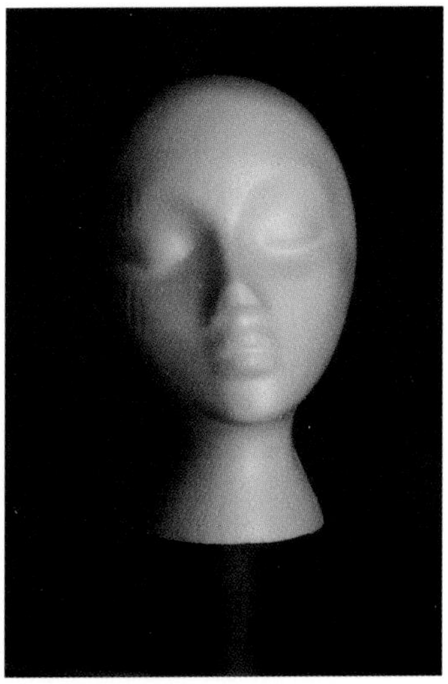

A 42x72-inch light panel. The transitions are softer and there is less shadowing.

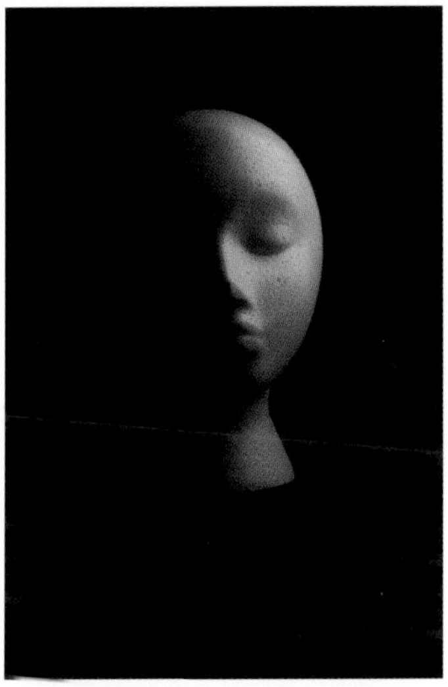

A 12x18-inch softbox was positioned 1 foot from the subject. There is a long gradation, particularly on the forehead.

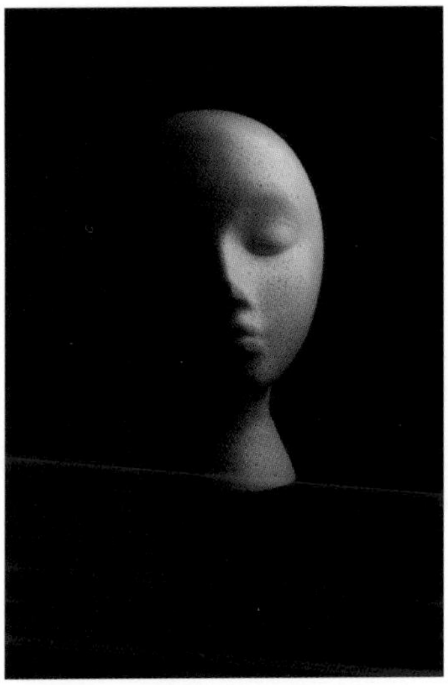

Here, the softbox was placed 3 feet from the subject.

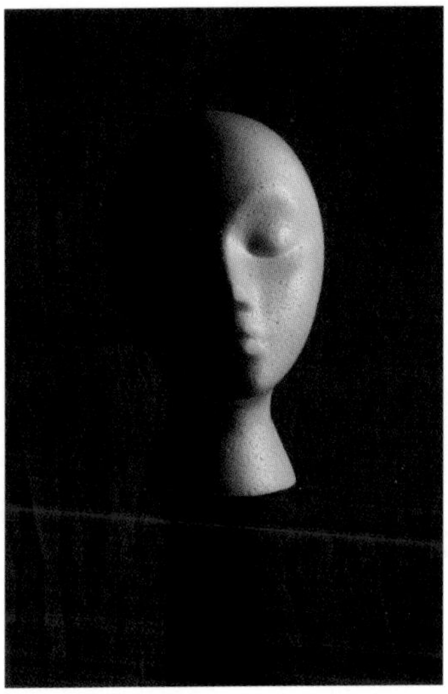

Here, the softbox was placed 5 feet from the subject.

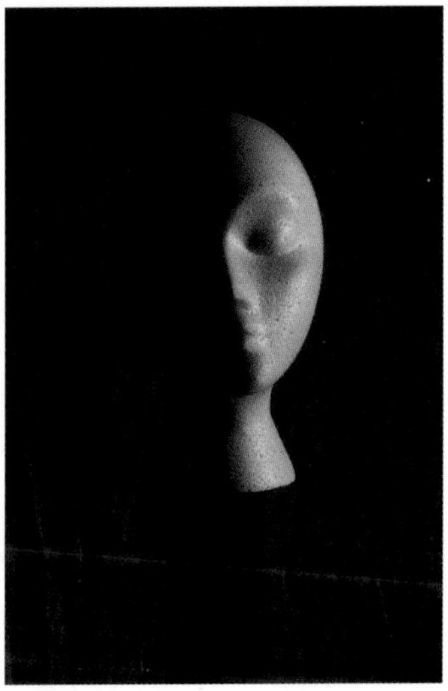

Here, the softbox was placed 7 feet from the subject.

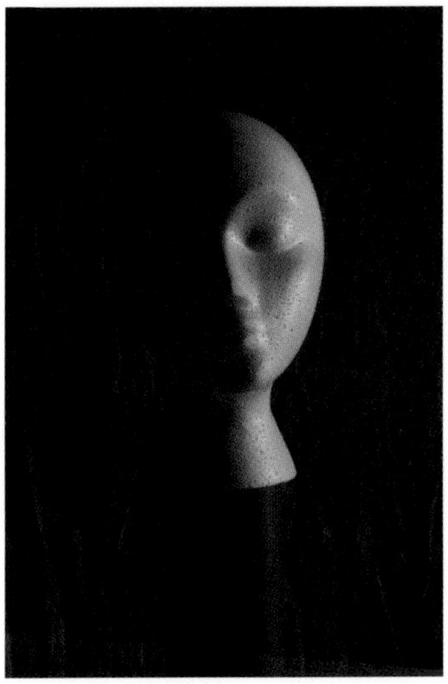

Here, the softbox was placed 9 feet from the subject.

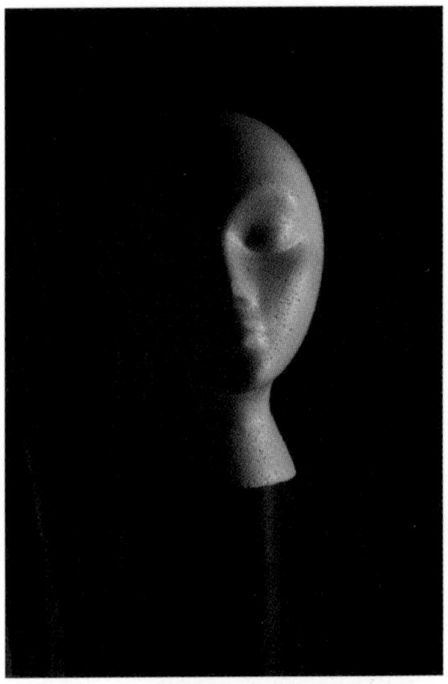

Here, the softbox was placed 11 feet from the subject. The light is much harder.

source rather than the primary source. Having a sufficient quantity of light gives you more control in lighting.

Value. A light's value is the relationship between its cost, functionality, and endurance. If a light is inexpensive but doesn't last, it has low value. One thing to consider with lights is they don't change much over time. I am still using lights I bought more than twenty years ago. This really adds to the value of a light.

Versatility. Versatility refers to the ways in which we can modify a light to suit our vision for the shot. Most lights are designed to work with accessories that make the light act larger or smaller and control its position. In choosing a light, it is important to be sure that the light is able to perform.

Ease of Use. Ease of use involves issues like weight and portability, as well as how easy it is to control the light to fulfill your ideas for the shot.

STROBES MAKE LIGHT BY RUNNING A SPARK THROUGH A TUBE FILLED WITH XENON GAS.

LIGHT UNITS

Strobes. Strobes are my favorite lights, and they score high on the standards I just described. Strobes make light by running a spark through a tube filled with Xenon gas. Although this takes a lot of power, the spark only lasts for a fraction of a second, so strobes are efficient to work with. Since strobes are only on for 1/1000 second or so, they will stop action. Other lights only stop action if used with a high shutter speed.

Strobes have a spectrum that matches daylight. This means that you can mix strobes and daylight without concern over color casts. These lights can provide a huge amount of light for the fraction of a second that they are on; they can be many times brighter than full daylight. This means that you can make the strobes the brightest light in the shot. I have used some of my strobes for more than a quarter of a century without problems—they are a very good value. Strobes can be repaired, if necessary.

Different strobes may take different accessories, but most will take all the accessories described in this book. Many accessories, such as the softbox,

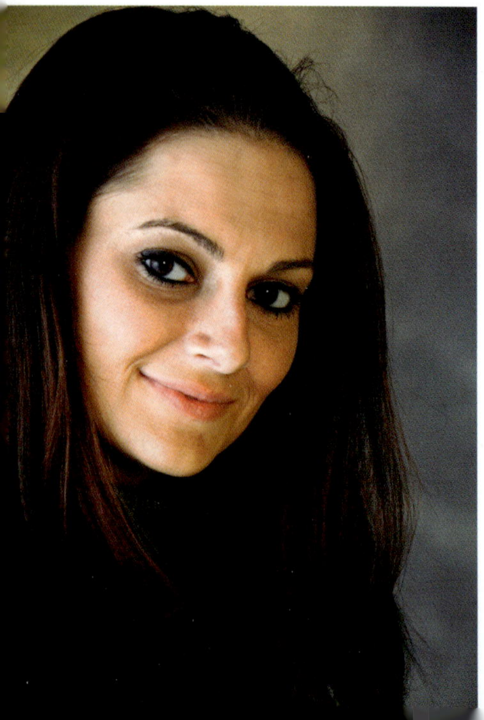

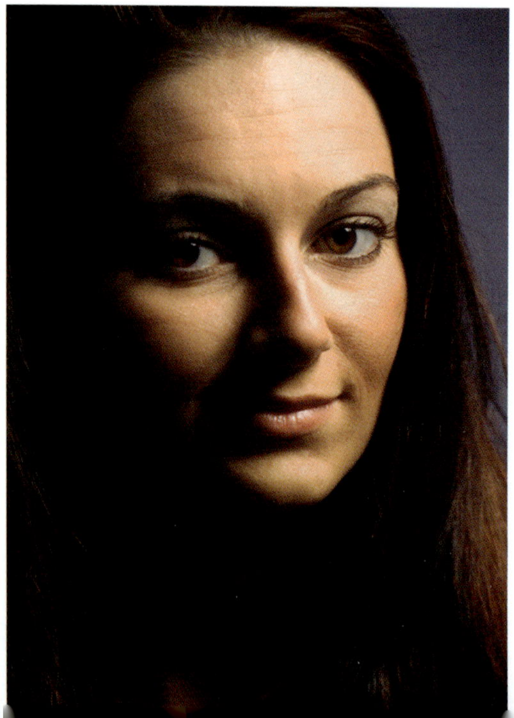

Left—Soft light seems to come from all directions. This image was made with a light panel/umbrella combination. This makes a light that is about 4x6 feet. A second light was used, mostly to create a catchlight in the subject's eyes. **Right**—In this shot, the directional light gives additional shape to the face and provides a sense of shadow. The position of the light (a 22-inch beauty dish) is important.

PREVISUALIZATION

Ansel Adams used the zone system and filters to understand how the finished image would look before he ever pushed the shutter button. We do much the same thing with lights—we pre-visualize the way that light, shadow, and color will render a person, place, or thing in the final image. In order to use these tools effectively, you will need to practice. Photographers often assume that what is important is their way of seeing. While this is true, your skills are every bit as important as your eye, and your skills improve with practice. People assume that musicians will practice; photographers should practice as well. Get a styrofoam wig head and work with that when nothing else is available. Wig heads really show you how light can affect shape.

This book is designed to enable you to work with light. That means learning why things work, the way they work, and how to take advantage of that understanding. It does not mean that there are recipes for lighting, main light, fill light, hair light, and so on. The problem with approaching light as a dinner menu is that there are so many ways to customize your light for the shot you're making. If you rely on cookie-cutter lighting diagrams, you will miss these options. There are places that are appropriate for this way of working: weddings and production studios. In these areas, you don't have enough time to customize. Remember, if you expect to be creative, you need to be able to customize your work and match your work to the project.

were introduced for strobes. Still, before you buy a strobe, it is a good idea to determine what accessories are available for it. Some things like a snoot (used to concentrate light) will only be available from the strobe manufacturer, but umbrellas (used to broaden light) can be purchased from a wide range of manufacturers.

Strobes are lightweight in relation to the power they give you. However, as they give you a lot of power, they do actually weigh more than many other lights. I have a 750 watt-second monolight that weighs about 7 pounds. While this isn't bad, a complete kit can be a challenge to haul around.

The biggest problem with strobes (any instantaneous light, whether on-camera flash or studio strobe) is previsualization. While most studio strobes have modeling lights that are on continuously, they do not provide exactly the same light that the strobe tubes do. If you understand how light works, strobes will be easy to use. If you don't understand why light behaves the way it does, using strobes will be difficult. Because strobes rate so high in quality, quantity, value, and versatility, it certainly pays to understand light.

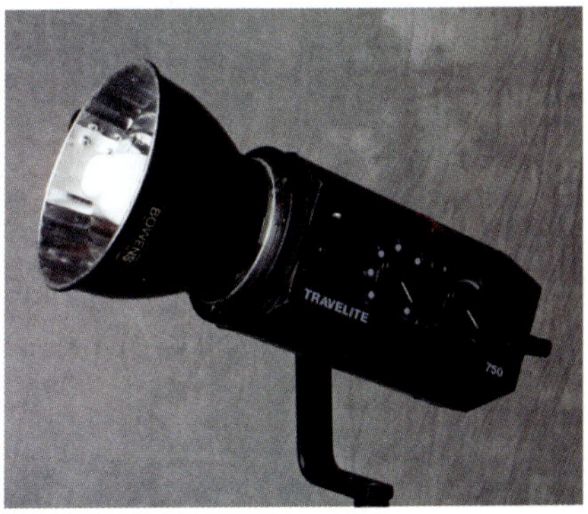

This is a monolight strobe. It is a self-contained unit.

Watt-Seconds and Guide Numbers. A strobe's power is measured in one of two ways: watt-seconds or guide numbers. Watt-seconds are used to measure the amount of power output to the strobe tube of medium to large strobes used off camera. Unfortunately, the measurement is not standardized across brands: 300 watt-seconds might be twice as powerful on one brand as on another. In general, a strobe with more watt-seconds is brighter than a strobe with fewer, but this is not always the case.

If you have a strobe with 800 watt-seconds, then you are at ½ power at 400 watt-seconds and ¼ power at 100 watt-seconds and ⅛ power at 50 watt-seconds. Note that the light modifiers photographers use with their strobes change the spread and efficiency of the light, so if you bought a strobe that had high power because of one special reflector, it wouldn't tell you much about how the bare strobe would light the subject. If you are looking for a strobe for portraits, tabletop, or architectural photography, choose a unit with at least 500 watt-seconds. This will usually provide sufficient power.

Guide numbers are used for small strobes that are generally used on the camera. These units have built-in reflectors, so they can be compared in terms of light output. The guide number is usually figured as the aperture value for the light at 10 feet from the subject multiplied by 10, at ISO 100. So if a meter positioned 10 feet from the strobe indicates that the aperture should be f/5.6 at ISO 100, then the guide number would be 5.6x10 or 56. If the meter said f/11, the guide number would be 110. There are times when guide numbers are figured in meters or at ISO ratings other than 100. Of course, this changes the guide number significantly and can make things more confusing.

Virtually all strobes have the ability to raise and lower power over a range of several stops. Most strobes adjust continuously over their range. This is incredibly useful, allowing you to control the light balance of your shot easily. The other lights I will discuss don't have this capability. This is a really important part of your creative control over light.

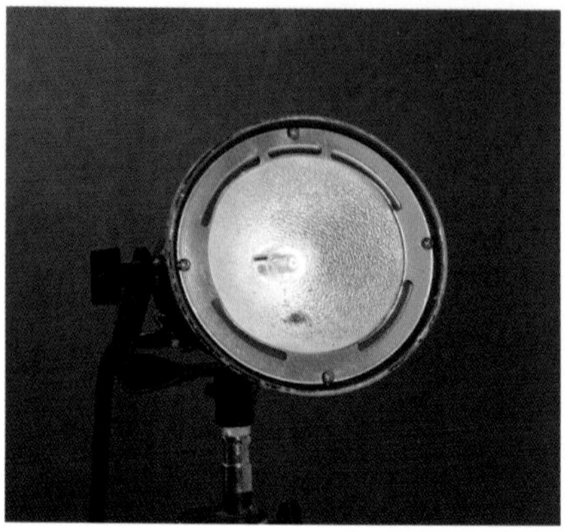

This is a 600-watt quartz light.

Quartz Lights. Quartz lights are basically movie lights, but they can also be very effective for still photography. They do have one significant problem not associated with other lights: extreme heat. If you have several quartz lights in a small studio, the studio can become very hot. This can make portrait work very difficult. Still all of the old Hollywood portraits were done with these lights, so high-quality work is very doable.

Quartz lights produce light in much the way a standard lightbulb does: hot wire inside an enclosure. The real difference is that the bulb is made of fused quartz so it can run much hotter than a standard bulb. As a result, you'll see quartz bulbs with wattages from 600 to a couple of thousand watts, which is why they run so hot. Although the spectrum is continuous, it is redder than daylight. So if you want to mix these lights with daylight, you will need to filter either the daylight or the quartz lights to achieve a color balance. Obviously, there are quartz lights available that are powerful enough to match or even overwhelm daylight, but unless you are working on a movie set, you may not see them in use. A 600-watt quartz light has enough power for making a portrait in a studio, but you will have significant problems working with sunlight.

IF YOU HAVE SEVERAL QUARTZ LIGHTS IN A SMALL STUDIO, THE STUDIO CAN BECOME VERY HOT.

Quartz lights are generally a good value. The bulbs last from ten to thirty hours, and the cost is not outrageous. A good quartz light will cost between $75 and $250 and will last for many years. Because of heat and other factors, quartz lights do not take as many accessories as strobes, but there are specialized light fixtures. So you can get broad lights, spot lights, optical spots, and so on. Most softboxes won't work with these lights because of the heat.

If you are working in an environment where heat is not a problem, quartz lights are very effective. Since you are looking at the light your camera is shooting, it is possible to make very precise adjustments in the light. As a result, quartz lights can be very good for shooting products, including jewelry. These lights can also be very useful for artists, particularly those who work in three-dimensional media. Certainly, you do not need to develop as high a degree of pre-visualization skills with these lights.

Quartz lights are a type of tungsten light. There are also many other tungsten lights made for photographers. These are usually quite inferior. The bulbs, which look like regular lightbulbs, change their color, often in as little as four hours. The fixtures are often hard to adjust and control. While these lights are cheap, they often have little or no value. One other thing about quartz lights: they are very bright—of course, they need to be in order to provide enough light to shoot at a good combination of aperture, shutter speed, and ISO. Quartz lights have significantly less flexibility than strobes because you cannot adjust the power of a quartz light. You can find dimmer switches to work with quartz lights, but making the light dimmer will cause the light to appear more red.

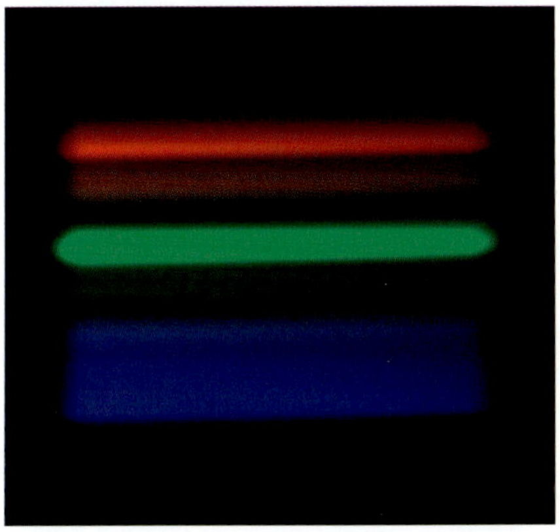

The spectrum of a fluorescent tube designed for photography.

Fluorescent Lights. There are a number of lights that use fluorescent tubes as the light source. I suspect that these lights are very effective with video, but they present problems for still photography. Most of these problems exist because of the way a fluorescent tube makes light: ultraviolet light is created in the tube, and this makes the chemicals on the outside of the tube glow with visible light. This results in a spectrum that has bright and dark spots. Also, the color can vary as the alternating current (AC) cycles, which it does sixty times a second in the United States. So if you want the color to be more consistent, you should use a $1/30$-second shutter speed, since this gives you two complete cycles. The result of these problems is that you can easily have problems with inconsistent and inaccurate color. Another problem is that they don't produce much light, so you'll have problems with quality and quantity.

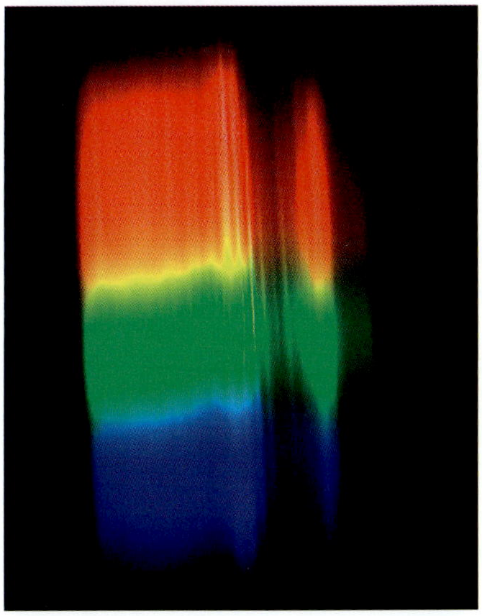

The daylight spectrum.

Still, the tubes provide a softer light than that from an unmodified quartz bulb or strobe. The lights are easier to arrange than a strobe because you can see the light you're shooting. Finally, fluorescents don't have the heat problems of quartz lights. I used them with an early digital system that required continuous light, and while I would not want to rely on them, they could be useful for doing large amounts of small- to medium-sized product photography in a production setting.

There's no question that I prefer strobes to other light sources for most applications. Not only do they have advantages in flexibility and durability, they are daylight balanced. Strobes also allow you more flexible control over the relationship with other light sources, and they stop action. Strobes will require you to learn to pre-visualize your images, but that skill will pay off in all your photographs.

2. INTRODUCTION TO STROBES

Your choice of lighting gear depends on the power, flexibility, and portability you need—and of course, your budget. Before you shop for strobes, you'll need to determine the kinds of photographs you want to make with lights. For instance, if you want to shoot portraits of children in a home studio, you might need three strobes. You might also want a system that can be ceiling-mounted, as children can be dangerous around light stands. If you want to shoot weddings, you'll probably want a couple of proprietary strobes or other dedicated strobes. These allow you to work with minimal concerns about exposure, which is important with the fast pace of a wedding shoot. Although I will offer some general recommendations, I can't offer suggestions for every possible kind of work.

This shot was done on location. Most of the light came from a monolight with a 60-inch umbrella, positioned at camera left. There was a second light with an umbrella on the right. This light had much lower power.

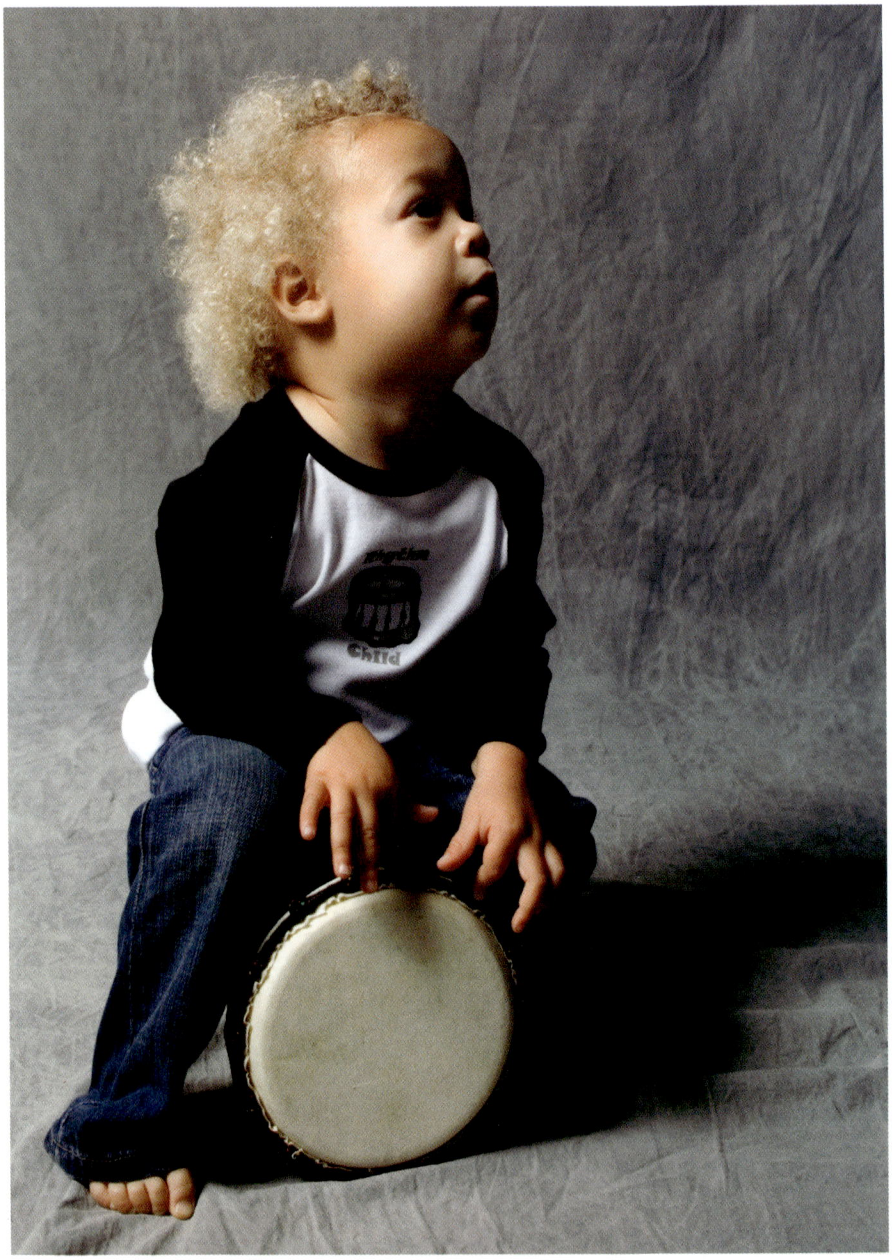

DEDICATED STROBES

Dedicated strobes are those units that are designed to work automatically with your specific camera. When you use these lights, your camera takes a through-the-lens reading of the flash output and turns the flash off when enough light has been emitted to create a proper exposure. These are a great choice when you need to work quickly and in varied environments and, for this reason, they are a great choice when photographing parties and weddings. They are also an especially good choice for adding fill flash when working outdoors, as

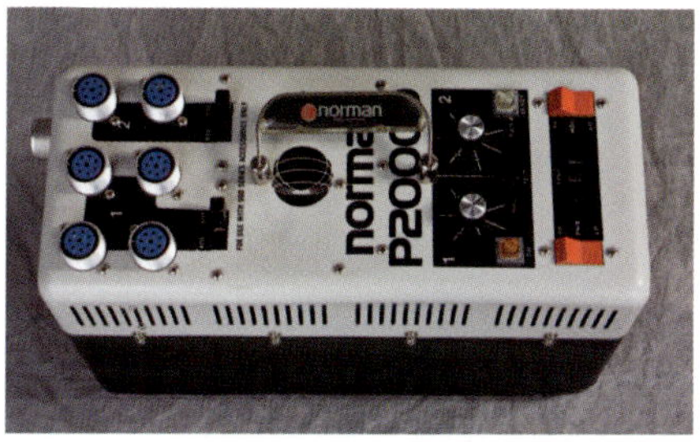

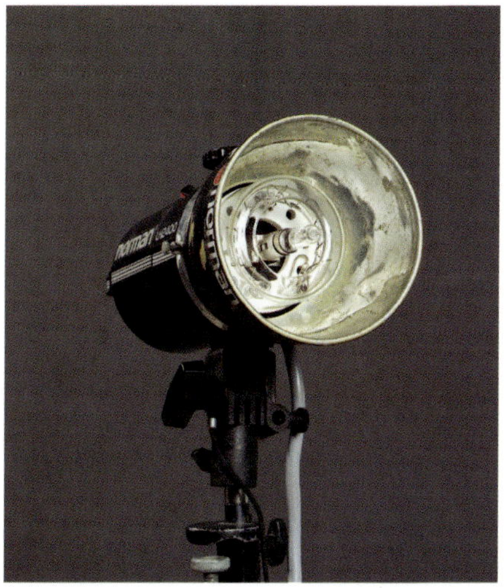

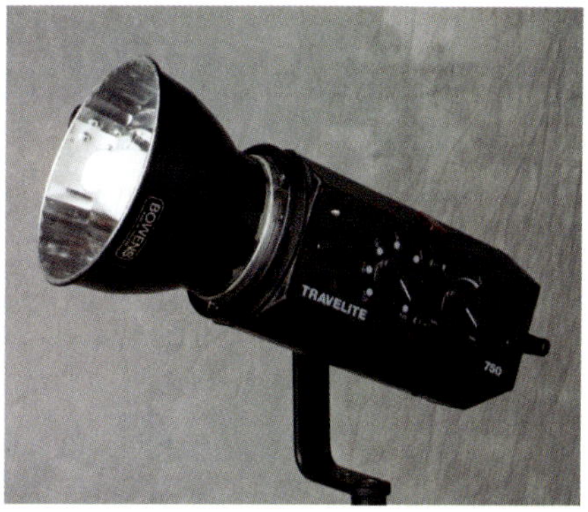

Left—A Norman power pack. It only works with Norman strobe heads. **Center**—This is the head of a studio light. It must be plugged into a power pack to work. **Right**—This is a monolight strobe. It plugs directly into the wall. Monolights are really useful tools.

they can react to small changes in ambient light. Despite all of these positive points, there are some downsides to using dedicated flash: They do not have modeling lights, which help you pre-visualize your image; because they run on batteries, they can take significant time to recycle (i.e., be ready to be used again), especially after they have run for a while; and they do not take standard accessories (however, there are devices available that will allow you to mount most accessories).

STUDIO STROBES

Studio strobes are units that must be plugged into a power pack. These units provide a real advantage with large subjects that require a lot of light (e.g., a car or an architectural subject). One real advantage of studio strobes is that they are often available used at very reasonable prices. So if you are on a budget, it makes a lot of sense to check out used strobes, particularly the big units from Norman and Speedotron. I have several Norman units, which continue to serve me well. Strobes can certainly be used outside of the studio. No matter where you use them, though, be sure that the running cords are taped down, as they can be a safety hazard.

HOT TOPIC

Many strobes, especially monolights, are equipped with a built-in fan. Many older strobes, especially those that used separate power packs, took a fan as an accessory. The fan can be critical if you enclose the strobe, as there are problems with heat from the modeling light. If your strobes take accessory fans, use them. If your strobe does not take an accessory fan, it probably doesn't need one. Units that have no modeling light generally do not need fans.

MONOLIGHTS

Monolights do not need a power pack, as they plug directly into the wall. This makes them very easy to use in any situation where you have access to AC power. In addition, most monolights can be used with accessory battery packs so that you can use them without a wall socket. The cost of monolights is reasonable, and some manufacturers make powerful lights that cost less than proprietary strobes. Since each unit is independently powered, it is easy to add to your system. These units are effective in the studio and on location, but as we'll discuss in the chapter on exposure, monolights and studio strobes require manual exposure.

HOW MANY LIGHTS DO YOU NEED?

Whether they are working on location or in a studio, most portrait photographers will use three lights—a large light source and a couple of lights to fill or create detail effects. You will also need tools to sculpt the light (e.g., a light panel to broaden the light, barn doors to control light, and a snoot to produce a harder spot of light). I also like to have a couple of colored filters for the lights so that I can add color to the subject's face or background.

If you are shooting architectural interiors, you will want several strobes—maybe six or seven. When I go out to do a magazine cover for a trade magazine (strictly low budget), I'll bring three or four lights. If I am working for a hotel, I'll have seven or more lights. When I light an interior, I pay a lot of attention to the existing lighting in the space (hopefully, someone designed it). I use large umbrellas as often as I can, but I also use direct light, bare bulb, and shoot-through umbrellas. Since architectural lighting is complex, it helps to have a big bag of equipment to position and control the light. If I were using a DSLR, I'd want to use monolights. If I were using a large format camera, I might choose studio strobes.

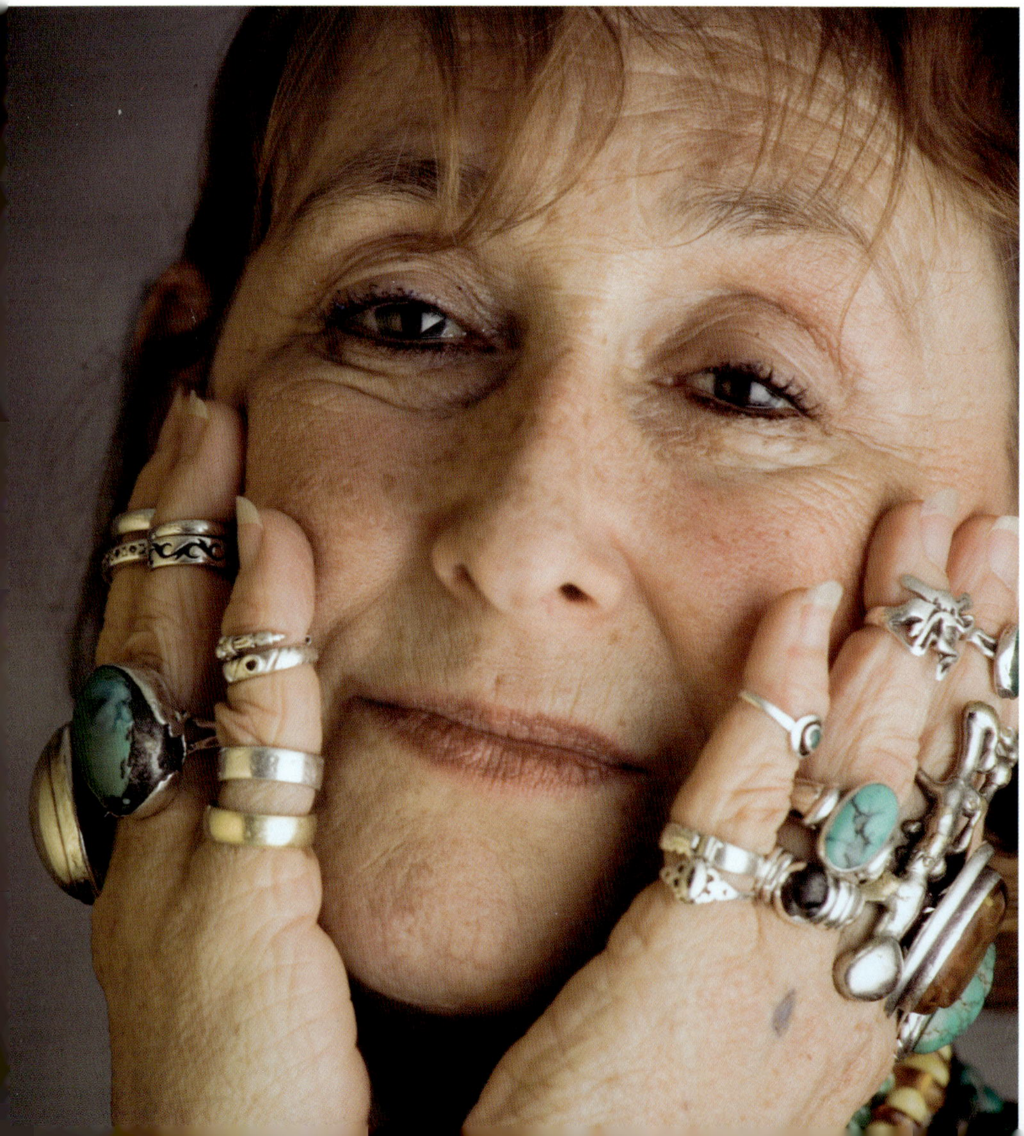

This image was made with one light and an umbrella/light panel combination. I also used a large reflector.

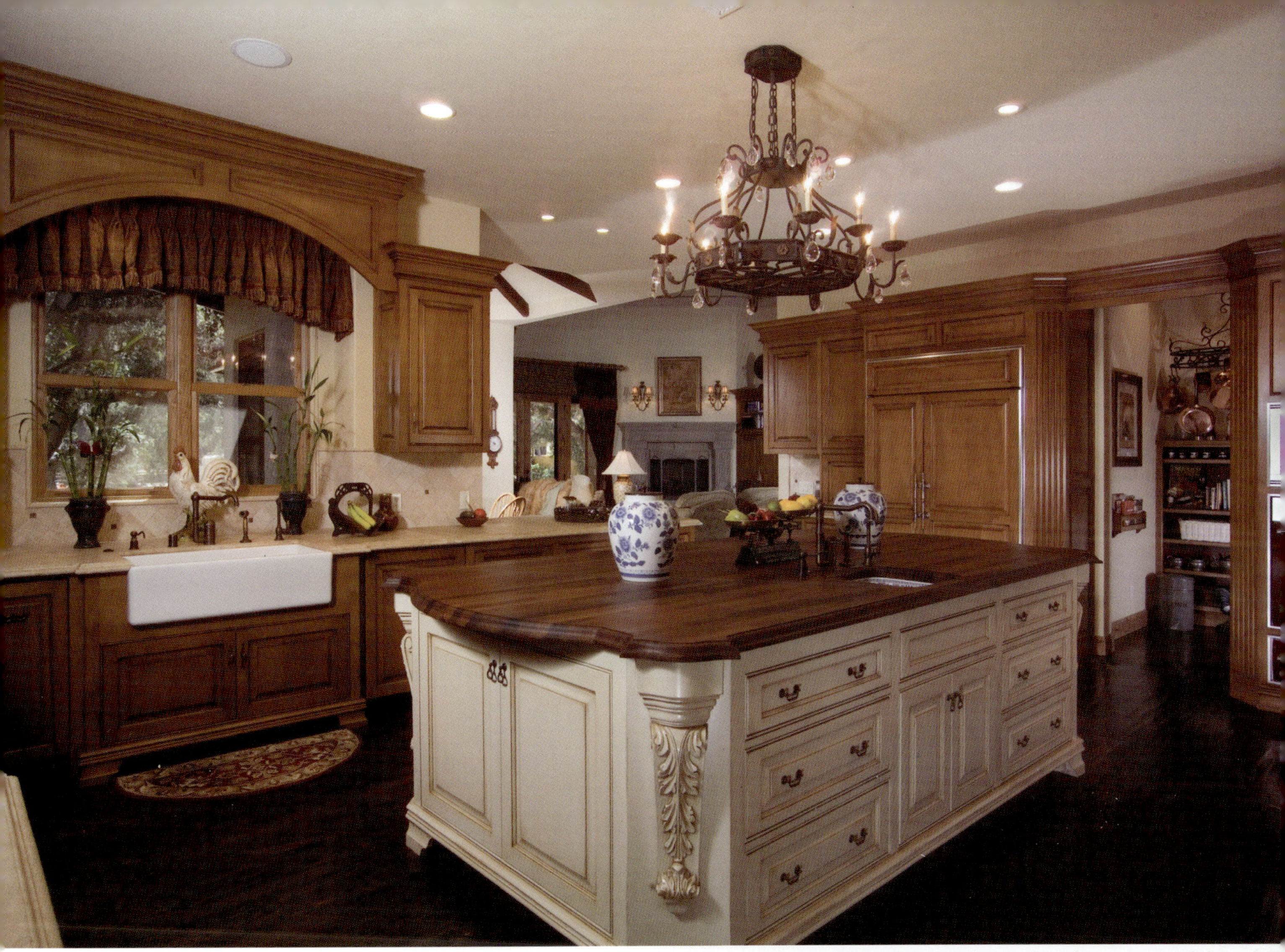

Above—This image had six lights spread between the kitchen, pantry, and living room. It can take quite a while to make natural-looking light in an interior shot! **Right**—I used two lights with light panels to make the light for this shot. Curved surfaces, like the cover of these watches, can reflect a large area, so you need big light sources, placed close to the product.

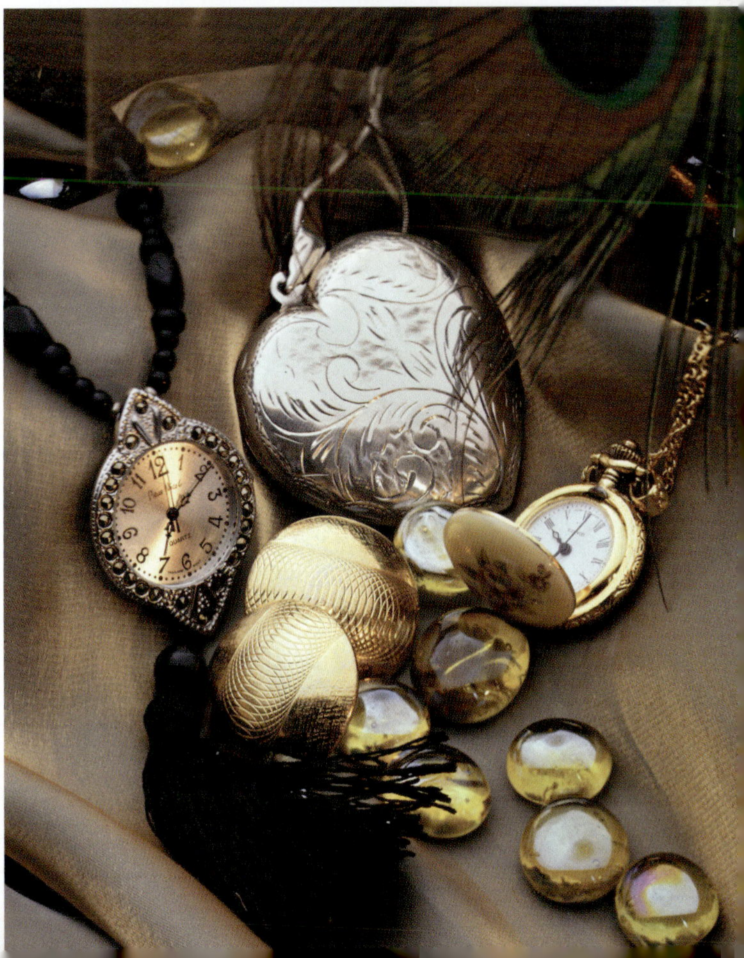

For product or tabletop shooting, I would use at least two strobes—more if I were shooting a large product. Either studio strobes or monolights work well here. Although an umbrella can usually do the job, a softbox can often reduce the amount of cleanup you need to do on the image. I think light panels can also be incredibly useful for this kind of work.

For small reflective work like jewelry and watches, you might also want a light tent (described in chapter 10). For more creative tabletop work, you might also want a Kodak slide projector or two. The projector gives you unbelievable control over the light.

I want to suggest a kind of basic kit here. This is primarily for portraits but would be a good starting place for other kinds of work. Start with one strobe rather than buying everything at once. It is difficult to understand how lights interact in the beginning.

LIGHT STANDS

Light stands are among the heaviest and least portable items in a lighting kit. Since you will be using them to support expensive equipment, I recommend that you go to a retail outlet and select stands that are strong, stable, and not too difficult to carry. Second-quality stands can be used to hold reflectors and other light modifiers.

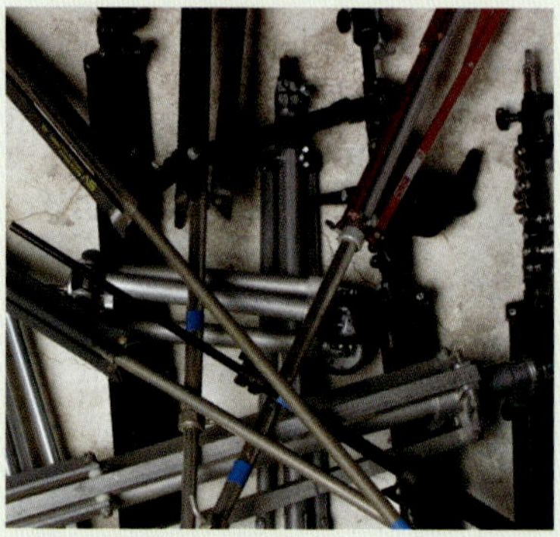

Light stands are heavy and take up a lot of room.

THE BASIC KIT

- A monolight (500 watt-seconds minimum)
- A clip-on reflector (generally about 60 degrees)
- A 45-inch white satin umbrella with a removable black back (a ribless umbrella would be better)
- Two light panels with cotton or nylon covers, plus a black cover and a silver cover
- A light stand (8 feet tall minimum)
- A set of background stands and a neutral muslin background

When you get a second light, which might be lower in power than the first, you should get:

- A clip-on reflector
- Barn doors and/or snoot
- A light stand
- An umbrella that matches the first one you purchased
- A 60-inch umbrella
- A very short light stand

If you add a third light, you should get:

- A clip-on reflector
- A second light panel (should have a gold cover and a white cover)
- A light stand
- Barn doors or a snoot if you didn't get it before
- A 45-inch umbrella

3. MODIFYING LIGHT

Light modifiers fall into two basic groups: those that broaden light and those that concentrate light so that you can affect just one part of a photograph. I use more light-broadening tools than light-concentrating tools, and I think most others do too.

LIGHT-BROADENING TOOLS

As mentioned in chapter 1, light that comes from the sun on an overcast day is soft and diffuse. The light rays come from many areas and angles, not just a small part of the sky. When we are working with artificial light sources, we use bulbs. By default, they produce a hard, more direct light. Fortunately, there are a number of tools available that we can use to modify that bulb's light. Remember that simply using a light-broadening tool will not ensure that you achieve the effects you are after. If the tool is tiny and/or the modified light source is placed far from the subject, the source can still appear hard. For instance, a tiny softbox or umbrella, like the ones made for camera-mounted flash, placed 6 or 7 feet from the subject won't do much for your shot if you're trying to produce soft light.

Bare Bulbs. In certain situations, the strobe tube or quartz bulb, by itself, will be your best lighting tool. The advantage is that it spreads light everywhere. Because the light source is very small, it produces very hard light. It can be useful to aim a bare bulb into a corner of a room to bounce light back

POWERING UP

Many modifiers, especially the light-broadening type, reduce the output of the light, so it is good to have powerful strobes.

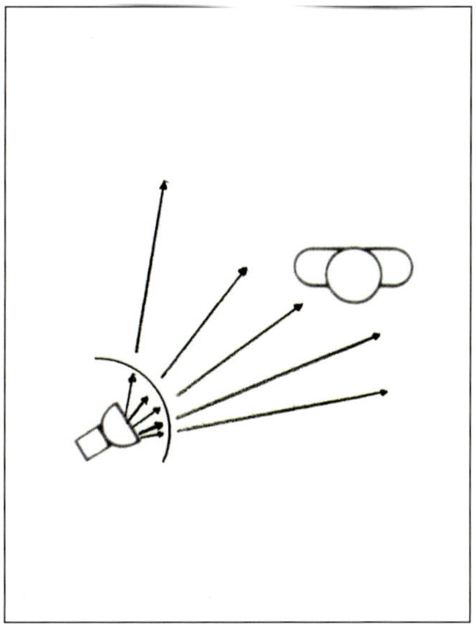

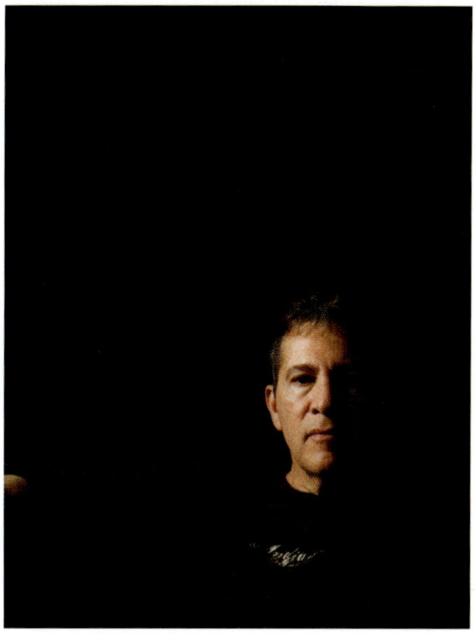

Left—Spreading light with a diffuser doesn't change the quality of light on the subject very much, as the light comes from the same direction. **Right**—Only direct light was used to create this shot. A snoot was placed on the strobe to control the light.

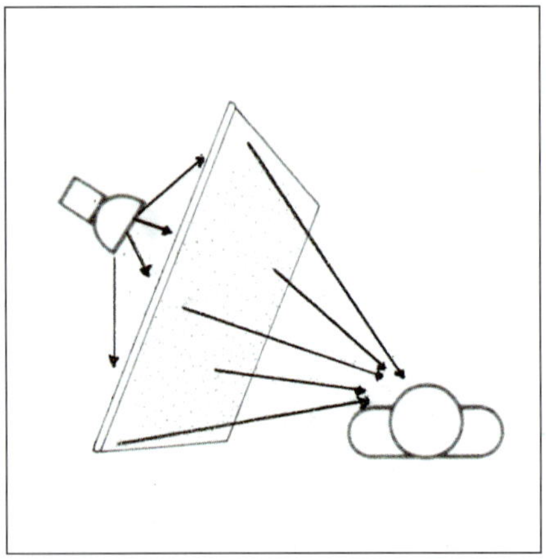

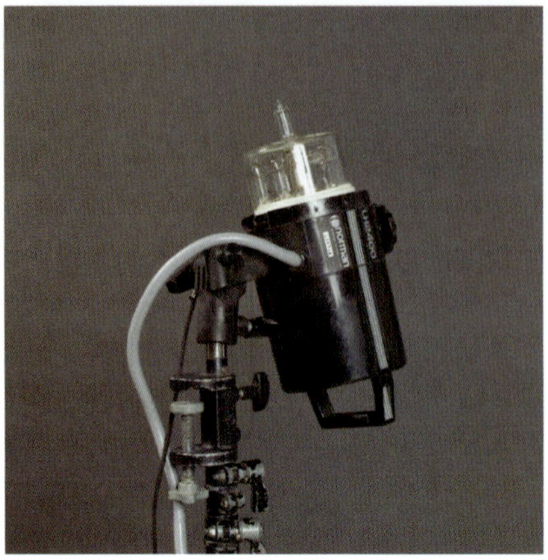

Left—Umbrellas, softboxes, and light panels broaden the source of light, allowing the subject to be lit from more angles. When the light comes from more angles, it has softer transitions and less shadows. **Right**—The bare strobe tube can be useful in lighting a tight space. **Bottom left**—This shoe covering does a great job of bouncing light and makes the light source a little larger. It collapses into a small space, making it highly portable. You can buy a package of these at a hardware store for less than $4.00.

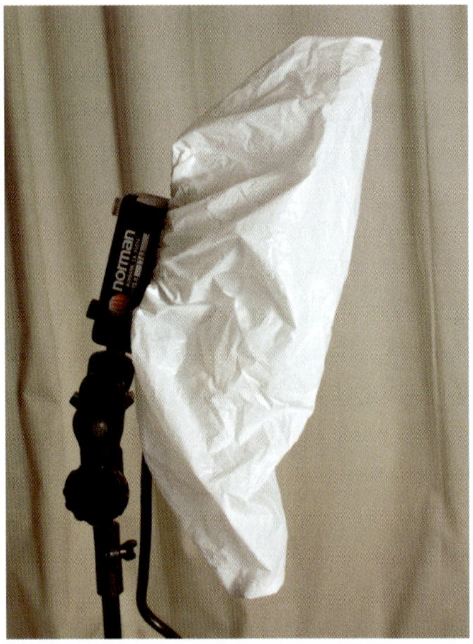

onto your subject (unless you have colored walls that will create a color cast). Bare bulb lighting is generally not useful outdoors, as much of the light goes where it isn't needed.

There are many devices on the market that can be used to broaden the light from a camera-mounted strobe or a strobe that is being used in a small space. Unfortunately, many of them cost hundreds of dollars. As an alternative, you can put a translucent plastic bottle over the bare bulb to soften the light a little. I have been using shoe coverings over my strobes rather than plastic bottles. They are very inexpensive and collapse into a very small size. Get white shoe covers from your local hardware store. The blue ones are only good for covering shoes.

UMBRELLAS ARE WONDERFULLY EASY TO SET UP, AND THERE ARE SEVERAL WAYS TO USE THEM.

Umbrellas. Umbrellas are concave light modifiers that are lined with a reflective white, silver, or gold material. When the strobe fires into the umbrella, the beam of light is made broader and softer. Some umbrellas, called shoot-through umbrellas, work a little bit differently. They allow you to direct light through the fabric. This can really come in handy when you're working in a small room, as you can use the light that goes through the modifier as you intend, and the light that is reflected from the inside of the umbrella can be bounced off the wall and back onto your subject.

I first learned lighting using umbrellas. I still find them to be one of the best tools ever created for lighting. Umbrellas are wonderfully easy to set up, and there are several ways to use them. Shoot-through umbrellas permit you to aim the light through the white fabric, instead of bouncing off the inside of the umbrella. If you are lighting a small room, you can use light from both

SILVER AND GOLD

An umbrella with a silver lining reflects more light, but the quality of the light is harder. An umbrella with a gold lining will help correct a color imbalance between daylight and tungsten (as will a blue umbrella if you can find one), but for my tastes, the light it produces is too yellow.

sides at once. The light from the back of the umbrella will bounce off the walls and into the shot. Unless I am pressed for space, I prefer to bounce light off the umbrella, as this method produces less spill light and allows for more control.

There are a variety of design variations that can allow more control over your umbrella. A bigger umbrella will produce softer light than a smaller one. I use umbrellas with a removable black back, so that when I bounce light there is no light spilling from the backside. This improves my control over the light and contrast. I also like to use umbrellas where the fabric is in front of the ribs; it makes a cleaner reflection. I refer to these umbrellas as ribless umbrellas. Finally, enclosed umbrellas are now available. These umbrellas, called brollyboxes or octaboxes, are sort of a cross between an umbrella and a softbox. They are like a shoot-through umbrella without the spill out the back.

There are pros and cons to using umbrellas. On the minus side, the reflections they produce look like white, round umbrellas (if you use ribless umbrellas, the reflection may be less objectionable); they are difficult to use outdoors, especially in high wind; and they spread light everywhere, so you won't have subtle control. On the plus side, they are easy to set up, heat is not a problem because of the standard umbrella's open design, and most strobes have built-in umbrella holders.

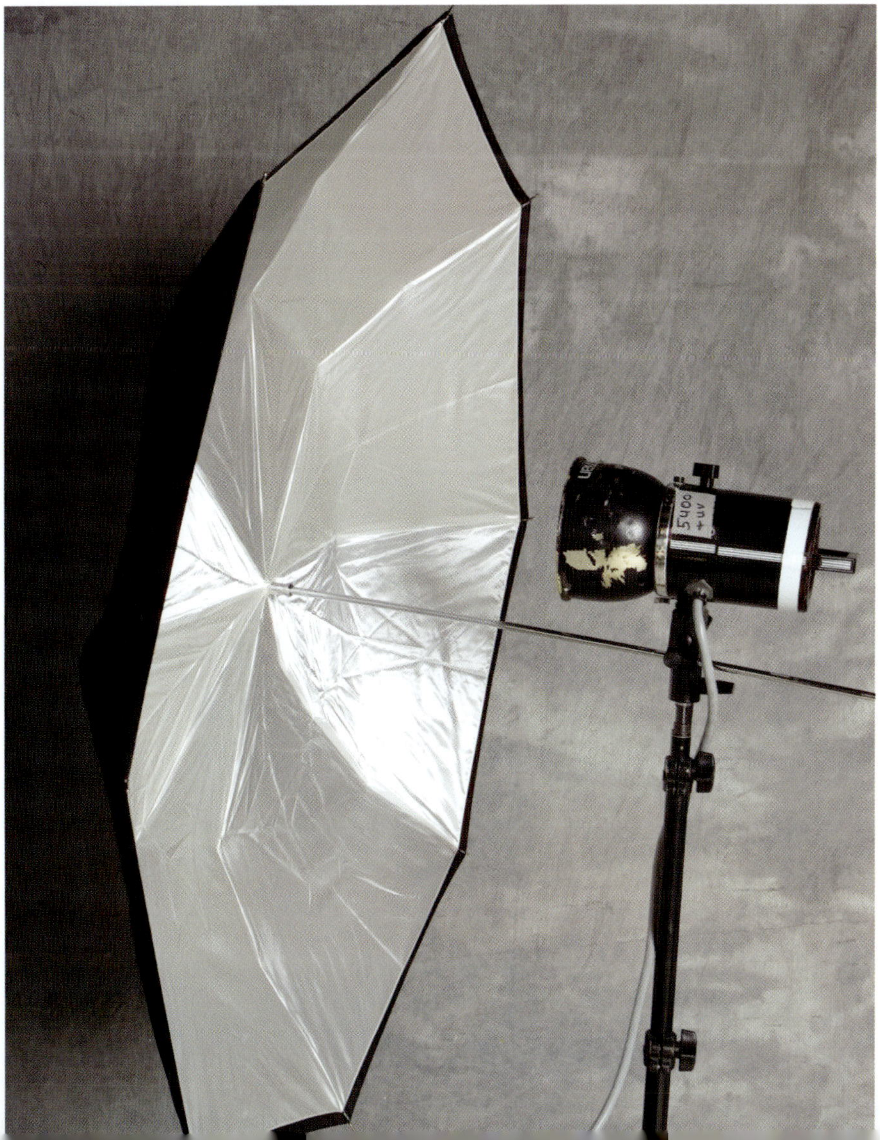

This is a ribless umbrella with a removable black back. It's a very useful and adaptable tool.

Softboxes. The basic design of a softbox is something like a dome tent. I find both dome tents and softboxes annoying to set up and take down. They have rods that have to be under tension to keep the shape. Once set up, they provide a good, even light source. Softboxes offer more subtle control than an umbrella, especially at the edges. If you can get a softbox that has a cover with a round or rectangular hole in the front, you can choose a round reflection as well as the rectangle the box normally creates. This might be more useful than getting an octabox or a brollybox. Note that most manufacturers make adapters to fit popular models of strobes.

Large softboxes produce softer light than small ones. I have one that is about 3x3 feet. I also have one that is about 12x16 inches. It is great for putting reflections in bottles, but not much else.

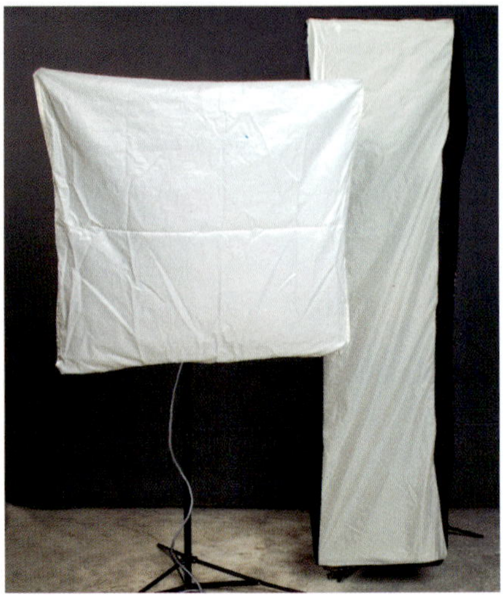

Softboxes are available in different sizes and shapes. This image shows my 3x3-foot softbox and my 6x2-foot strip light.

Light Panels. A light panel is a large white fabric panel inside of a frame. You can purchase a light panel or make your own (this way, they are very economical). The wonderful thing about the panels is that there are so many ways to use them. You can put a lamp behind them and use them to make a

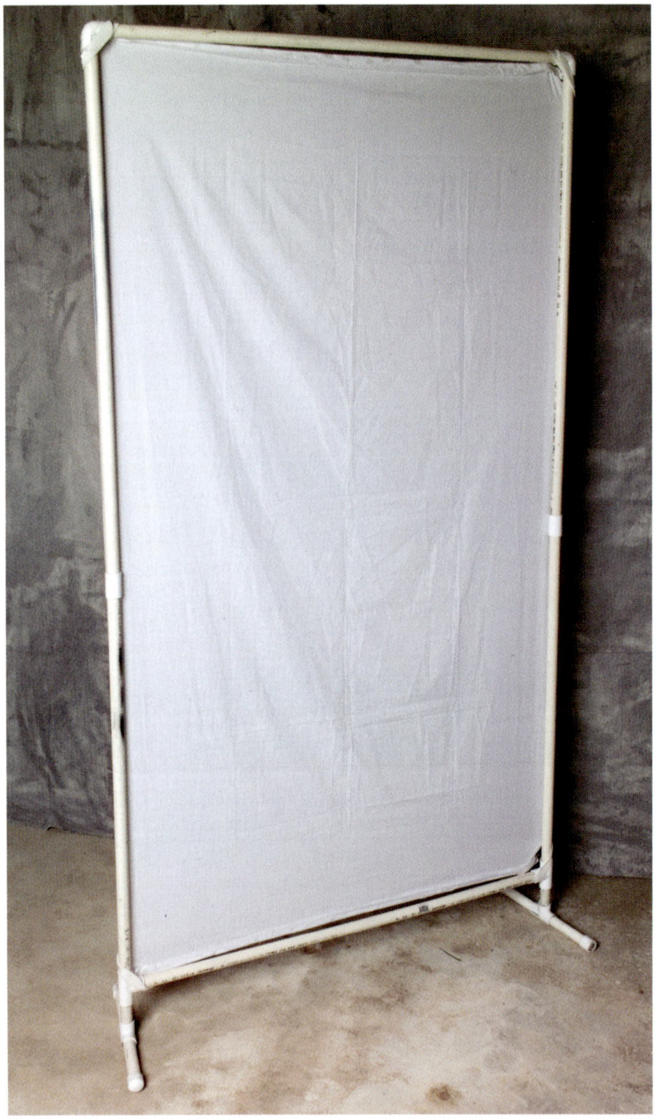

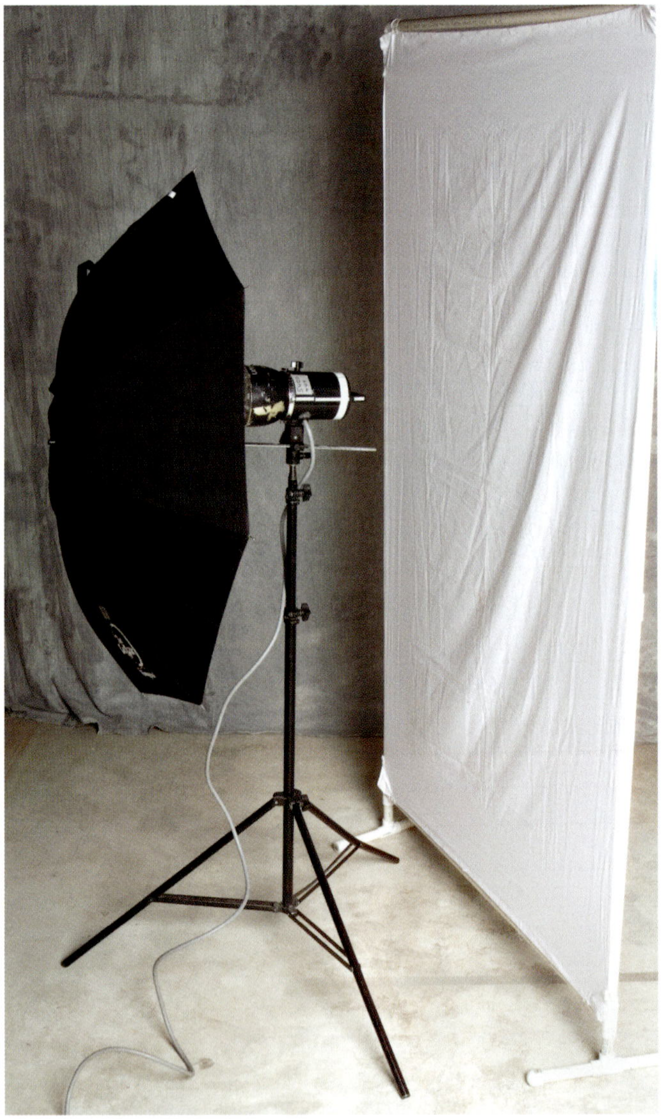

Left—This is a light panel. You can find them at a photographic supply store or can make your own using the instructions on the facing page. **Right**—When you bounce light off an umbrella, it diffuses the light over the surface of the light panel. This provides a very large, even, and soft light source.

BUILDING A LIGHT PANEL

You are going to want some of these light panels. They help me to create large, shadowless light sources.

Materials

You can get all of this stuff at most hardware stores:

3 pieces 10-foot PVC pipe, 3/4-inch schedule 40 (the thick stuff)
4 pieces T connectors
2 pieces straight connectors
2 pieces corner connectors
4 pieces end caps
7 feet of white cotton broad cloth, 42 inches wide. You can use nylon as well. You may also want gold, silver and black covers.
2-foot elastic strip
PVC glue (use outdoors)
white glue or wood glue

How to Assemble

Cut the PVC into the following lengths:

2 pieces 42 inches
4 pieces 36 inches
2 pieces 6 inches
4 pieces 10 inches

Glue one side of a PVC connector to a pipe (except on the feet). If you do this, you will be able to break down your panel. You can glue all the parts on the feet (see image A.2), but don't glue the feet to the panel. It is best to assemble the panel once before you start gluing.

Attach two corner connectors to the same piece of 42-inch PVC. Make sure the openings point in the same direction.

Attach one straight connector to a piece of 36-inch PVC and a T-connector to the other side. Make two of these. You should have two pieces of 36-inch PVC without any connectors and two pieces with a connector on each end.

Put the 36-inch piece with no connector into the straight connector on the other 36-inch piece. The 42-inch connector with the corner pieces will fit on the top and the other 42-inch piece will fit across the bottom. You should be able to assemble these pieces into a rectangle 42x72 inches. When you are through, it should come apart easily. You should be able to put everything into an equipment bag.

The feet will fit into the open holes at the bottom of the 36-inch pieces with connectors on both ends.

Take two of the 10-inch pieces of PVC and glue them into the straight through sides of a T connector. Glue an end cap onto each of these. Glue a piece of 6-inch PVC onto the open side of the connector. This will fit into the bottom of the frame you just made.

Now the fabric. You will want to finish up with a piece of reflective gold, silver, black, or white cloth that is tight in the frame, so measure the frame! For the shoot-through white, either cotton or ripstop nylon fabric works well, but it is easier to glue hems on the cotton. Glue hems on the top and bottom of the fabric. *(Note:* If you buy fabric that is 42 inches wide, you will not need to hem the sides.) Sew pieces of the elastic ribbon on each corner. This will hold the fabric on the frame.

You have just made an important lighting tool.

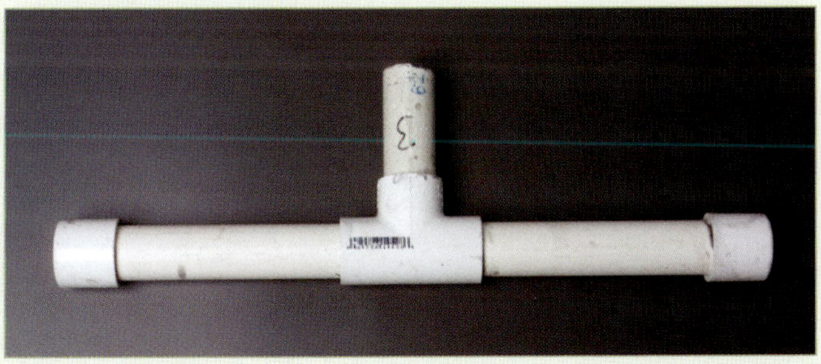

__Above__—This image shows how to assemble the foot for the light panel. __Right__—The elastic will hold the fabric onto the frame.

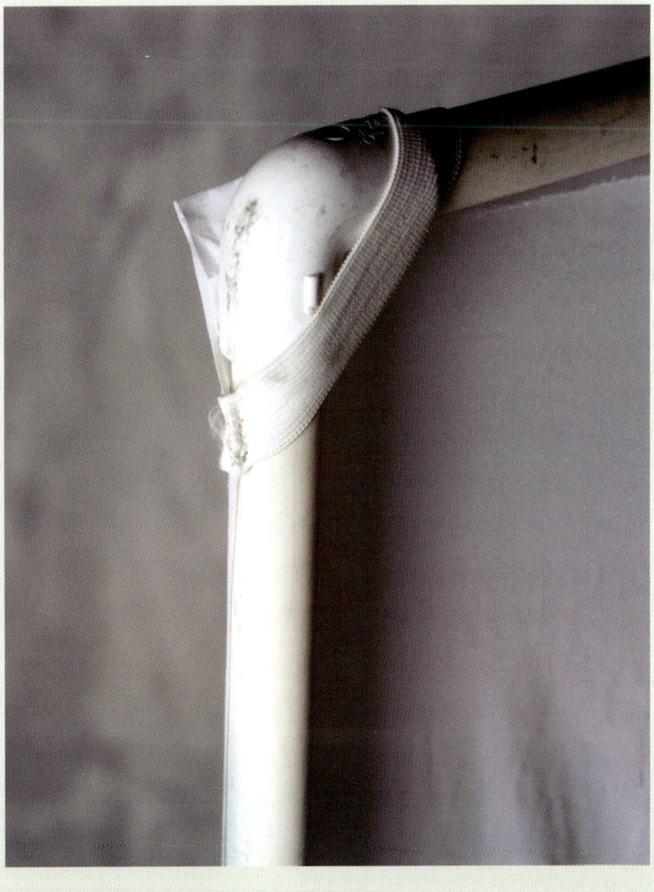

large, diffused light source. In this case, you can use the lamp straight, you can rake it across the surface or, if you want very soft light, you can bounce the light off an umbrella before it goes through the panel. You can put a reflective silver or gold cover on a panel and use it as a reflector. You can even reflect off the white cotton cover that is generally used to transmit light. Finally, you can put a black cover over the panel and use it to block light.

Beauty Dishes. A beauty dish is a wide and shallow bowl-shaped reflector that is fitted onto a strobe. It works like a small umbrella or round softbox, but with a defined shape. The one shown on this page is 22 inches across, a good size for portraiture if placed close to the subject. I really like to use them to create catchlights in the eyes.

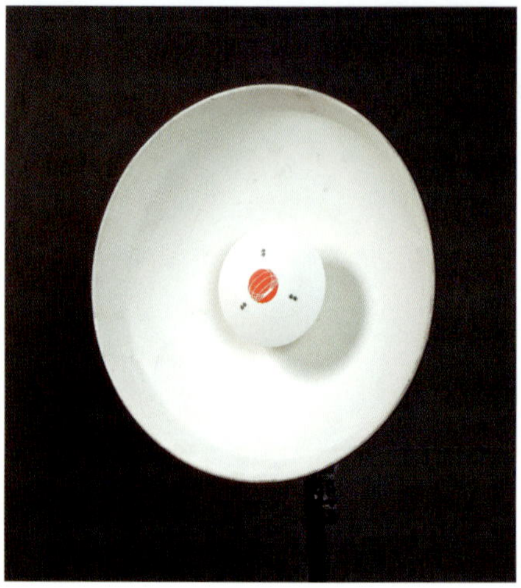

Beauty dishes create a nice, even, round reflection. The light has about the same quality as any light source of the same size.

LIGHT-NARROWING TOOLS

On a sunny day, the sun comes from a small area of the sky and produces hard, distinct shadows, sparkling highlights, and you can really see texture. When working with strobe lighting, we can mimic the effects of harsh sunlight. Each of the tools described below make light cover a smaller area. The resulting light, called hard light, creates hard shadows and fast transitions from light to dark.

Clip-On Reflectors. A clip-on reflector is a simple dish that attaches to the end of a strobe or is built into a tungsten light. This offers control, especially compared to a bare bulb. Most strobe manufacturers make clip-on reflectors of various sizes that offer different light spreads. These reflectors are only available from the strobe manufacturer.

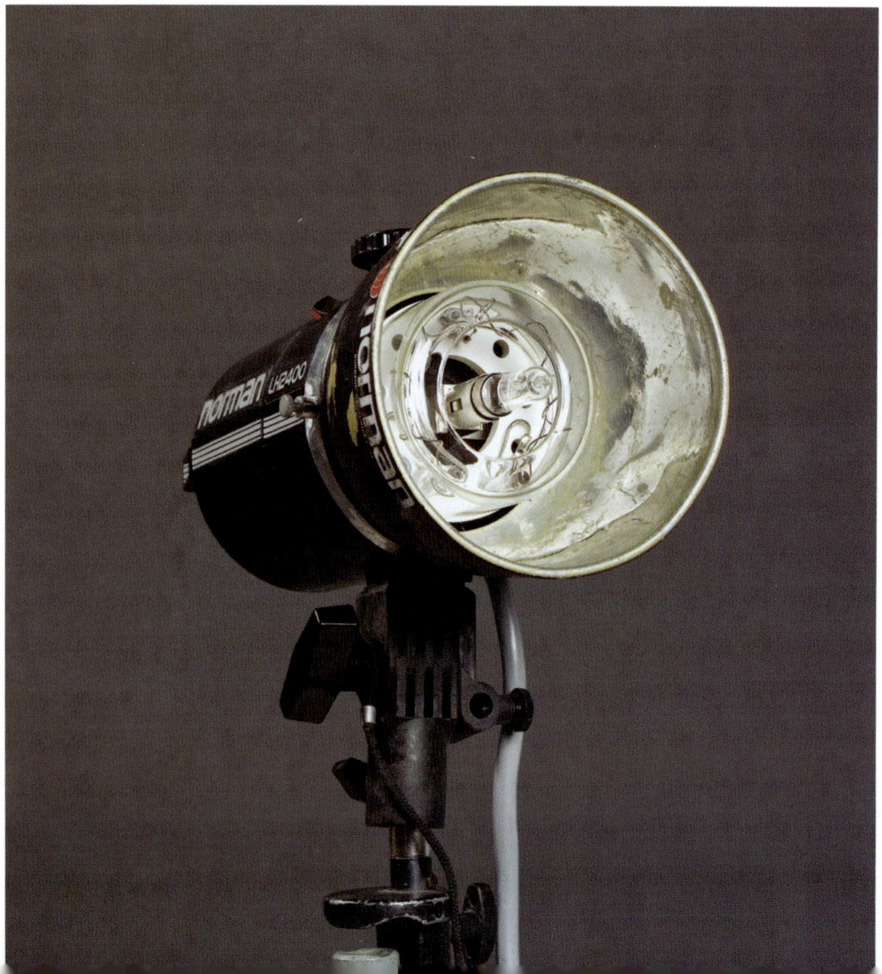

This shows a 60-degree clip-on reflector on a strobe. Reflectors give some control over the direction of your light.

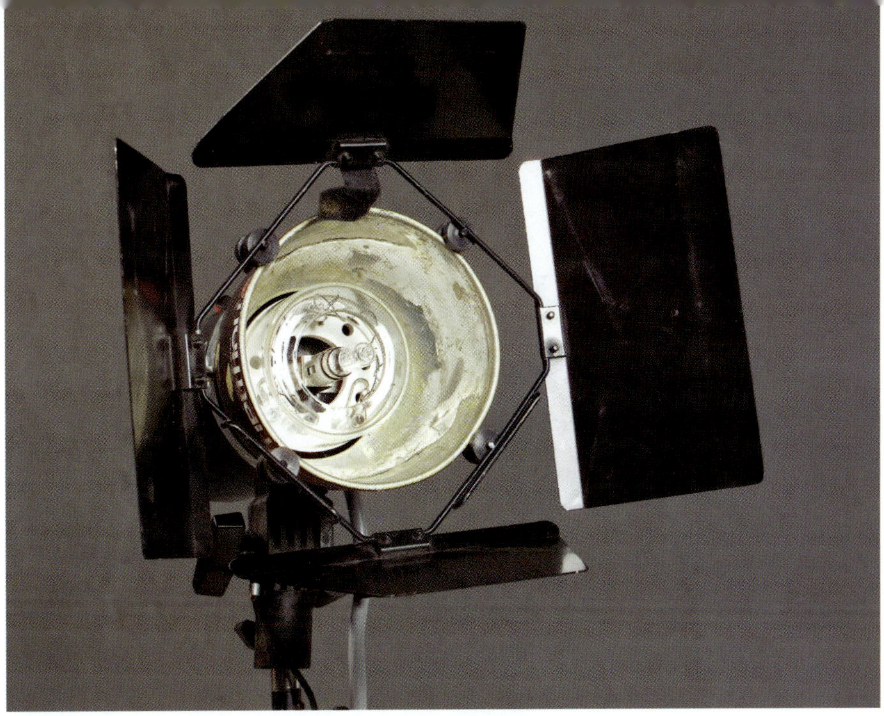

This strobe has a clip-on reflector and a set of barn doors. The doors enable you to control the spread of the light.

Barn Doors. This is the most flexible of the light-condensing tools. Two or four metal blades are attached to a clip-on reflector, and in some models, the shape of the blades can be changed. By moving the blades, you can control the spread of light, from wide open down to a small strip of light. Keep in mind that the metal blades become extremely hot in use. It is easy to forget and get burned. Barn doors offer more control over the light than do snoots and grids but do not limit the spread of light to the degree that those tools do. Also, light tends to leak out of the sides of the barn doors. This light can bounce around the studio and create some fill light on your subject.

Snoots. A snoot is a tube-shaped modifier that slips over a light. It reduces the spread of light dramatically (but not as much as a grid can) and is designed to throw a small round light at your subject. I like using a snoot because the light transitions from light to shadow very quickly, resulting in very contrasty lighting. Light spreads when it leaves the snoot, so the size of the light changes depending on the light-to-subject distance. Because a snoot prevents light from spilling from the sides of a light unit, there is no reflected fill light. Snoots are available in different sizes. The one shown in the image on the left is a stovepipe snoot; its opening is about 4 inches across.

Grids. A grid is a metal honeycomb that goes over the light. It reduces the spread of the light more than any of the other tools. A gridded light placed 6 feet from the subject may light an area that is less than 1 foot around. Grids are rated in degrees (e.g., 10 degrees, 20 degrees, etc.) The smaller the number, the more narrow the spread of light. This also makes a small round light, similar to the snoot, but since the light goes through a honeycomb-shaped series of tubes, the light doesn't spread as much. A grid spot is just the thing for adding a very small highlight. This makes a strobe act more like a small optical spot. These lights are extremely useful for adding sparkle and

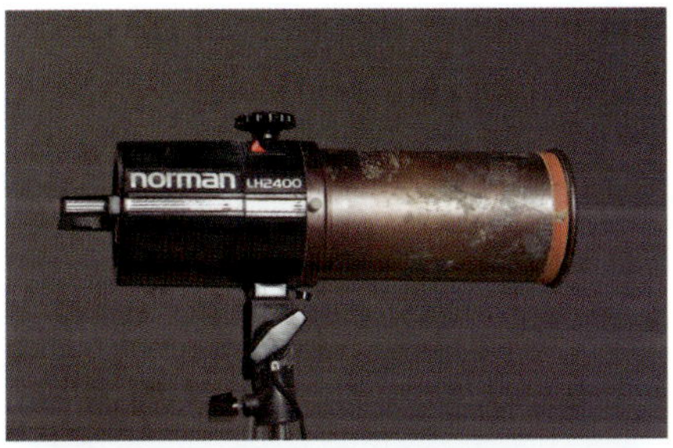

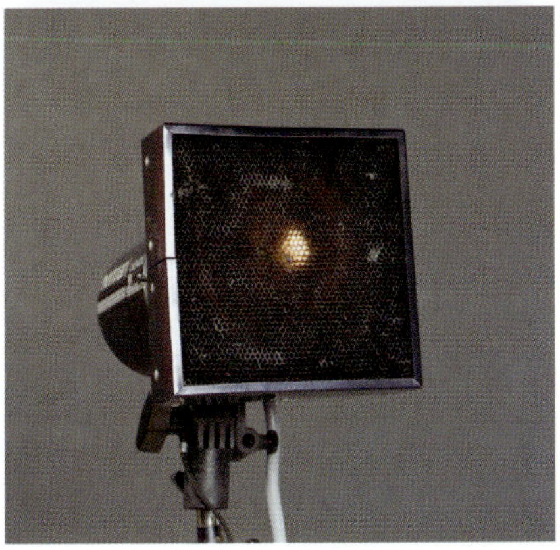

Top—A snoot keeps light from spreading, allowing you to bring out one part of an image. I used this snoot to create the portrait in the beginning of this chapter. **Bottom**—The grid spot allows you to put very small highlights into a shot with considerable accuracy.

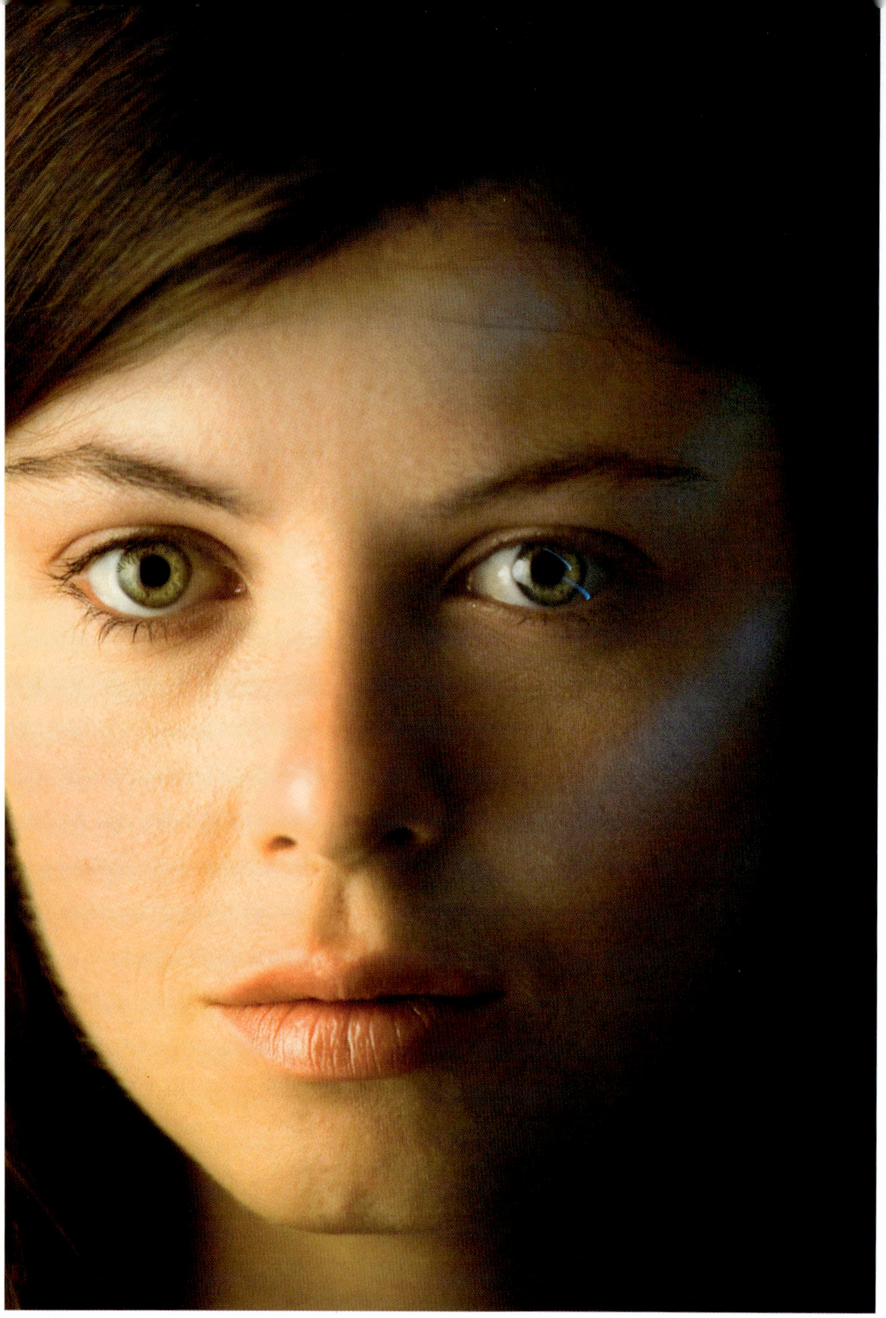

I used a Kodak slide projector, a cookie, and a blue gel to create this shot. The large light source was an umbrella/light panel combination. 1/4-second exposure.

KODAK SLIDE PROJECTOR

There is one other tool that I like to use for controlling light: the Kodak Slide Projector. This is a continuous light, so you often need long exposures. You have fantastic control over the light. You can make tiny spots of light or add a piece of Cinefoil with cutout patterns where a slide would normally be inserted to project patterns of light and shadow. You can add a colored gel in the slide holder—or even use a slide of a pattern. The most recent Kodak projectors have better color: earlier ones are green. All of them are basically a tungsten light balance. I like to use rear curtain sync when I use the projector. This way, the strobe comes at the end of the shot, which makes the model less likely to move during the shot.

drama to a shot. You can mix them with soft lights to add highlights that you wouldn't get from a large light source. You can mix a soft light and a grid spot from the same direction. This can create a very effective light: sparkle from the grid and soft light from the larger source. The grid spot shown on page 27 has 1/4-inch holes and fits a 6-inch, clip-on reflector. The grids are available for larger reflectors and have different sized holes. The differences control the size and spread of the light. A bigger grid with bigger holes throws a bigger spot that spreads faster. It is often useful to have several different grids.

Cinefoil. Rosco Cinefoil is a matte black aluminum foil that soaks up light. It won't burn, so you can use it to make custom light control devices for your specific needs. Keep in mind it will get hot and the black coating may smoke. You need to be careful when shaping it on the light. Cinefoil is really a useful thing to have around the studio.

DARKENING TOOLS

Flags, Gobos, Scrims, and Cookies. Flags, gobos, and scrims can be used to subtract light from a scene. A gobo (short for "go before optics" or "go between") is a device (usually black) placed between a light source and the subject to modify the way the light falls on the subject. A flag is a kind of gobo used to shield an area of the subject from light or prevent lens flare. A scrim is a device placed in front of a light source to reduce its intensity.

The closer the darkening tool is to the subject, the better and more precise the light-blocking is. When the device is moved farther from the light source, there is smoother transition from light to shadow.

These tools can also be used to keep light from bouncing back into a shot.

A cookie is an opaque device with a cutout pattern that, when placed in front of a light source, will cast shadows over the subject or backdrop. They can be purchased or made from Cinefoil. I use them with the slide projector.

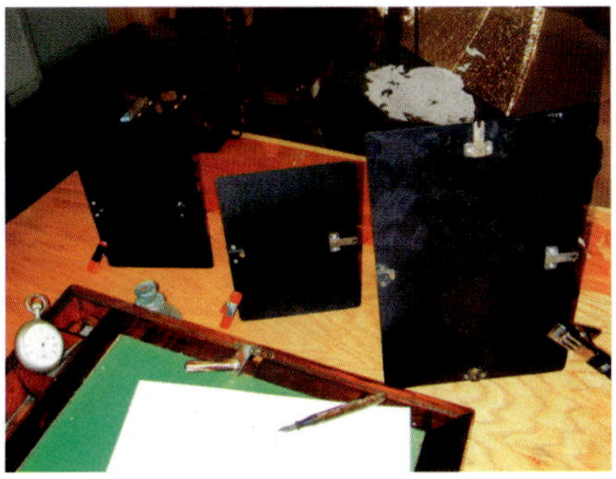

The final shot (right) and the setup shot (above) show how darkening tools were used to create a light with character for this shot. In addition to the three darkening tools, you can see the filters I used to help create the mood of this shot.

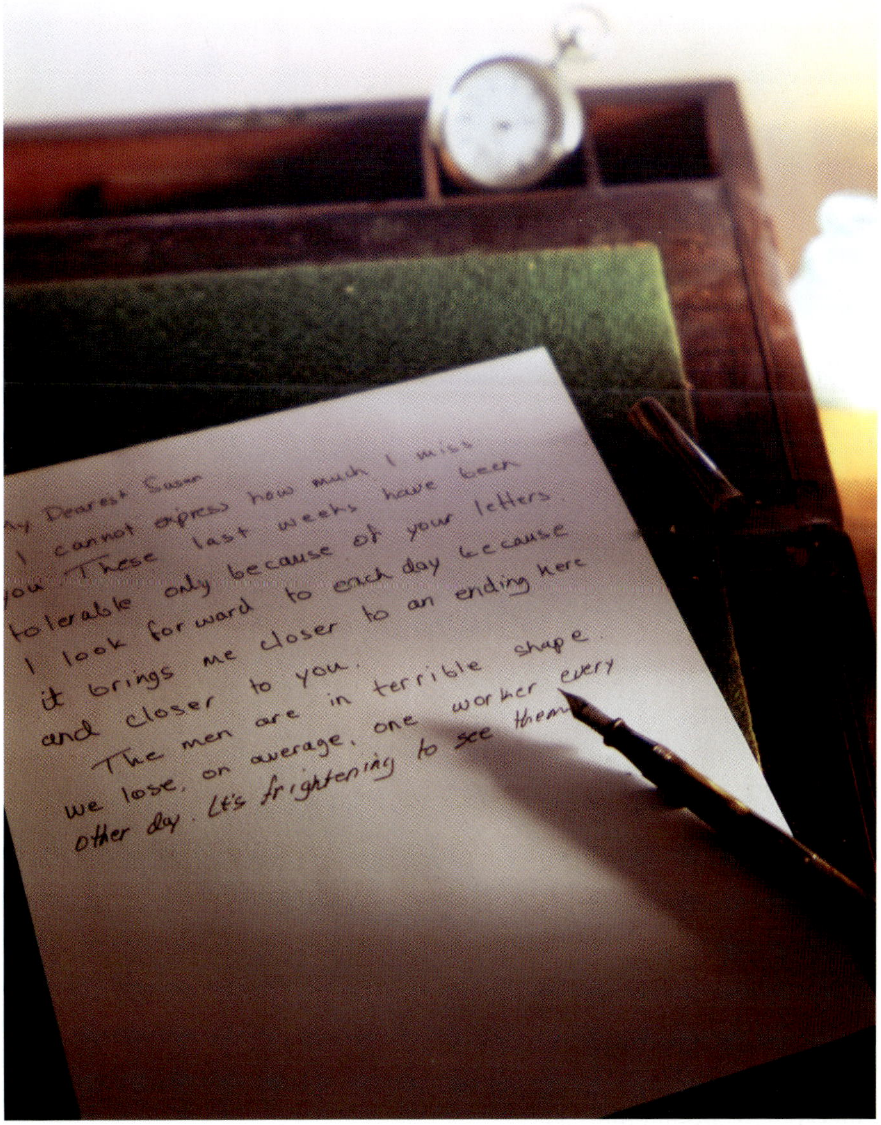

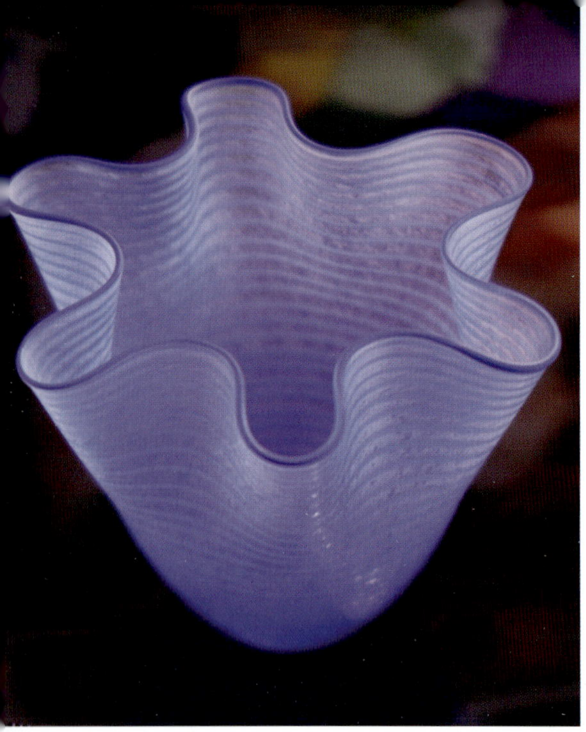

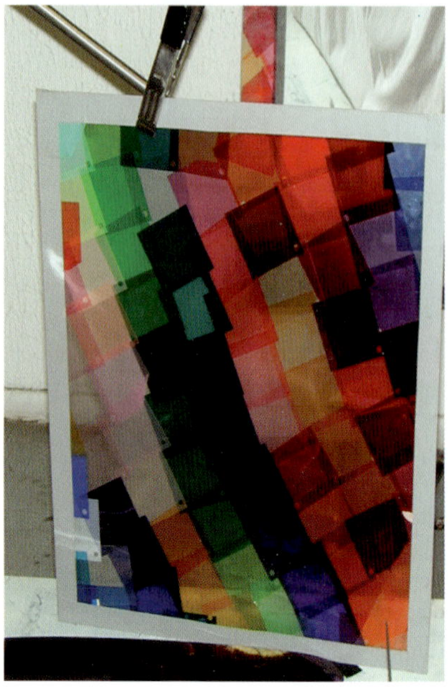

I used a piece of glass covered with filters (left) to reflect in the shiny black paper at the base of this shot (right).

FILTERS

Filters are flexible plastic sheets that can be used to control the light from your strobe or change its color. I get filters from Rosco. These filters are designed primarily for the movie industry. This is an advantage because the filters are designed to withstand heat without burning. The modeling light in a strobe can get quite hot, so a random piece of colored plastic could be dangerous. I use several filters to control color:

- Full Orange (CTO/3407)—Converts daylight or strobe to tungsten color balance.
- Half Orange ($\frac{1}{2}$ CTO/3408)—Makes strobe or daylight much warmer.
- Quarter Orange ($\frac{1}{4}$ CTO/3409)—Makes strobe or daylight a little warmer.
- Full Blue (CTB/3202)—Converts tungsten to daylight. Makes color temperature cooler.
- Half Plus Green (3315)—Makes strobe or daylight look more like fluorescent light. (This doesn't always work.)

FILTERS ARE FLEXIBLE PLASTIC SHEETS THAT CAN BE USED TO CONTROL THE LIGHT FROM YOUR STROBE OR CHANGE ITS COLOR.

These filters are available in sheets and rolls. The rolls of half orange are very useful for covering windows. The material can be reused until the color fades.

MOVING FORWARD

It seems that I've described many tools, but as I mentioned earlier in this book, we are going to write with light, so we will need the tools that work best for each scenario. Having the ability to carry out the shots as you've conceived them is tremendously rewarding!

4. GETTING THE RIGHT EXPOSURE

Many people believe that there is one right exposure for each image. That is not true. Often, the right exposure is subjective. Sometimes no exposure seems correct for your shot because the light does not suit the subject or the contrast is too great.

Most photographers believe that they need to rely on a light meter—whether handheld or built in—to ensure a perfect exposure. Unfortunately, the best a meter can do is give you a starting point. When I am working with strobes, the first thing I do is set the camera to manual. When you're working with strobes, your camera's meter is useless (unless you're using dedicated strobes). I do not use a handheld meter, either.

The best way to ensure accurate exposure for your image is to rely on your eye, the image's histogram, your LCD screen or, if you are working with a DSLR tethered to a laptop, the image you see on your monitor. Using these tools can make it much easier to design your lighting.

I am often asked how I controlled my lights when I was shooting film. People have the idea that photographers relied on meters. For complex shots, we used Polaroid backs to produce test images. I used to use thousands of dollars of Polaroid materials in a year. I did not rely on a meter.

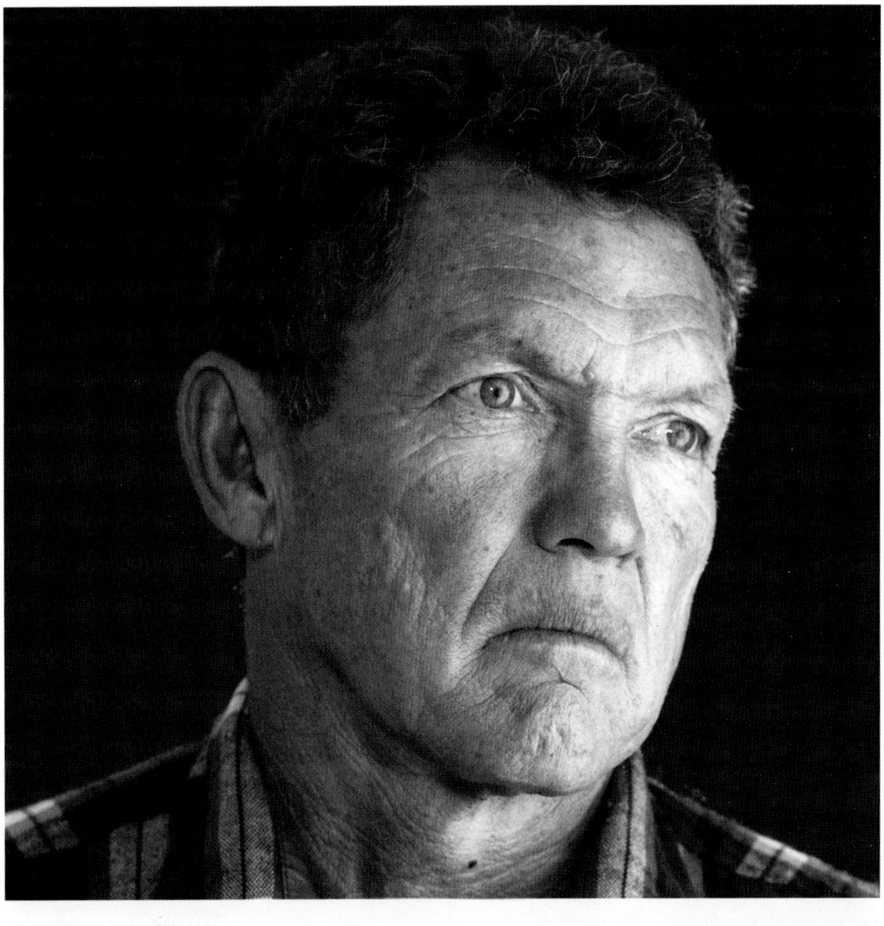

Meters often have a tough time properly interpreting contrasty light.

BUILDING A COMPUTER TABLE

Start with a piece of plywood or paneling about the size of the bottom of your laptop. The next thing you need is a T-nut connector, size 1/4x20. The 1/4x20 is the size of a tripod screw. Drill a hole in the center of the plywood, just a little smaller than the center of the T-nut. Hammer the T-nut into the wood. This needs to be tight, and the sharp ends of the T-nut need to go into the wood. You now have a tabletop that can be mounted on a tripod. For security, you should put some elastic on the sides to hold the computer.

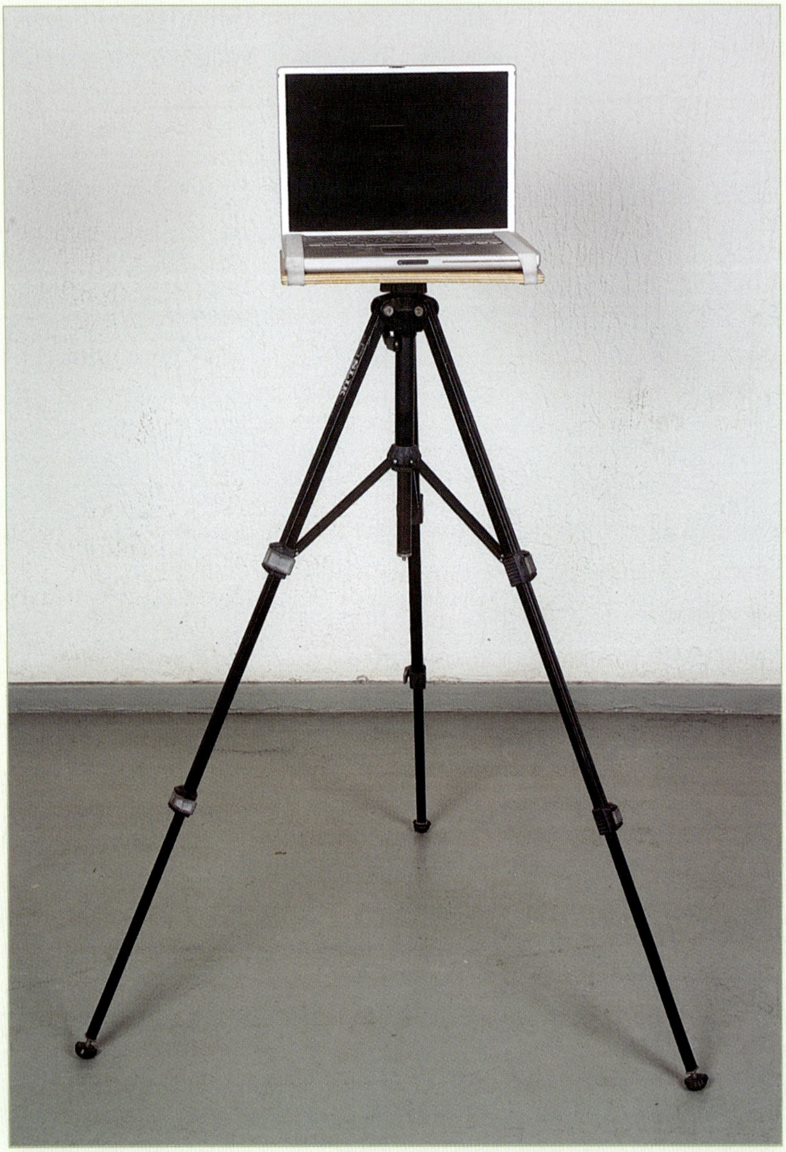

This is a portable table for a laptop. It uses a tripod base. It makes it easier to use the laptop on location.

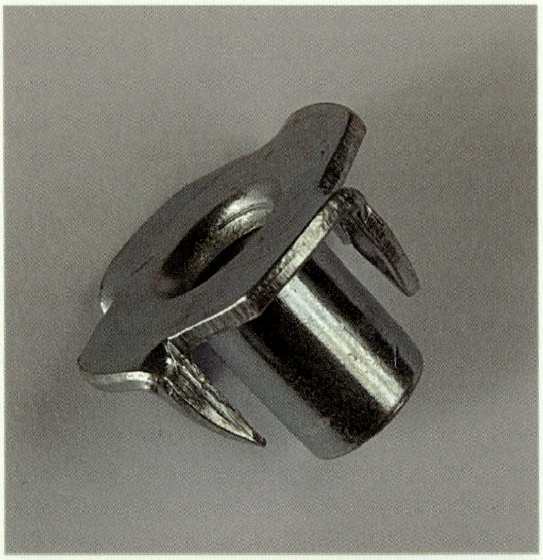

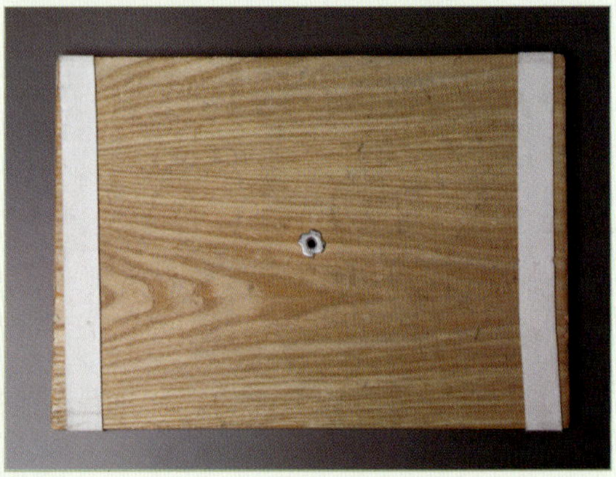

Top—*You can find T-nuts at hardware and home improvement stores.* ***Above***—*You can see where the elastic is attached to the tabletop.*

Top—In this shot, there is not enough light. The painting isn't featured by the light. The image doesn't really have an intimate feel. **Center**—In this image, we get a good sense of the subject. The snoot gives the painting a lot more light. Of course, we see less of the room, but the light on the room is better. **Bottom**—This shows the position of the lights. Since the light with the snoot is easy to miss, I circled it. There is also an overhead skylight.

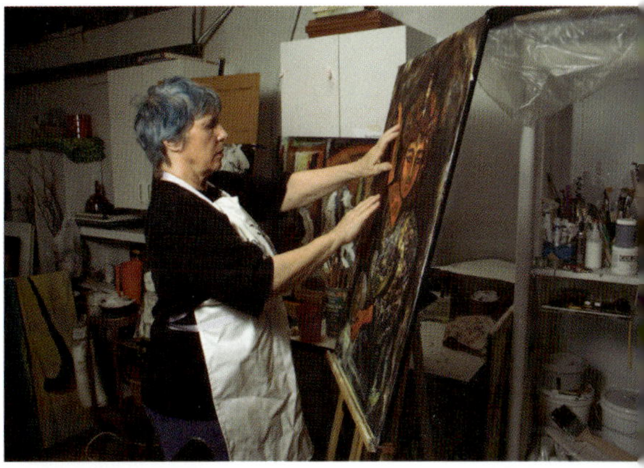

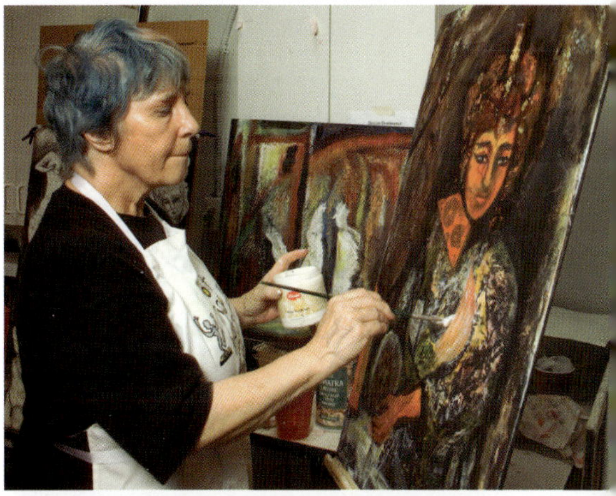

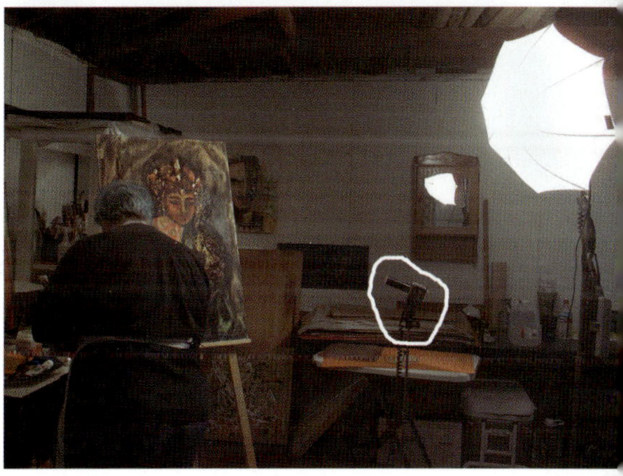

Let me recommend a plan for seeking the right exposure:

1. Set the shutter speed to the sync speed. The sync speed is the fastest speed you can use for your camera with a strobe. At any faster speed, part of the picture will be black. (More on this in the next chapter.)
2. Select the middle aperture on your lens (e.g., if your lens apertures range from f/2.8 to f/22, set the aperture to f/8).
3. Take a picture. It will probably be wrong.
4. Open up or stop down your aperture to let in more or less light based on your first test exposure. Look at the histogram to determine how much to change the aperture. The LCD/monitor image can tell you if you need to change a lot or a little.
5. If you are using more than one light, you may want to shoot each light individually so that you know what each light does.
6. Make additional test exposures and change each light's placement and power until the strobes are right.
7. If you want to incorporate existing light into the shot, make your shutter speed longer until you achieve a good balance.

If you practice this, you will be able to find the right exposure quite quickly. Keep in mind that musicians practice extensively. Photographers should too.

Let's look at a real-life example. For the image above, I wanted to light the whole room so that I could shoot from several angles, so I used a shoot-through umbrella. I was matching my strobes to the daylight from an overhead skylight. Also, it was about 90 degrees Fahrenheit in her studio. I used two lights: an umbrella and a snoot. The snoot was added to bring extra light and sparkle to the painting. To build the right light for the subject, I made the first shot, made changes, made a second shot, and so on.

The essential trick with strobes is to evaluate and change our images in search of the right levels for our lights and exposures.

WORKING IN THE RAW FORMAT

Always shoot in RAW. When you do, you have more extensive control over the exposure and the color after the shoot. If you shoot JPEG, you lose much of this control and get almost no advantage. The final picture is an expression of the file you capture, just as a recording of a cantata is an expression of the music the composer wrote. When we light a shot, our goal is to make the best possible capture, but the capture is not the picture. The picture is an interpretation of the capture. If you save as much information as possible in your capture, you will be able to make a better final image.

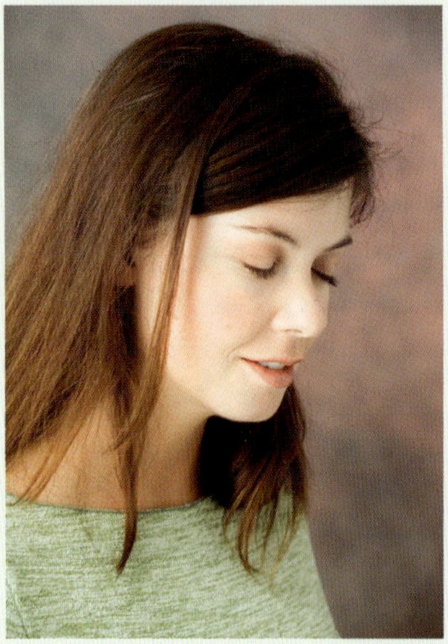

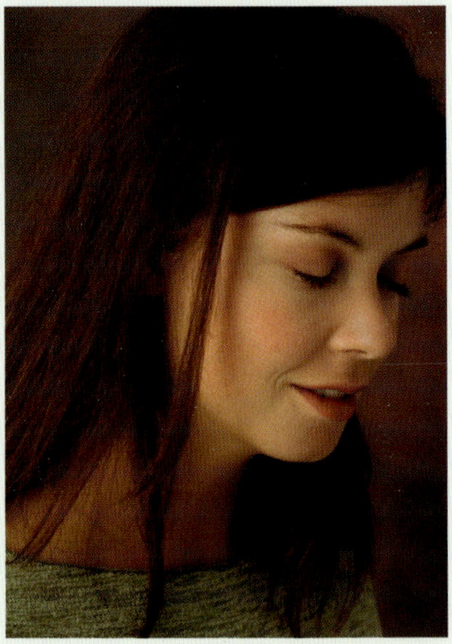

***Left**—The original image. Some of my captures are closer to the final image than others. **Right**—In this version of the image, I changed the contrast and exposure with the tools in Adobe Camera Raw. I also changed the color balance. A final picture is your capture plus your interpretation.*

THE HISTOGRAM

As mentioned above, using the histogram can help you ensure a great exposure. The histogram is a mathematical representation of the image file's exposure information. It shows the tonal distribution in an image. If you took a picture of a gray card without anything else in the picture, the histogram would show a spike in the middle of the graph and nothing else (the image would be comprised of only mid-tones). If you were to give the card more light, overexposing it, the spike would move toward the right side of the graph, because the right side represents lighter density pixels. If you removed light from the shot, the spike would move to the left, showing darker pixels.

What can we say about a shot with a lot of different density pixels in it? If the data does not extend to the very ends of the histogram, you can be sure that all of the information about the image was captured on the sensor. If the data runs to the very edges, you can rest assured that you will see areas of black without detail and white without detail in your final image. If you don't want to see white without detail in the shot, you will need to reduce the amount of light in the shot. If it is an existing light shot, adjust the aperture, shutter speed, or both to let in less light. If this is a strobe exposure, adjusting the shutter speed will not change the amount of light from the strobe. You need to adjust the aperture, ISO, or the power of the strobes. If the information in the graph is pushed against the left side, add light. With practice, it should take only seconds to evaluate a histogram and decide what to do. Here are three examples with an actual image.

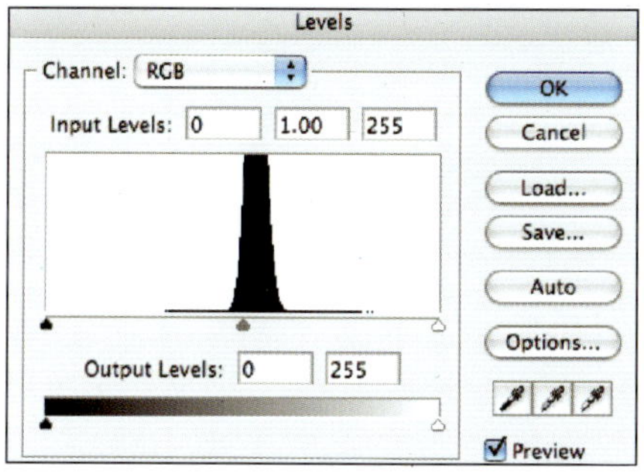

The above swatch is close to a middle gray, and the histogram shows all the pixels are in the middle.

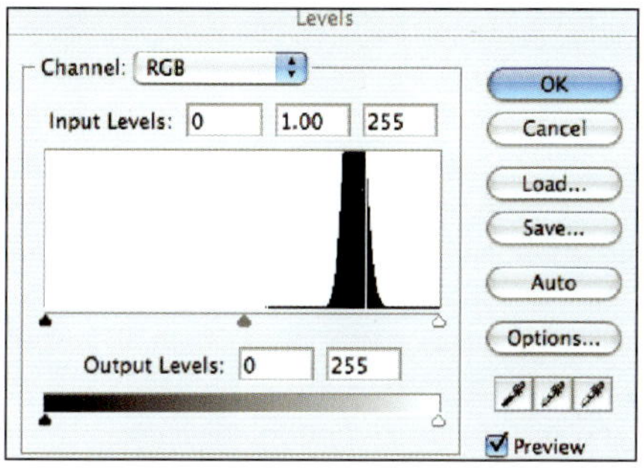

This is a lighter gray swatch, and the pixels have moved to the right.

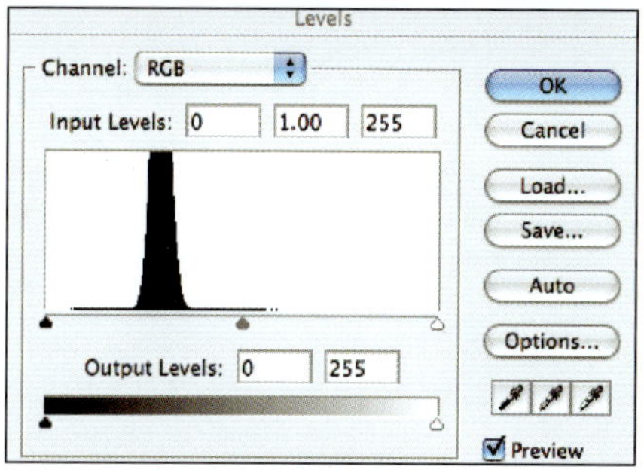

This swatch is the darkest of the three. The histogram shows the pixels have moved toward the left side of the graph.

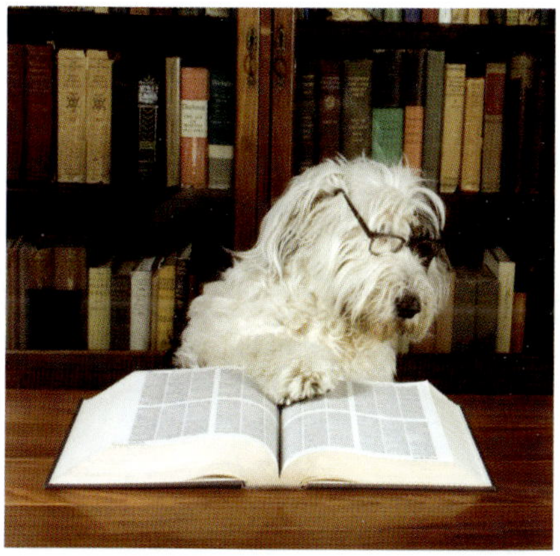

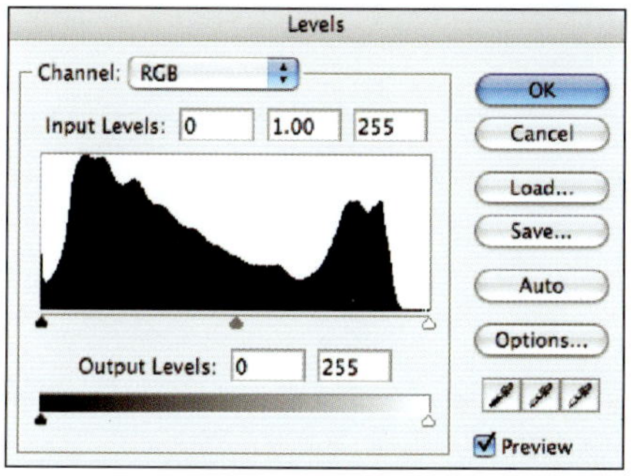

I like the exposure on this shot, but I lose a little detail in the shadows. I don't have bright whites, but that makes sense with this shot.

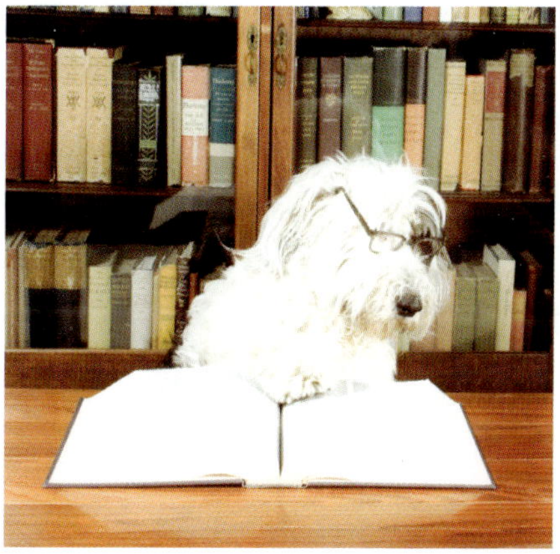

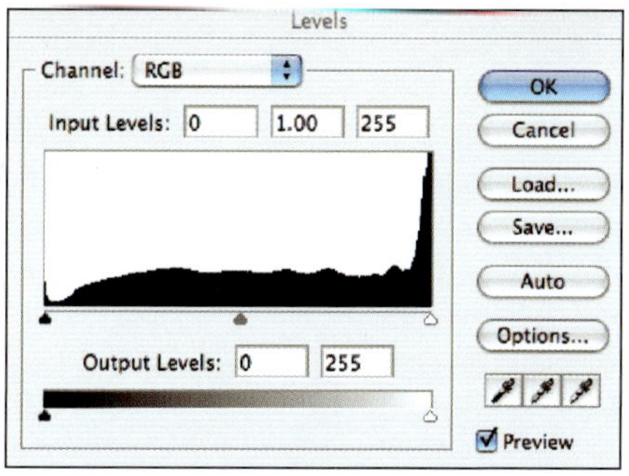

This version is too bright, and the information in this histogram is cut off on the right side.

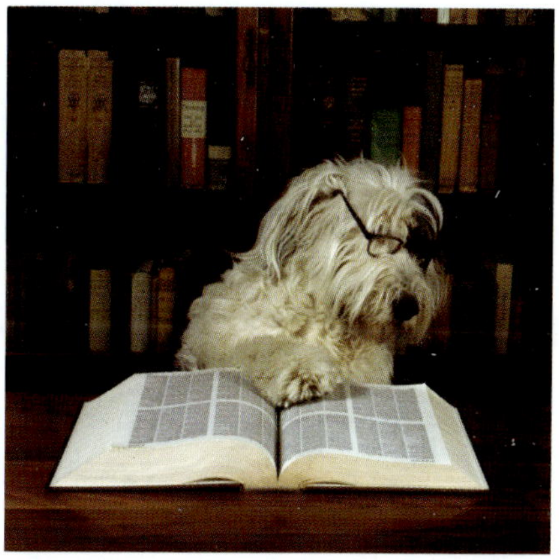

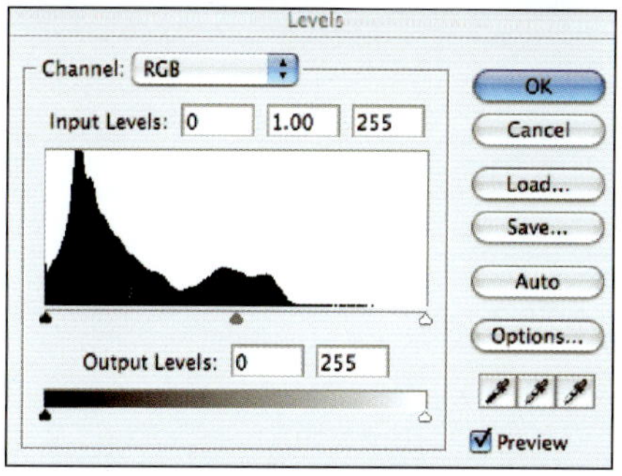

This version is too dark, and you can see the data in the histogram is pulled to the left side.

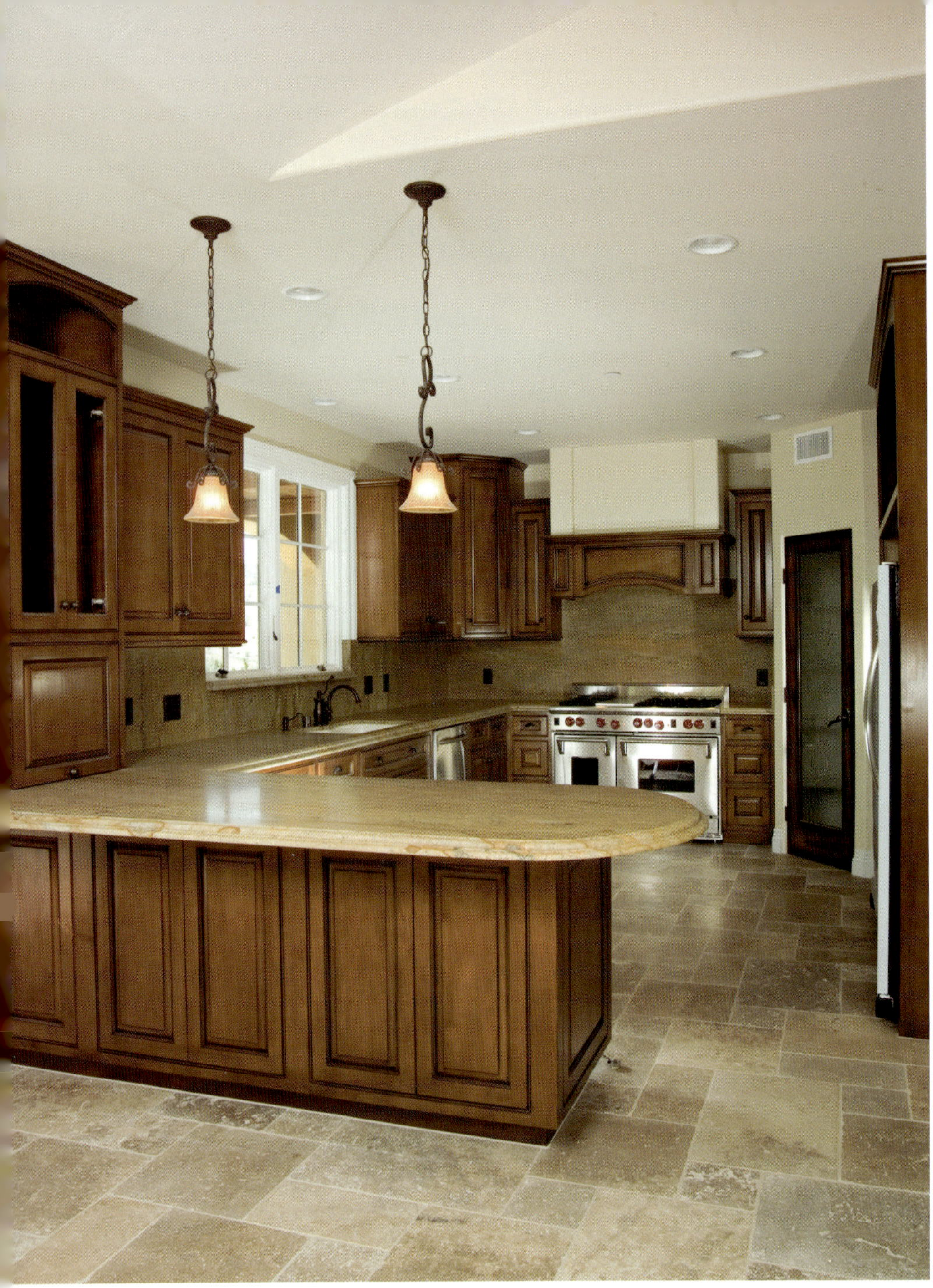

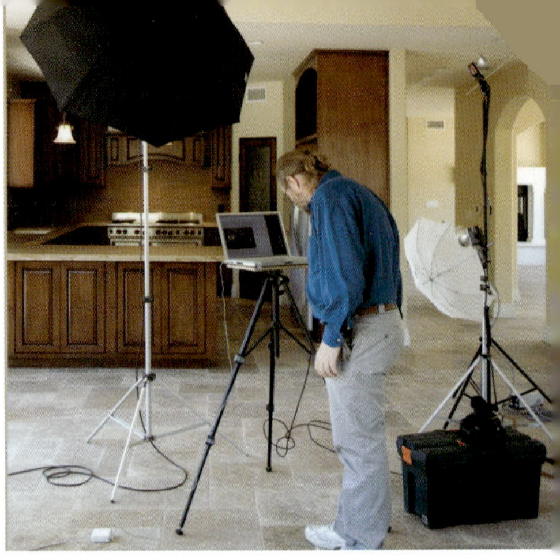

Left and above—Getting the light to work on this shot was easier because I viewed the image on the laptop screen.

TETHERING THE CAMERA TO A COMPUTER

Most DSLR cameras can be tethered to a computer. The advantage of this is that you can evaluate your image with the larger screen of the computer rather than the small LCD screen on the back of the camera. Also, some programs give you more information, like a histogram. This is critical when you are working with lighting. Personally, I am unable to evaluate the subtleties of lighting on a face—where the highlights are, how the light gradates across the face, how the catchlights in the eyes look—on a screen with a 3-inch diagonal.

Most camera manufacturers offer software and cables to allow for tethering the camera and viewing a histogram. There are also wireless options, but I haven't found a need for them.

When I am shooting architectural images, particularly interiors, I shoot everything tethered. I would do the same thing for a product shoot. When I photograph people, I do all my setup shots tethered, then capture the rest of the images on the memory card. This gives me the advantage of the additional information from the tethered system when I adjust the lighting and other aspects of my image. But, I shoot with the camera capture since it is faster, and I don't have a cord going to the computer.

Ansel Adams said that the negative is the musical score and the print is the performance. If you can perfect your capture, the final image will be the best it can be.

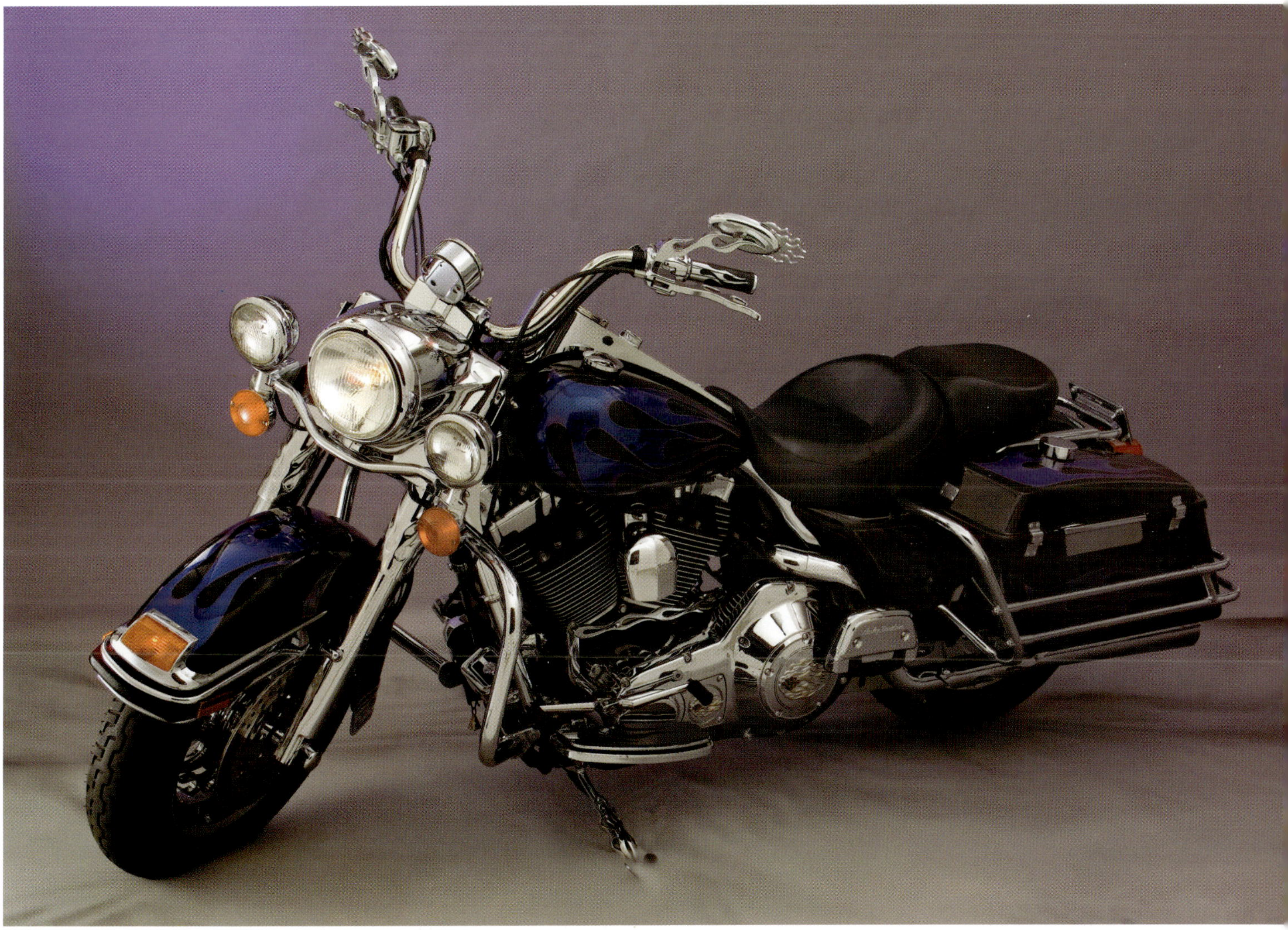

Doing a bike shot like this requires the right light, not just the right exposure!

5. STROBE CONTROLS AND SYNCING

STROBE CONTROLS

Let's take a look at the controls on a monolight. There are similar controls on studio lights. Strobes, except dedicated strobes, are all simple (but that doesn't mean easy). You may find that your unit's controls look different from this one (facing page), but there are only so many things a light can do.

A. On/off switch.
B. Power connection.
C. Modeling light switch. Modeling lights are designed to simulate the effect the flash will give when the flash is triggered. They don't always work very well as a pre-visualizing tool. They are much better tools when they are the only light source. The switch will set the modeling light to always on, always off, and on only when recycled. The last is best, since it lets you know when the unit is ready to shoot.

MODELING LIGHTS ARE DESIGNED TO SIMULATE THE EFFECT THE FLASH WILL GIVE WHEN THE FLASH IS TRIGGERED.

D. Slave switch. On most modern monolights, there is a device that will trigger the strobe if a neighboring strobe goes off. These triggers are called optical slaves. Some units have built-in radio slaves that are triggered directly by the camera. Slaves are useful because you have to set up fewer cables. Slaves are sometimes called cells, particularly on European-made strobes. (More on slaves later in this chapter.)
E. Sync socket. The wire from the camera or an external radio receiver goes to this socket. The only thing the sync does is tell the strobe when to go off. A monolight or studio strobe gives the camera absolutely no exposure information. Only dedicated strobes exchange exposure information with the camera through wireless devices. So, this is a very simple circuit: all it says is now.
F. Slave sensor. This triggers the strobe when another strobe fires.
G. Power output control. This controls the amount of power the strobe puts out. This is usually set up in fractions of full power: Full, ½, ¼, ⅛, 1⁄16, 1⁄32, and maybe smaller. The control is usually continuous, so you can set the strobe between ¼ and ½ power. If you almost always use your strobe on full power, it probably isn't powerful enough. You should have some reserve for really big jobs.
H. Modeling light control. This is a dimmer switch that is designed to make your modeling light match the power of your strobes. I do not feel that

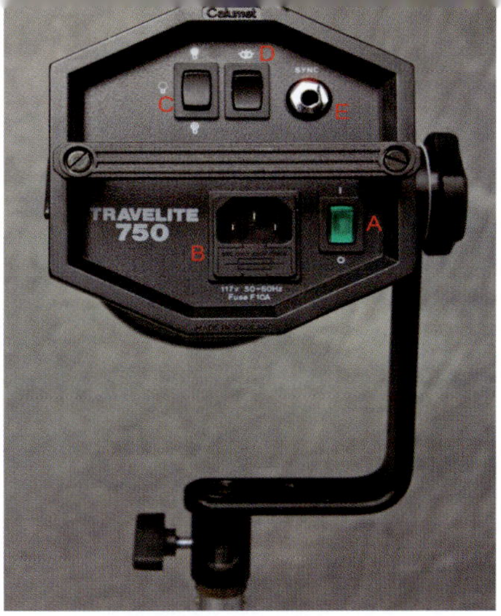

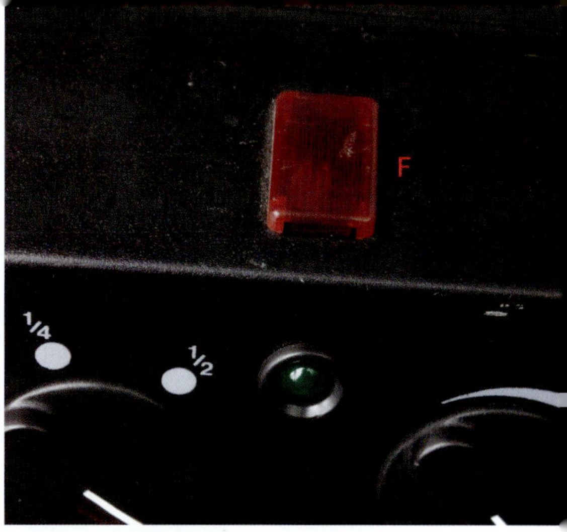

Left—This view shows the monolight's on/off switch, power connector, modeling light switch, sync connection, and slave switch. **Right**—This is the slave sensor. It can trigger the strobe when another strobe fires.

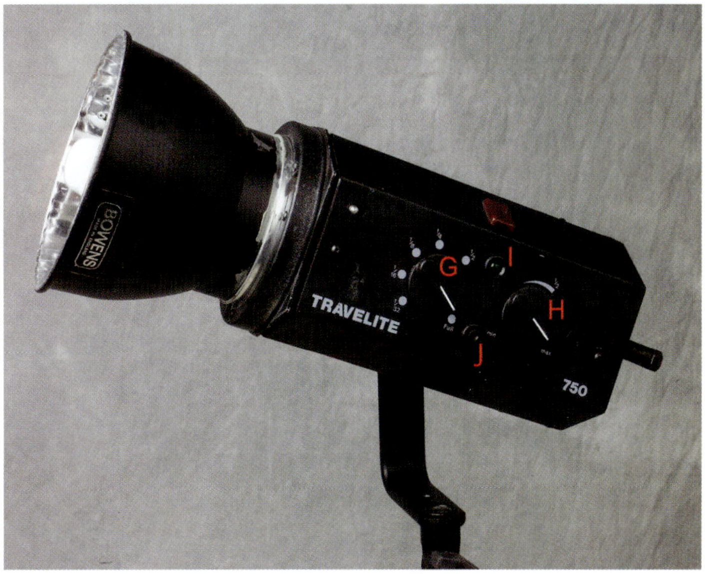

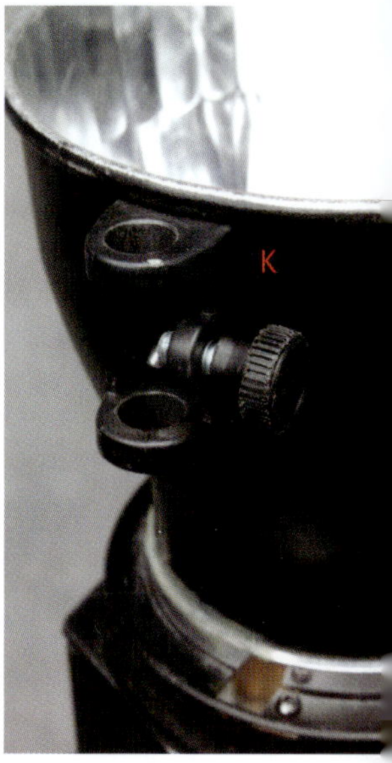

Left—This shot shows the power control, modeling light control, test button, and ready light. **Right**—The umbrella holder.

this concept works well, but I know people who swear by it. Sometimes the modeling light dimmer is coupled to the power control. The idea is if you have one strobe at full power and another at ½ power, you can set the modeling light to ½ power. That way, it will look more like the strobe.

I. Ready light. Tells you the strobe is recycled, you can also set the modeling lights to do this.
J. Open test button. This will allow you to trigger the strobe manually.
K. Umbrella holder. You can mount an umbrella to the strobe using this clamp.

That's it for the controls. They are all simple. Essentially, you can change the power of a light, and everything else you do with light modifiers.

Monolights are designed for use with AC power (wall sockets). Many of the current models have auxiliary battery systems that allow you to work on location. If you often have to work at locations without power, you may want to look at gear that was designed to work with batteries. Norman, Lumidyne,

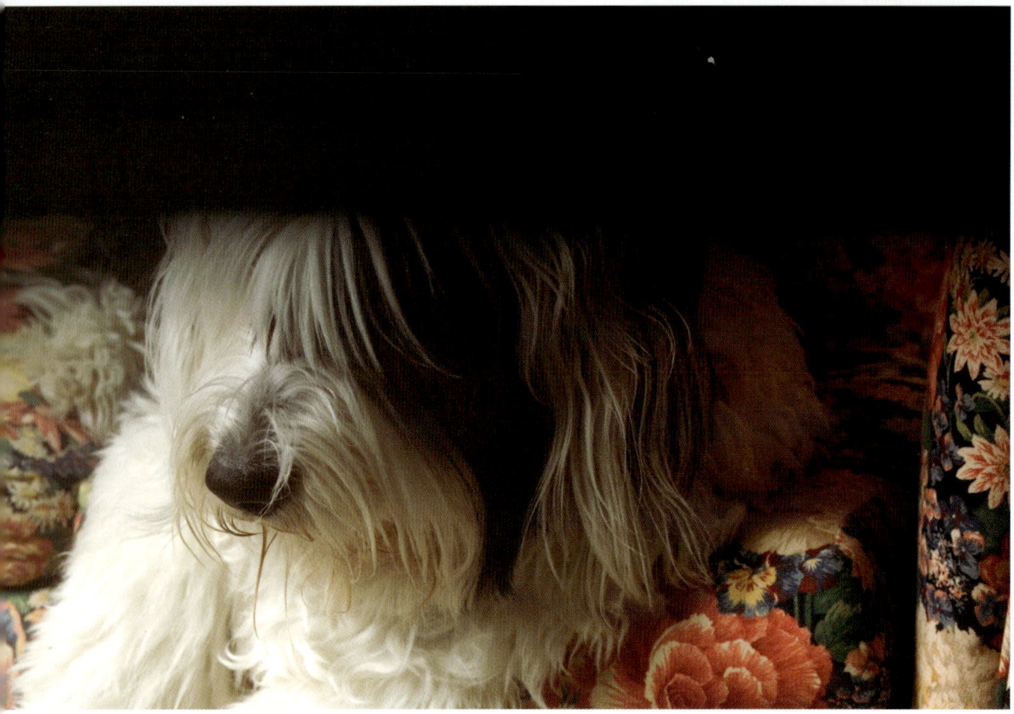

The second shutter curtain covers part of the sensor in this shot, so part of the picture is black. A longer shutter speed would have solved this problem.

Quantum, and other manufacturers make this kind of equipment. There is more information on this in the section about working on location.

SYNC SPEEDS

In a camera with a focal plane shutter, the shutter is comprised of two curtains—the first (front) curtain uncovers the sensor to start the exposure and the second (rear) curtain ends the exposure. When the front curtain of the shutter uncovers the sensor, the strobe is triggered. If the rear curtain has already started to cover the image sensor, part of the picture will be black. This happens when the shutter is set to a fast speed. For the light of the strobe to be properly recorded, the entire sensor has to be uncovered at the same time.

The shutter speed at which the entire frame is exposed when the flash is fired is called the sync speed. Your camera will sync at any speed longer than the sync speed, but not at a speed shorter than the sync speed. The sync speed varies from one camera to another, so check your user's manual to determine yours.

High-Speed Sync. A few cameras and dedicated strobes are set up for a high-speed sync. The nice thing about this high-speed sync is not stopping action but reducing the existing light in a shot. This gives you more control when mixing daylight and strobe—a technique called flash fill. Any modern dedicated strobe can do flash fill very well. The high-speed sync is not a necessary feature.

In addition to allowing us to take pictures with light from strobes, there are various ways to use sync to creatively mix existing light with strobes. We have

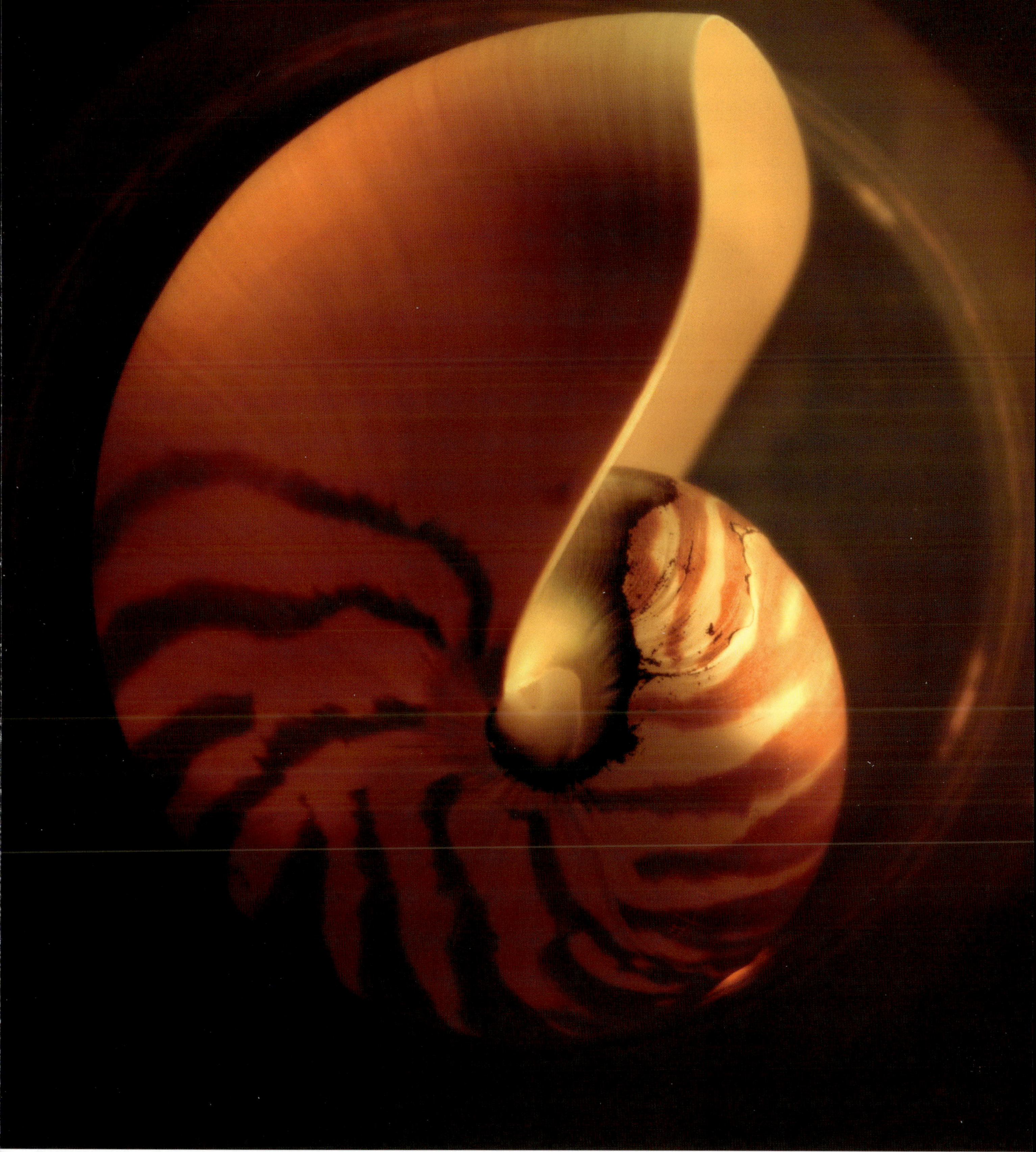

Most of the light in this shot comes from a grid spot pointed into the mouth of the shell. Some of the light from the grid spot was masked off with Cinefoil to make an even smaller spot. The shell is on a glass plate, and there is a very small amount of light coming from below the plate. The color was shifted using filters on the lights.

extra control because strobe lasts for such a short time. For instance, you can have a picture where the action is stopped by the strobe, while it is blurred by the existing light. The amount of blur is controlled by the length of the shutter speed. This effect shows a sense of movement and speed in an image.

If the strobes go off at the beginning of the exposure (this is called front-curtain sync), the blur will be in front of the image. If the strobes go off at the end of the exposure (this is called rear-curtain sync), the blur will follow the strobe. Both approaches can make good images.

TRIGGERING THE STROBE

To trigger your off-camera flash, you'll need to rely on a cord or slave. Let's look at these options.

Sync Cords. There are a variety of cords on the market that can be used to transmit the triggering information between your flash and camera. The cords connect directly to your camera via the PC socket (usually found opposite the shutter release button) or hot shoe (found on the top of the camera).

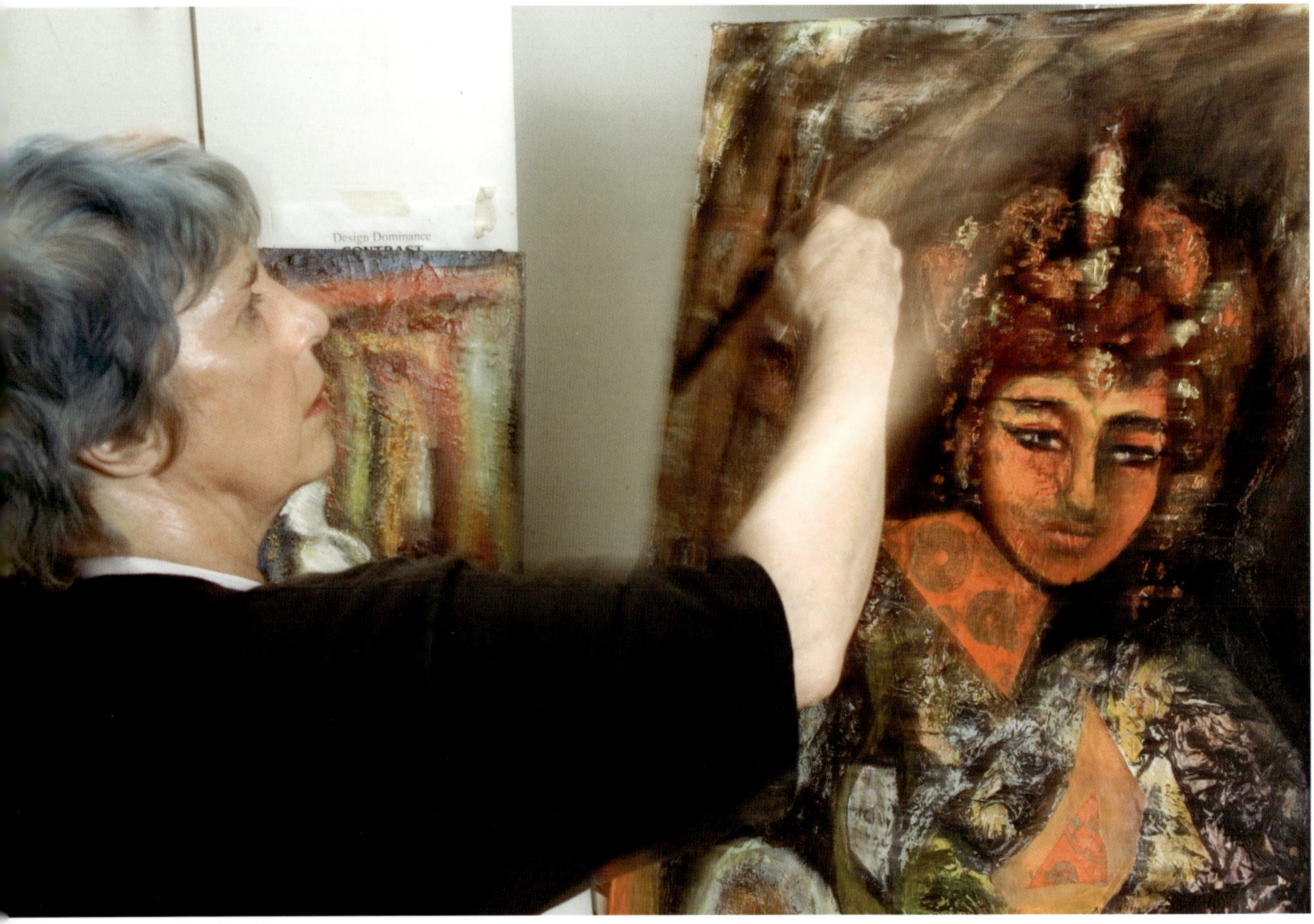

Long sync speed allowed the artist's hand to blur, creating a sense of movement.

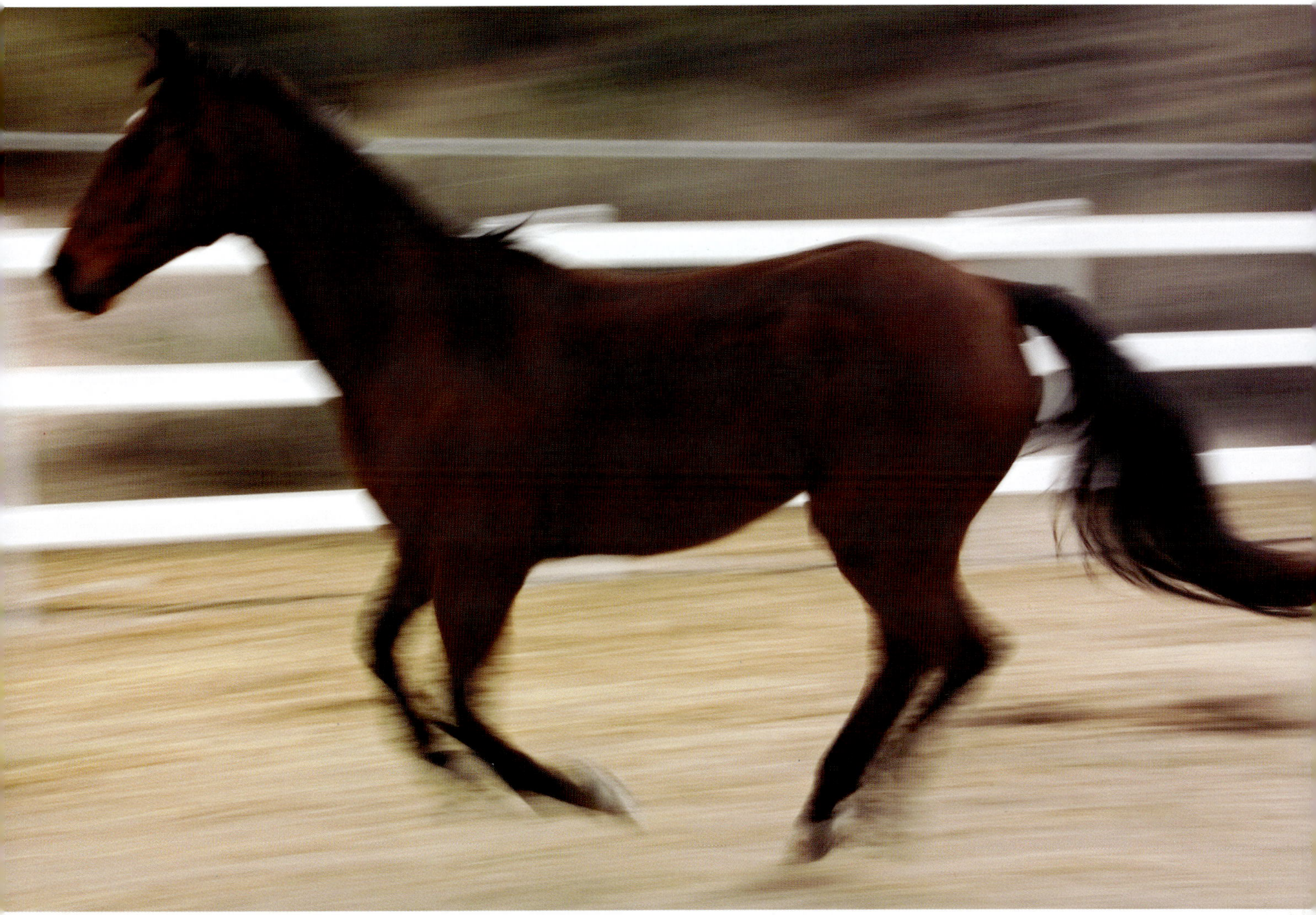

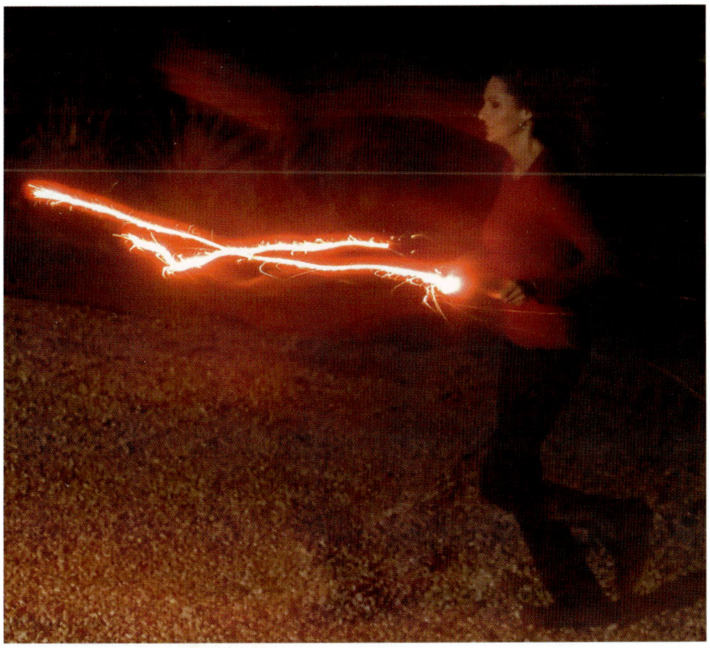

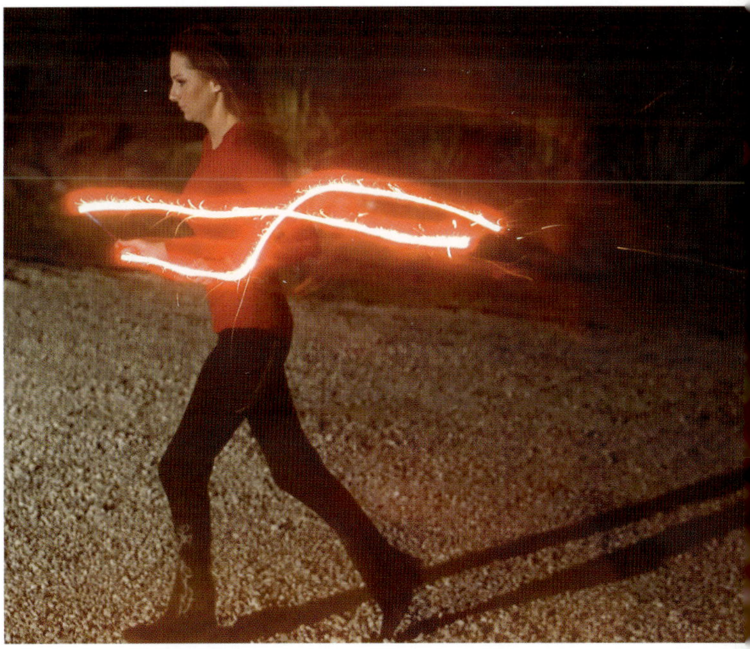

Top—The combination of strobe and daylight gives you a shot that presents a sense of speed. **Bottom left and right**—When the strobes go off at the beginning of a shot, the blur is in front of the sharp image from the strobe. When the strobes are triggered at the end of the shot, the blur trails the sharp image.

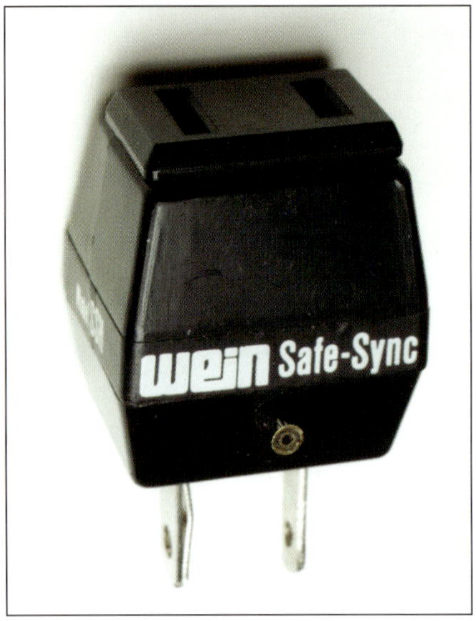

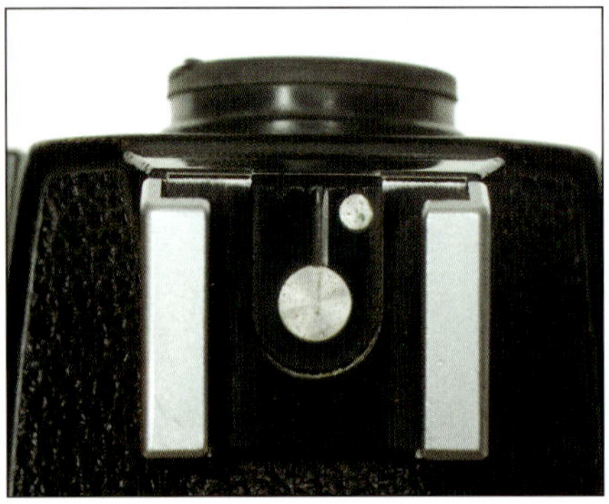

Top—A safe sync keeps high-voltage strobes from damaging your camera. This one is designed for a studio pack. There are other designs for different equipment. **Bottom**—A camera hot shoe. Modern ones have more contacts.

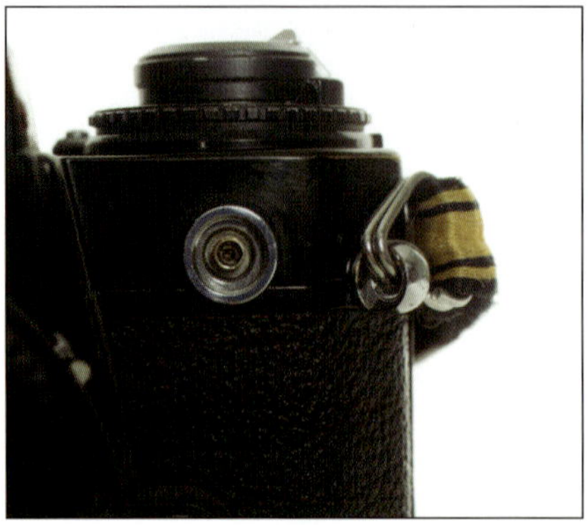

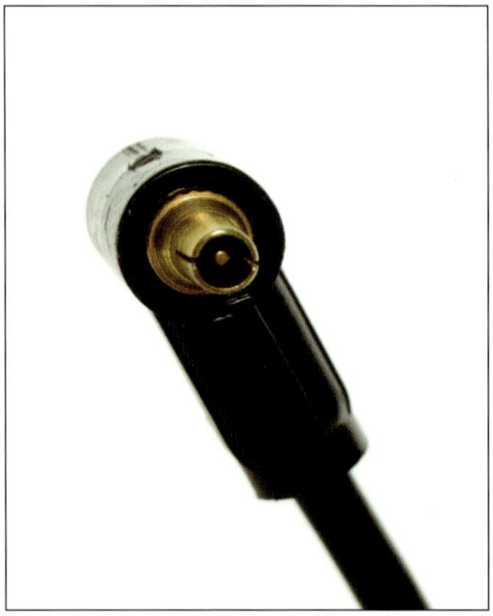

Top—A PC socket on a camera body. **Bottom**—This is the end of the PC cord that goes into the camera.

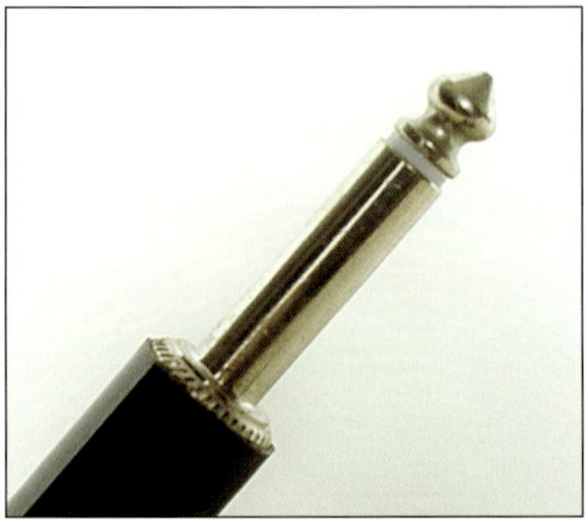

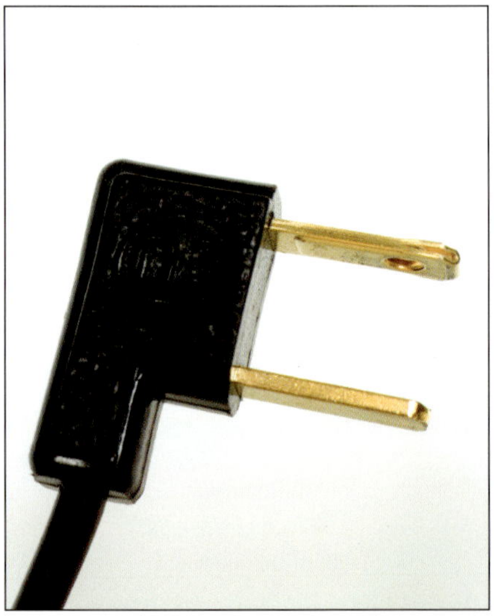

Top—There are a number of names for this plug. I usually call it a guitar plug. It was first used for telephones. **Bottom**—This is the same plug used in homes. Don't plug your camera into the wall socket!

Older flash units produce more electricity than newer models and can wreak havoc on newer cameras. Consider using a safe sync to protect your camera if you are considering using older strobes.

Sync cords tend to have one of two plugs. Most use a .25x1.25-inch plug, which looks like an old-style headphone plug. Others use a regular household plug, just as you'd find on a lamp or a blender. The problem with the household plug is that if you have a momentary lapse of thinking, you could plug it into the wall socket. This would be very bad!

Radio Slaves. A radio slave can be used to wirelessly trigger your strobe. This requires a transmitter that attaches to the hot shoe and a receiver that attaches to the strobe. With radio slaves, there is no long wire connected to the camera, which makes handling the camera easier. Also there is no potentially damaging high voltage being sent to the camera, which is very nice. There are several kinds of radio slaves on the market, and there is a wide range of costs. Units like the Pocket Wizard cost between $150 and $300. You can find units made in China and sold on eBay for $15 to $50. I have some of the Chinese radio slaves, and they work well.

Now, if you want multiple strobes to work together in a single shot, all units must be triggered at once. If you have multiple receivers for a radio slave, you can use them to do this. Because of the low price of some radio slaves, this is a good option.

Optical Slaves. Optical slaves are another option for triggering multiple strobes. These trigger the strobe they are connected to when they are hit by the light from another strobe. You can get external slaves that will trigger

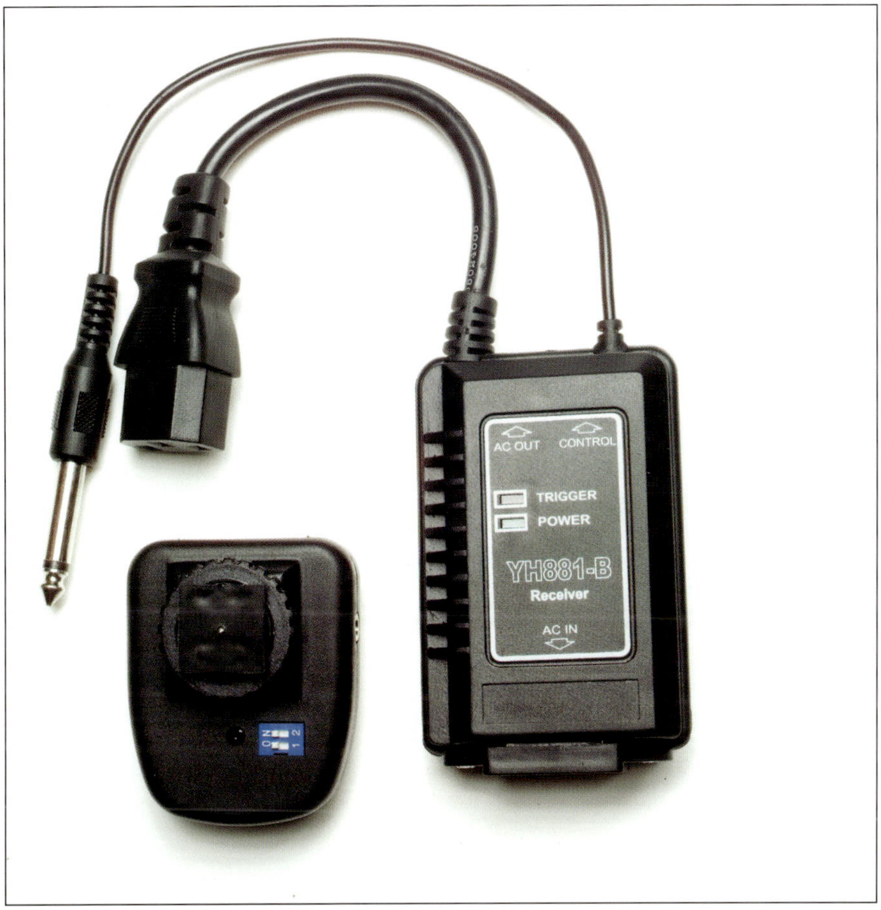

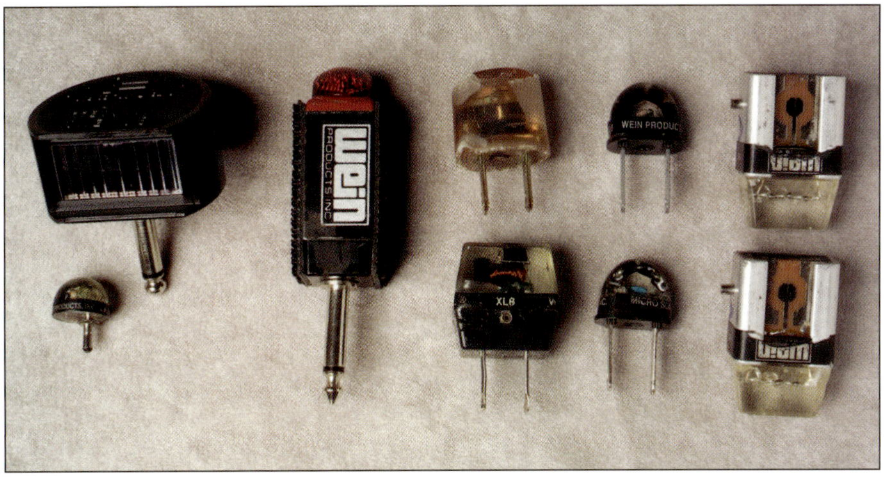

Top—An inexpensive radio slave. **Bottom**—There are hot shoe slaves, household plug slaves, and slaves for the guitar plugs available.

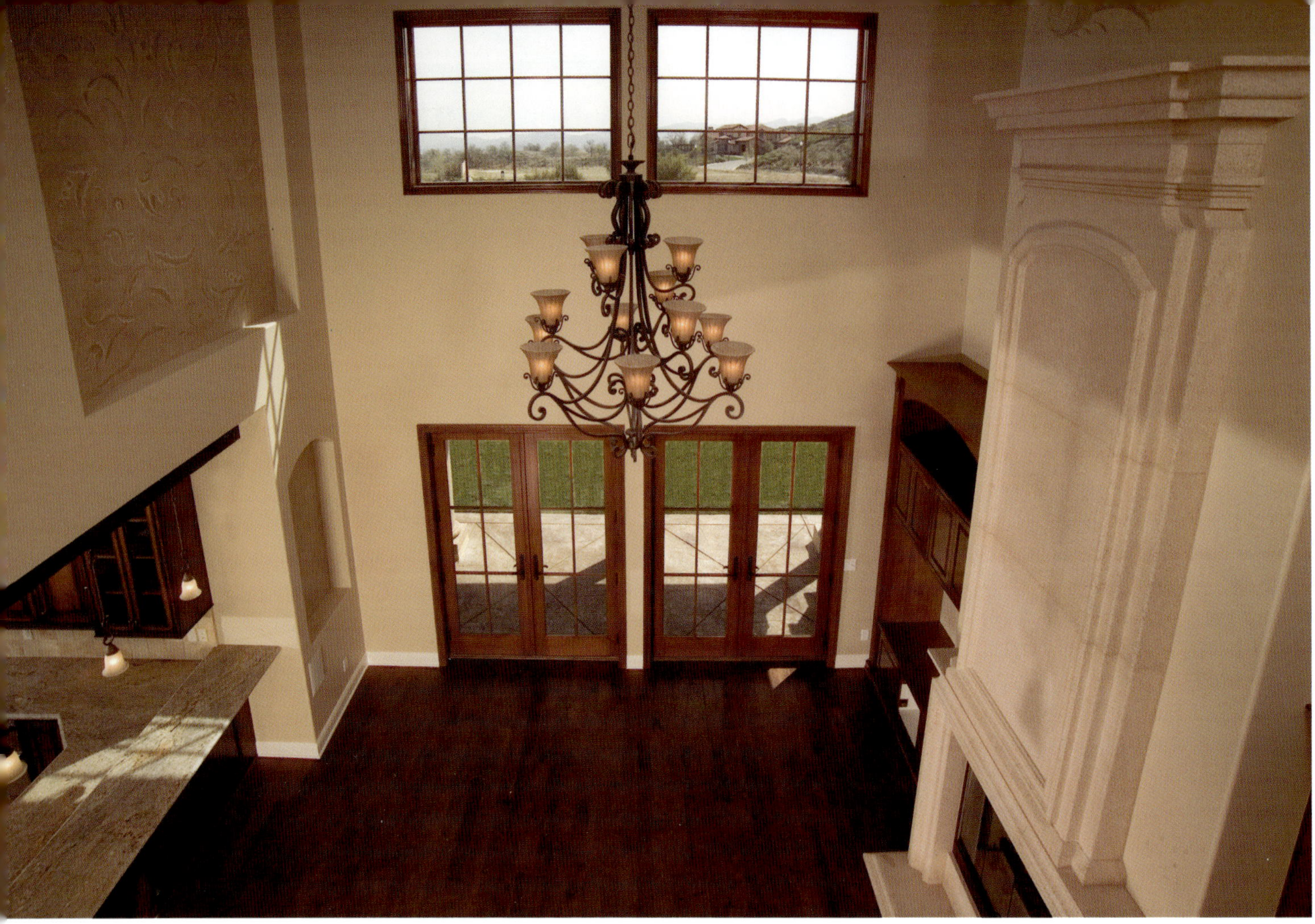

Optical slaves may be a little annoying, but a handful of them will make impossible shots doable! I balanced four separate strobes with daylight to get this shot. I couldn't have done it without optical or radio slaves.

equipment without built-in slaves. These can be simple tools and often cost as little as $15. Of course, more sensitive slaves cost more. These slaves are built into many monolights and some studio packs.

Infrared Triggering. There is another method for triggering strobes from a distance: infrared triggers. I tried the infrared triggering system for my strobes. The unit I chose was powered by AA batteries and took forever to recycle. I have expensive strobes that recycle in less than 2 seconds, but my trigger unit wasn't ready for at least 7 seconds. I don't like to wait. Also, the receivers were very sensitive to other light sources, so the strobes went off when I didn't want them to.

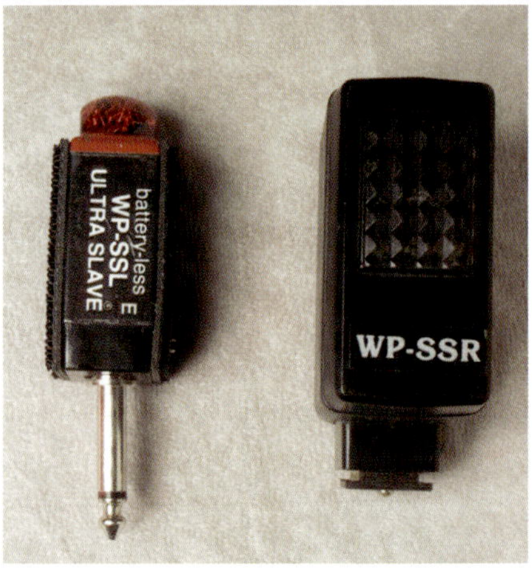

An infrared trigger and slave. I really wasn't happy with these units.

FINAL THOUGHTS

Sync is the key to controlling strobes, making them easier to use in your shot. It's not difficult to sync a strobe with your camera, but all these cords and slaves are subject to failure, so be sure to have a backup. Without sync, your strobes can't give you light!

6. WORKING WITH ONE LIGHT

There are several reasons to work with one light. One of the most important is so that you can understand how one light source works. If you understand the way one light works—how the size and position of the light affect the subject—it will be easier to add other lights to your shots. Other reasons for working with a single light are the ease, speed, and flexibility of your lighting setup. When I work, I want to be able to start with a powerful character light and move to a soft light without interrupting the flow of the shoot. I can do that with one light and a few simple tools!

In this chapter, I will be using just one light and the modifiers described in chapter 3 to demonstrate relatively simple strategies for portrait lighting and a more complex tabletop lighting setup.

JUST AN UMBRELLA

For the first shot in this exercise, I used a Norman LH2400 strobe head with just 250 watt-seconds of power, plus a 42-inch ribless umbrella. My aperture

Left—This image was made with a single umbrella. The light works, but it could be better. **Right**—For this shot, I placed one light on a stand and positioned it above the subject and to one side. It was a quick and easy setup.

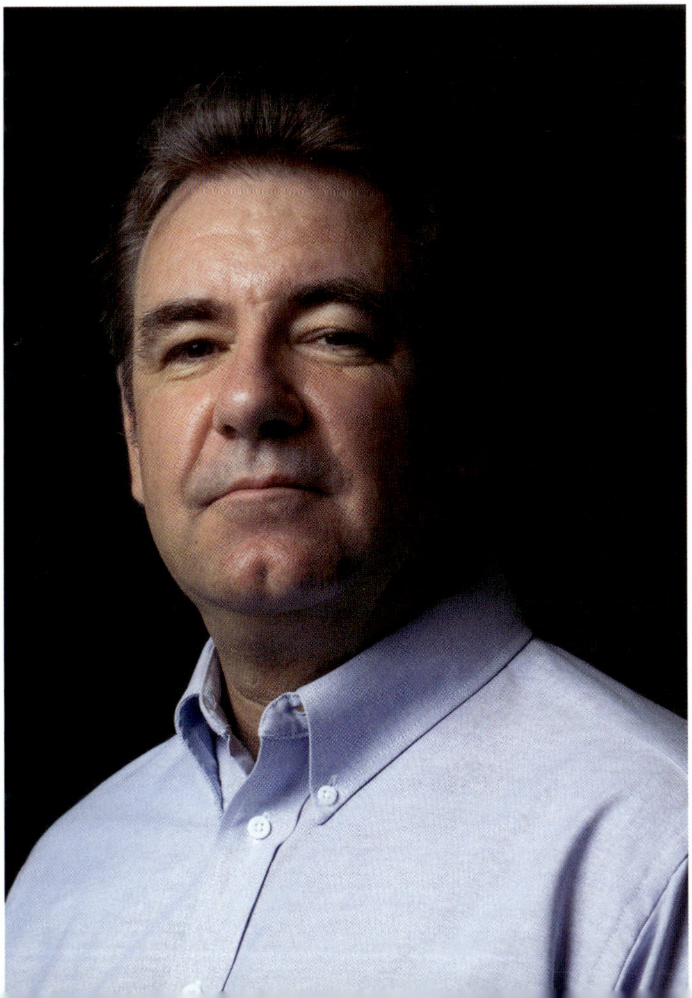

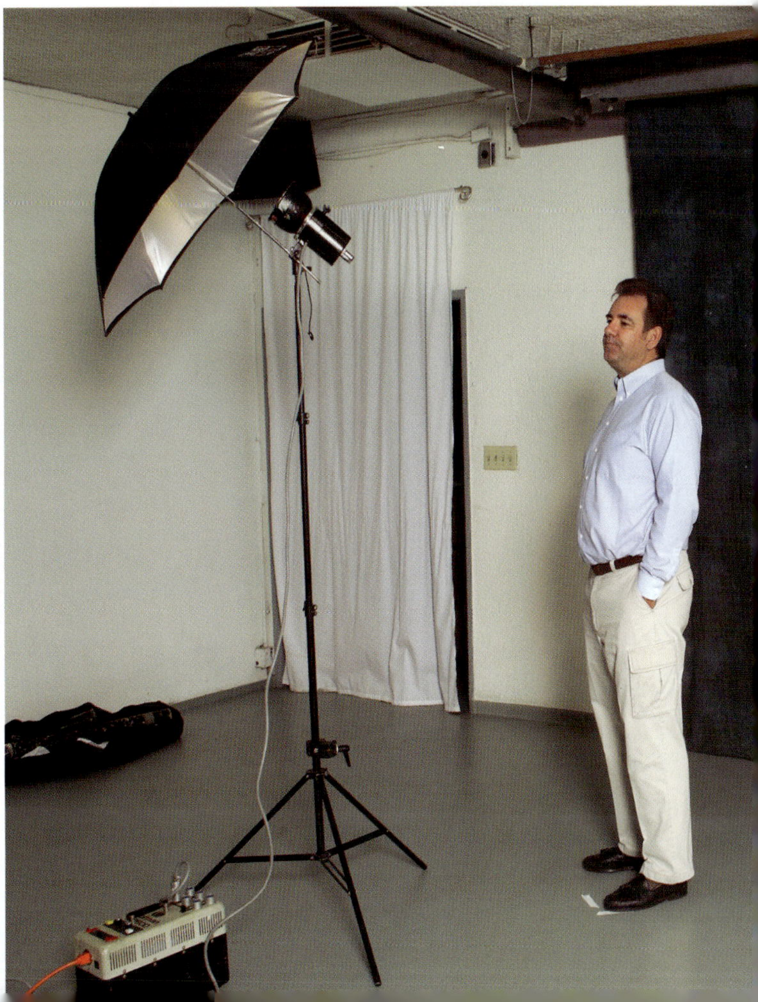

was set at f/11.3. Though umbrellas often create more even lighting, the effect here is a little harsh because the light is directional and there is no light filling in the shadows. (If you shoot in a small studio space with white walls, the bounced light will fill in the shadows.)

Using a setup like this is great for creating character shots, as texture and shape are well defined. The closer the light is to the subject, the less defined the character lines will be.

ADD A REFLECTOR

I added a large reflector panel to the first shot to create the two images below. I shot two frames—one with a silver reflector and the other with a gold one. Once again, this is a very fast and easy change. Much of the character of the first image is retained, but I've opened up the shadows. People often set up a portrait with the lights and reflectors at distances of more than 5 feet from the subject. This will greatly reduce the smoothness of the light in the image.

MAKE A LARGER LIGHT SOURCE

To create the next image, I added a light panel covered with white cotton broadcloth between the umbrella and the subject. This created a soft light the size of the panel. Compare the resulting image to the first shot in this chapter: you can see that the diffused light has yielded softer highlights and there is a smoother transition from highlight to shadow. This light is more flattering, as the wrinkles are not as well defined.

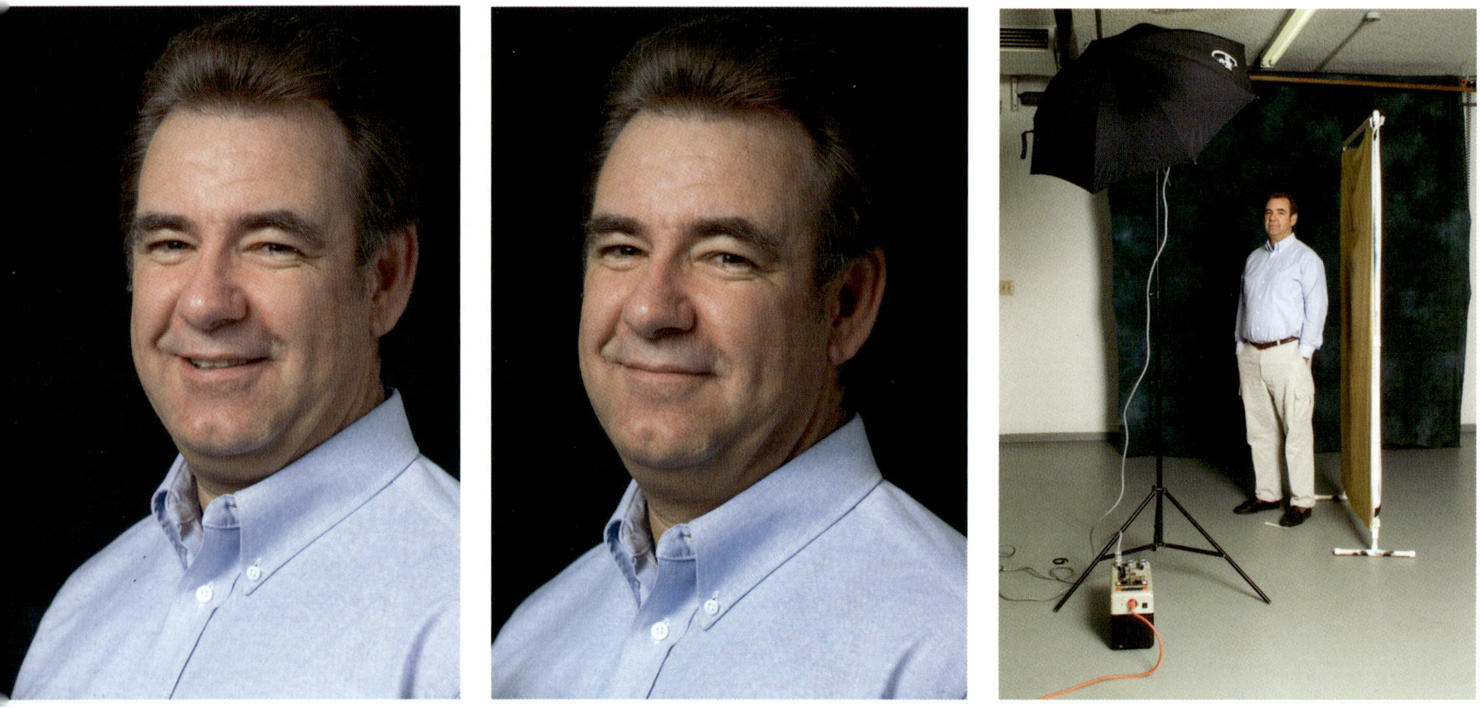

Left—Silver reflector. **Center**—Gold reflector. Note that the gold reflector warmed up the shadows. **Right**—I added a reflector to the original setup to open up the shadows.

Left—To create this shot, I positioned a light panel between the umbrella and the subject. **Right**—Here I used the umbrella/light panel combination. I use this setup a lot.

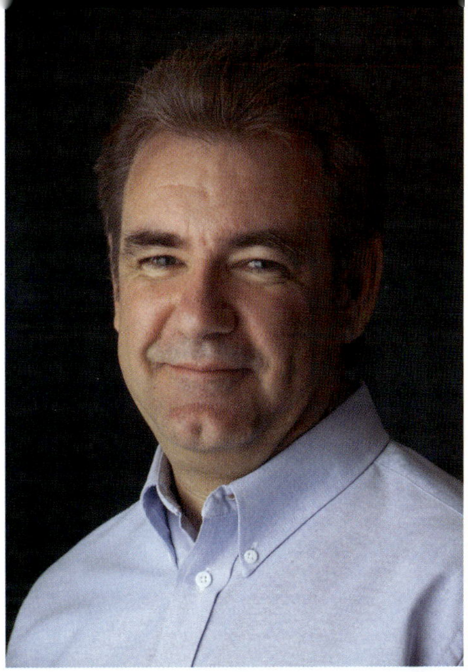

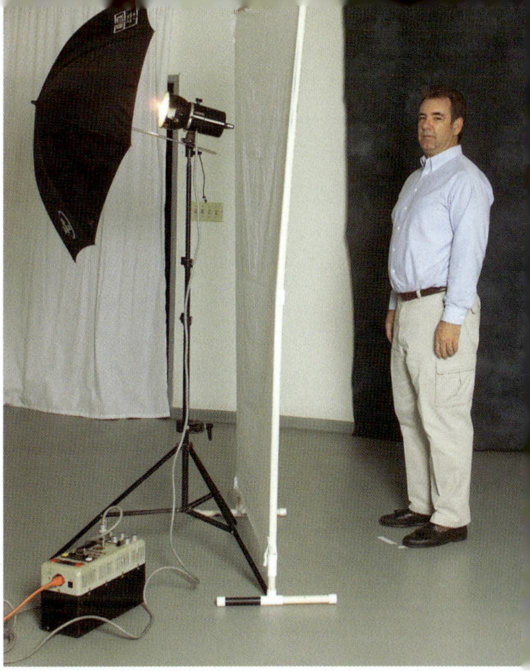

Left—Adding a silver reflector allowed me to fill in the shadows on the right side of the frame, building light that is even softer than that produced by the umbrella alone. The result is similar to the image above, but there is more fill. **Right**—Here is the setup.

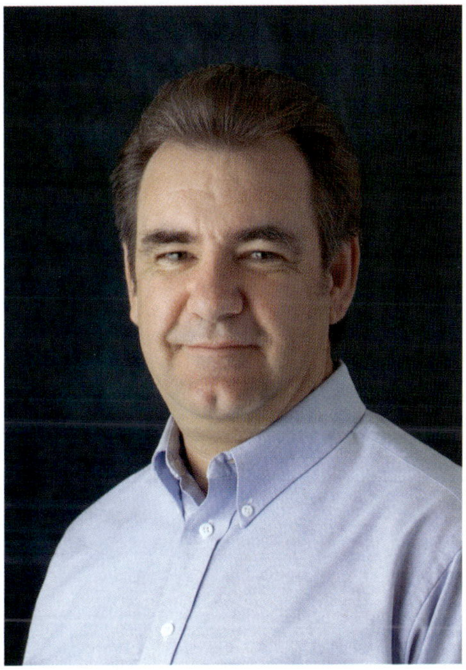

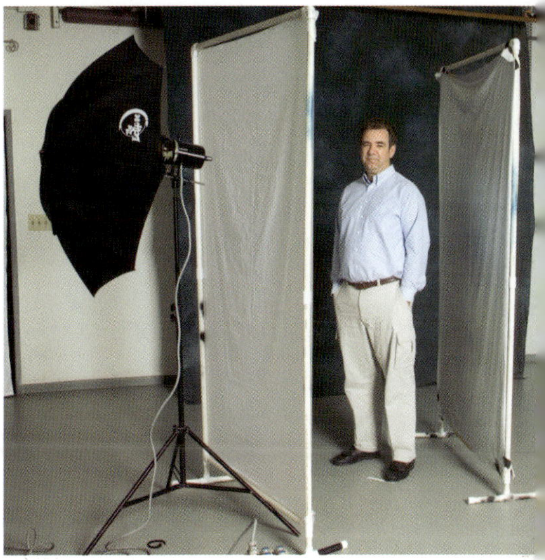

The light panel sucked up some light in this rendition of the subject, so I added more light to achieve a similar aperture.

BRING BACK THE REFLECTOR

For the next image, I added a silver reflector, just like I did in the second image. It was placed opposite the diffuser, creating two walls of light. The result is similar to the previous image, but there is more fill. The character lines are softer. That makes many people happy. Because I haven't changed the light source, there was no change in the exposure. Remember, you can opt to use a gold or white reflector to vary the color of the reflected light if you choose.

You can position the reflector so it gets more light directly from the umbrella, rather than just through the light panel. This makes the reflector

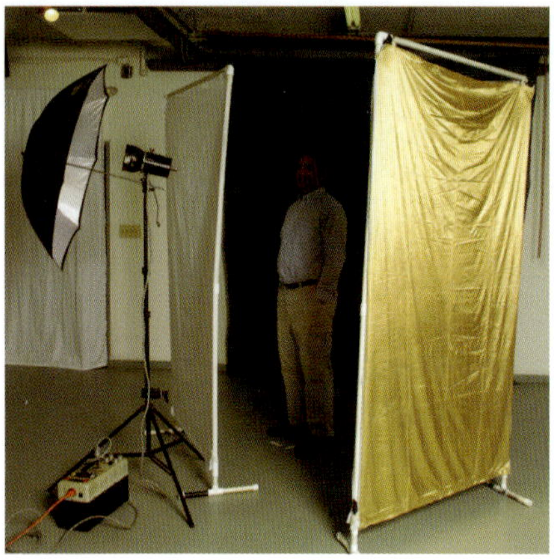

Above—For this shot, I positioned the reflector to pick up more light from the umbrella than from the panel. **Right**—The light on the subject's face is very even in this shot. The silver reflector added some highlights, and there isn't anything filling in from the subject's left side.

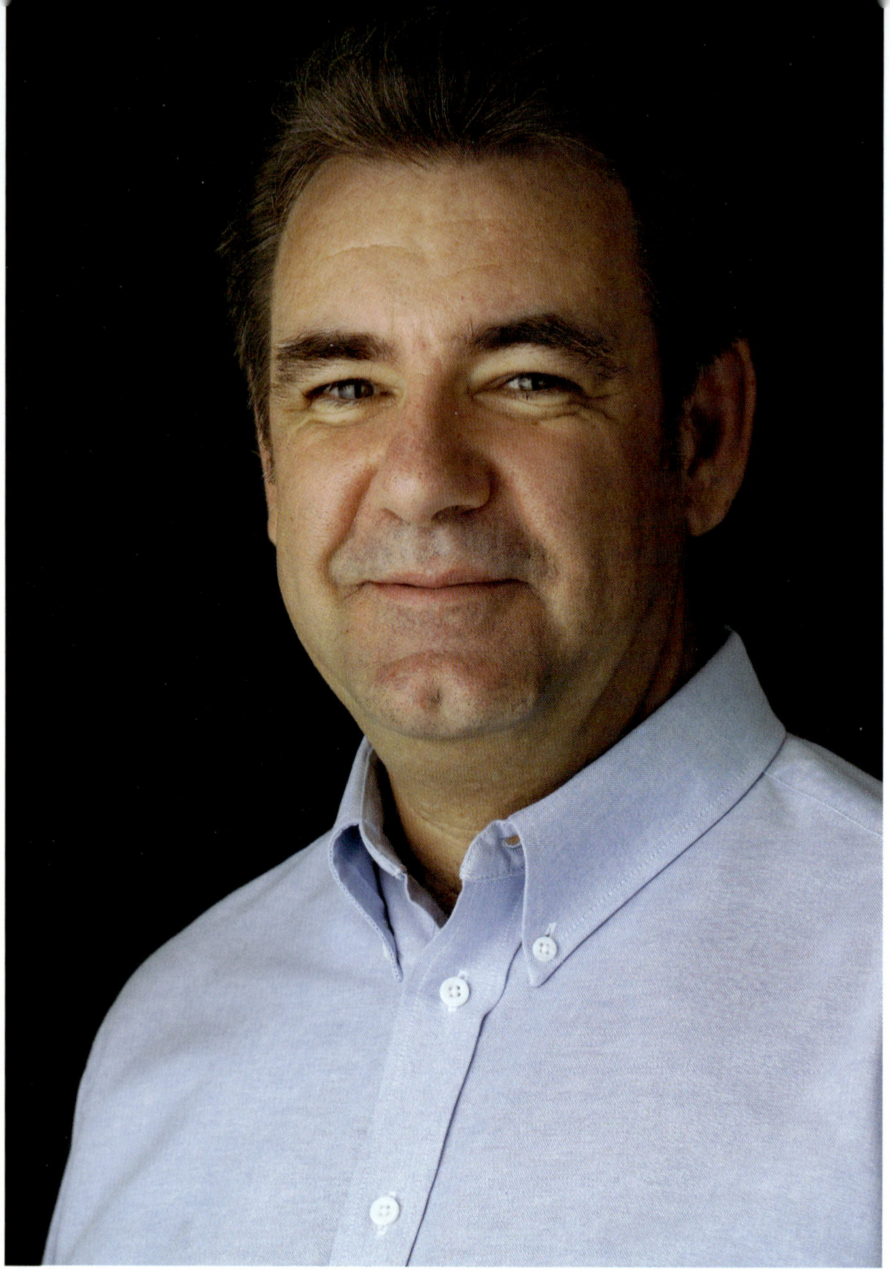

brighter compared to the side of the shot with the light panel and gives you a very soft, even light, like a tent. This will change your exposure a little because you are going to have to adjust the reflector and the light with the umbrella. I use this when I need a quick setup for a shot.

MORE PRACTICE

Single-light shots are an excellent way to practice lighting. In this case, I used a sculpture model as a subject. Styrofoam wig heads can be very useful practice subjects. This shot uses several light modifiers. It is a lot easier to gain experience with these tools when you aren't using a live subject.

When I set up a shoot, I first establish the relationship between the subject and the camera. This prevents putting a light where I want to place the camera. When photographing this model, my first concern was to hide its wire support. I also wanted to set the depth of field to create an increasing softness closer to the model's feet in order to make it appear more human sized. Since I shot this with a Toyo 4x5 camera and a 210mm lens, the f/11 aperture I chose produced very little depth of field, which was perfect for this shot. If I had done the same thing with a digital camera, I might have chosen to work at f/4.

Using multiple reflectors is the best way to make a one-light image look like one made with several lights. For this shot, I chose to use a continuous quartz light. It would have been difficult to set up this image with strobes, because it is harder to work with all of the small reflectors.

Before you set up your reflectors, of course, you must know where your light source will be positioned. It is important to place the light in an area where it can be accessed from different directions. I decided to place the light above the subject. This enabled me to use mirrors to reflect the light in from the sides. Then I pointed the light into a ribless umbrella. The black cover on the umbrella kept the light from spreading. The umbrella is marked "A" in the diagram.

I put a light panel with two layers of white ripstop nylon between the light source and the subject. I used two layers because I wanted to reduce the amount of light from above so that the overhead illumination would not overwhelm the reflected light. I placed a blue Rosco Cinegel on top of the diffuser to further reduce the amount of light from overhead and create an overall, low-level blue light on the set. The light has a subtle effect overall, but it is more evident on the upper area of the model's camera-right arm. The gelled light panel is marked "B" in the diagram.

Next, I placed a piece of black duvetyn fabric opposite the camera to absorb light and prevent it from bouncing into the shot. I added a large black card to the right side of the set for the same reason. The light panel and duvetyn are

This is an exercise in using one light. The object is to use reflectors and filters to make an interesting light. The diagram shows how I approached the image. The light was placed above the set and diffusers and reflectors were used to modify the quality of the light. The purpose of these tools is described in the text.

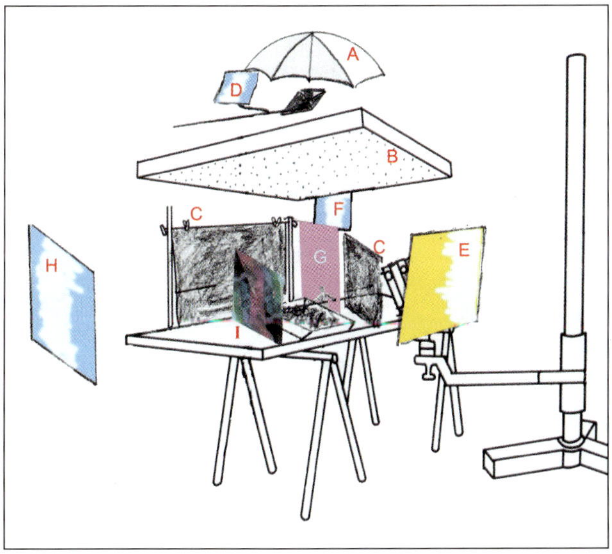

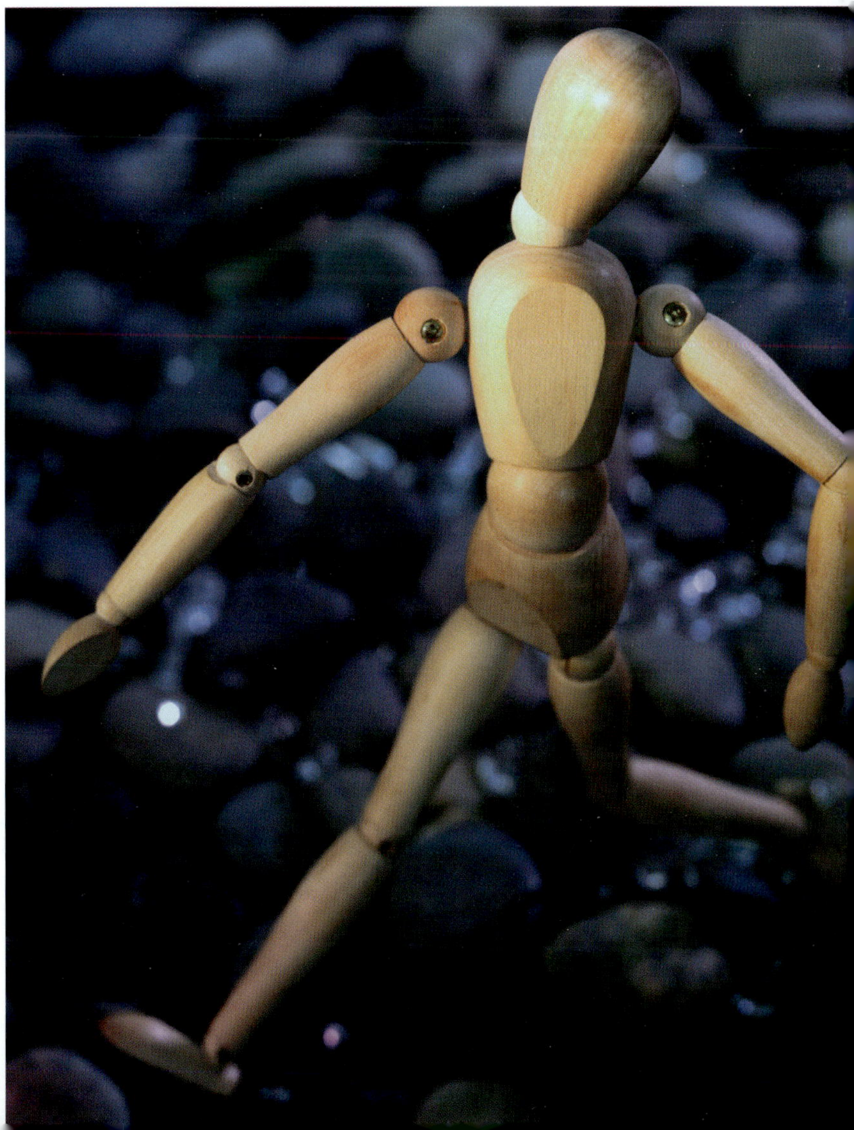

as important as adding light: they add shadow and create shape. Even lighting produces a flat look. Shadows help produce a feeling of three-dimensionality. The duvetyn is marked "C" in the diagram.

Now to direct some more light onto the front of subject. When I conceptualized the shot, I imagined a direct light hitting the top of the model. If I used a large light source for the front illumination, I would lose the three-dimensional effect in the head and chest of the model. I also wanted to add a warm color to this light to help offset the blue light from overhead. This color difference helps to make the model stand out from the pebbles in the finished piece. In order to do this I used a Lowel Tota-flector to bounce light directly from the Smith-Victor light before it hit the umbrella. The Tota-flector (marked "D" in the diagram) is part of a system that mounts both reflectors and flags onto flexible shafts. In this case, I mounted the flexible shaft onto the boom arm that the light is mounted on. I bounced the light onto a piece of gold Plexiglas mirror (marked "E") and then onto the model—something like a two-corner bank shot, but it's easier to get the light where you want it than to make that bank shot on a pool table—you just move the second reflector. Once you know where the reflector needs to be, you can mount it on a light stand. Keep in mind that we are bouncing light from the quartz bulb, not the umbrella, so the light is potentially much brighter than the light coming from above the model. Because the light was reflected off of gold Plexiglas, there is a considerable amount of color, warmth, and contrast in the lighting.

I set up two more reflectors to further adjust the light on the model. The first, an 8x12-inch silver Tota-flector, was positioned behind the set (marked "F"). This reflector bounced light from the umbrella into the back and side of the model, helping to separate the subject from the background by creating a more defined edge. The light from this reflector appears more subtle in this case because it was reflected from the umbrella. This light was filtered through a lavender Cinegel (marked "G"). This gave me the color and smoothness I wanted in the backlight. Another advantage of this light can be seen in the reflections in the broken glass: many of the shards were illuminated by this backlight. The color of the reflections in the broken glass is the tip-off to the source of the light.

The final reflector has some wonderful characteristics. The light goes through a simulated stained glass window! First let's pay attention to the mirror (marked "H"); it is about 18x24 inches, so it throws a big piece of light. A bigger reflector creates a larger light source that will have a greater tendency to diffuse over the subject. The mirror that creates this light is farther from the set than the other mirrors. The first reason for this is that the larger distance helps to balance the brightness value with the other reflectors. The other reason is that the light needs to go under the diffusion panel. The Plexiglas

Facing page—The job had to be done quickly, so I used only one light. The sunlight became an important part of the overall light.

EVEN LIGHTING PRODUCES A FLAT LOOK. SHADOWS HELP PRODUCE A FEELING OF THREE-DIMENSIONALITY.

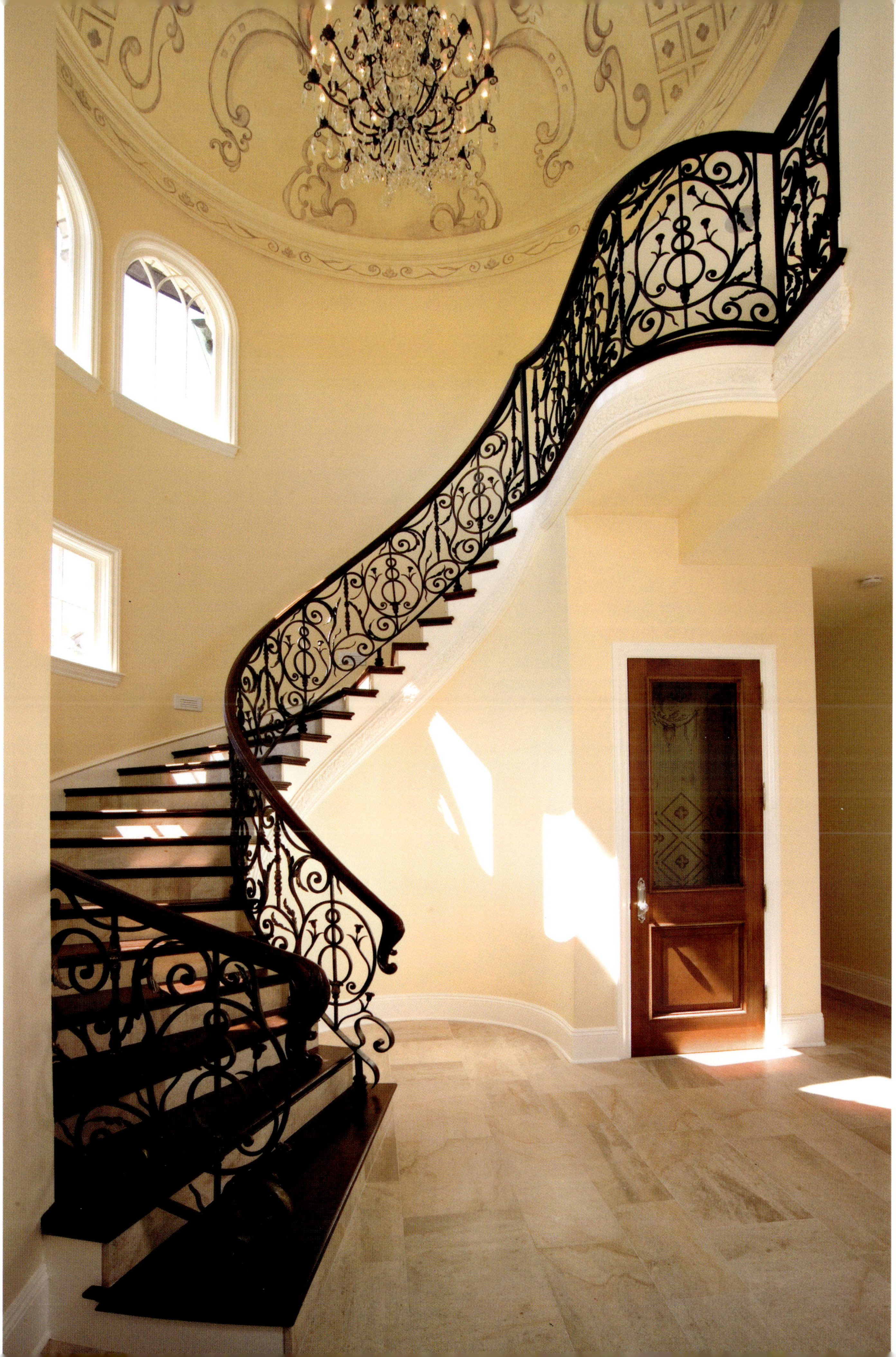

mirror is reflecting light from the Tota-flector at the umbrella (marked "D") that we used before. The final trick for this light is the filter (marked "I"). I took a sheet of glass and mounted the color gels from a Rosco Cinegel sample book to the glass with spray-mount adhesive. This glass acts as an irregular warming filter. It also creates some colored reflections off the broken glass (depending on the angle of the broken glass).

This method of using only one light is rarely the most practical way of doing a shot, unless you only have one light! The practical reason for doing such a shot is to improve your skills with lighting tools. Often we overlook the possibilities of reflected light. This exercise also encourages us to pay more attention to using black materials as flags and gobos to control the spill from our lights. So, in reality, this method of lighting is a very practical exercise of our lighting skills.

THIS METHOD OF USING ONLY ONE LIGHT IS RARELY THE MOST PRACTICAL WAY OF DOING A SHOT, UNLESS YOU ONLY HAVE ONE LIGHT!

Finally, a practical example: It's no surprise that some clients are on a budget. One way that I can keep the cost of a job down is to use less gear. I shot the image on the previous page for a client who makes custom staircases. I went to four locations in a half day. If I had packed and unpacked all of my lights, I would be there still. So I used only the 60-inch umbrella, just to the right of the camera. I had my 750 watt-second monolight in the umbrella. I used a long exposure so the daylight would help fill in my shot. I could have done more with more gear, but I kept the client happy and didn't break the bank.

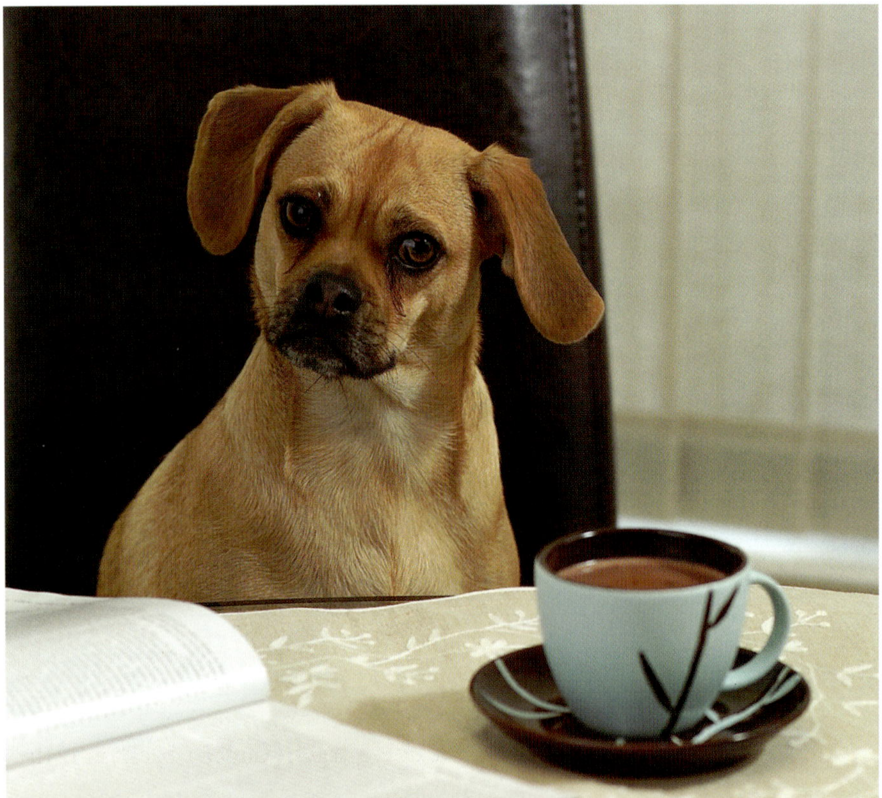

I photographed this dog with a single strobe with a 45-inch umbrella. Dogs don't like to sit still for a long time, so a simple setup can really help.

7. BALANCING LIGHTS

Whenever you work with more than one light source in a shot, even ambient light or continuous sources, you need to be concerned about how the lights relate to one another. Each time you add light to a shot, ask yourself some basic questions about the way that light should look. What part of the subject will receive additional light? Or will the whole scene receive more light? Should the light be hard or soft? Should the color of the light match the existing light, or do you want to add color? (Photographers often add light to a scene when what they really should do is change the color of the lights in the shot.)

Balancing your lights can be a simple matter of changing the power level of a strobe or adding a filter to change the color. If the basic quality of the light in the shot is good, balancing is just this simple. Unfortunately, much of the time you will have to examine all of the qualities of the light before you can make the lights work together in a pleasing way.

REDUCING SHADOWS

If you want to reduce the shadows from a light, it is more effective to make the light bigger than to try to add other lights.

WHERE SHOULD YOU PLACE YOUR LIGHTS?

As we discussed earlier, there are times when adding lights to your scene will help you create a more polished, professional result. By adding light, you can introduce or intensify highlight and shadow areas and heighten the sense of three-dimensionality in a portrait. You can also add a light to highlight your portrait subject's hair or create a rim light. There are many ways in which adding an extra light to your shot can work in your still life or product photography too.

The series of images shown on the next couple of pages show how a light can add definition to parts of a face. All of these shots were done with Norman studio strobes, but you could re-create these setups with any strobes. These are not the only ways to use light, but they are useful examples.

Portrait 1. The first pair of images show the basic lighting setup for the series. I used a single light with an umbrella/light panel combination on the left of the camera and a large reflector on the right side.

Portrait 2. I used the basic setup as a starting point to create the second portrait in the series. This time, however, I added a background light. I used the stovepipe snoot to light just the background. As you can see in the shot with just the stovepipe snoot, this light doesn't get bounced back onto the subject.

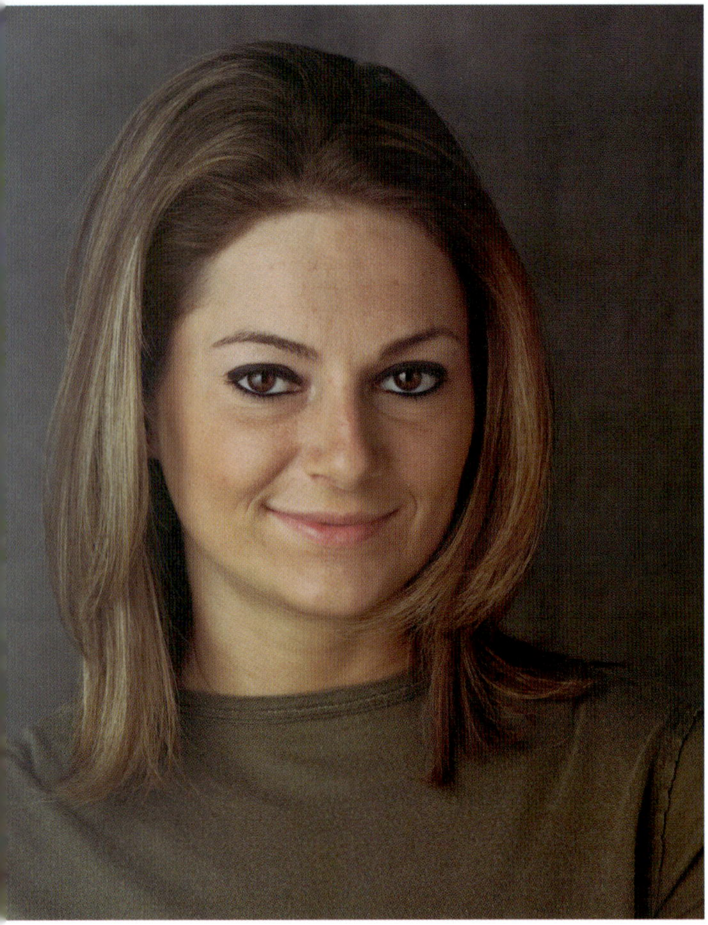

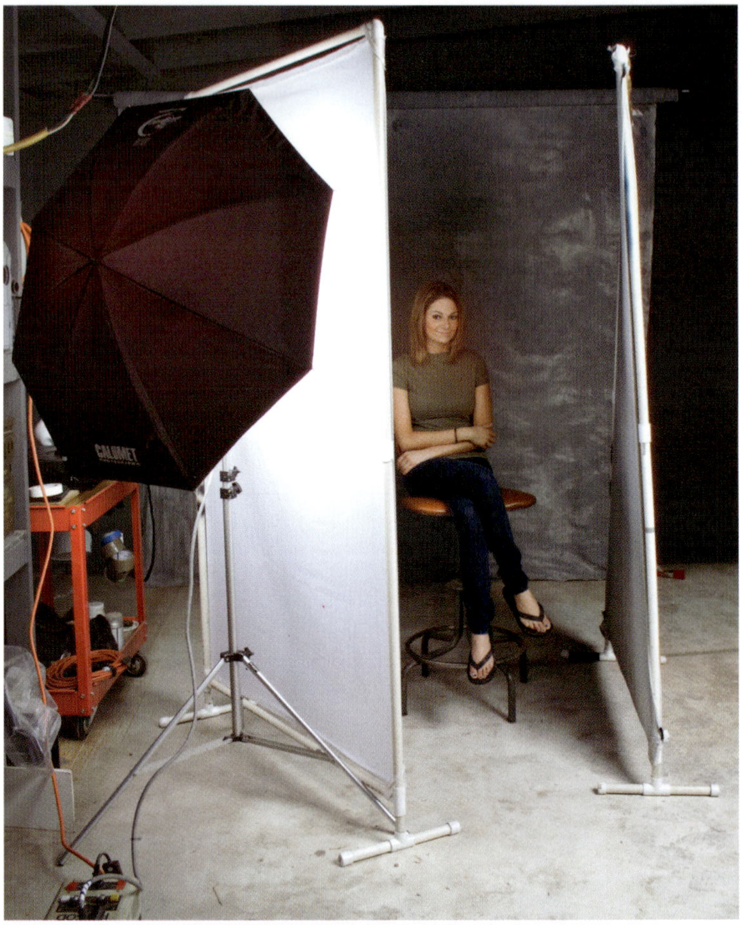

PORTRAIT 1. Left—This image was made to show the basic light that I used as a base for this series. **Right**—You can see the lighting setup here.

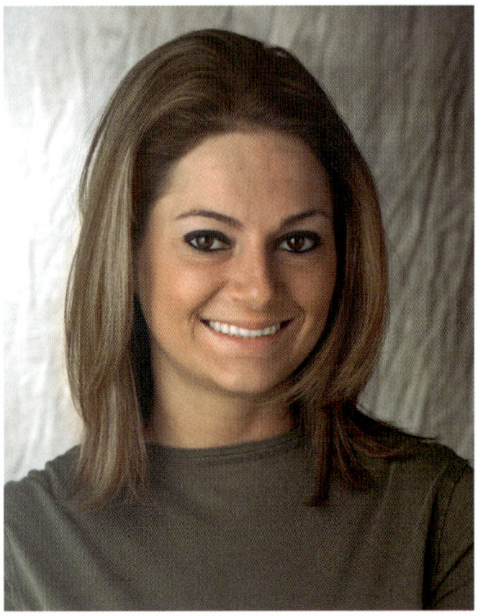

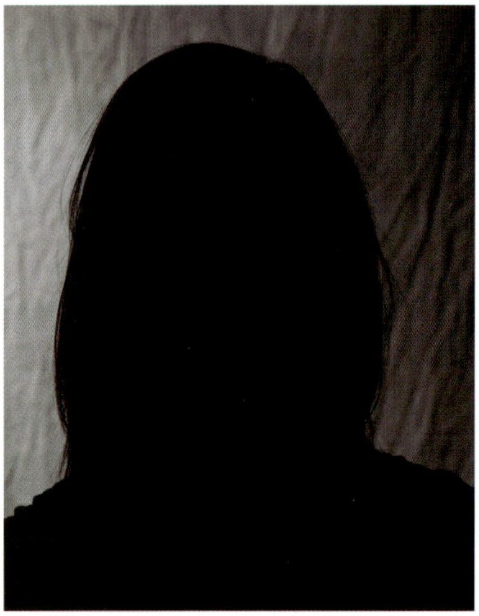

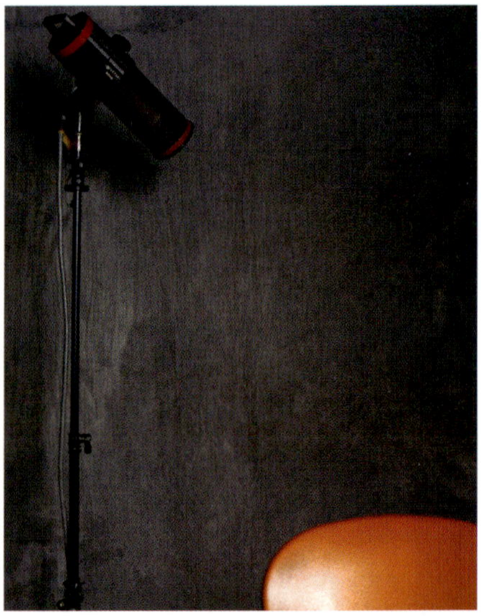

PORTRAIT 2. Left—To create the second headshot in the series, I added a stovepipe snoot to light the background. This image shows the effect created by the basic light and the snoot. **Center**—This image shows the lighting effect that results when the snoot is used alone. **Right**—This image shows the position of the snoot.

Portrait 3. For the third head shot, I used the snoot again. I placed it on camera right, behind the subject. This created a rim light on the edge of the subject and added a lot of light to the hair. When you use the snoot to light the subject, be careful about its placement: the snoot can add light to the wrong part of the subject, so it's important for the subject to remain in one place.

Portrait 4. For the fourth image in the series, I used a single light to add rim light and light the background. A bare bulb was placed right behind the subject's head. Of course, when you do this yourself, you'll want to make sure that the strobe tube is not visible in the picture. Note that you can put filter material over the light and move the light closer to the background to change the way the rim light or the background looks. The bare bulb creates a lot of bounce light in the room, so it fills in the subject more than the snoot does.

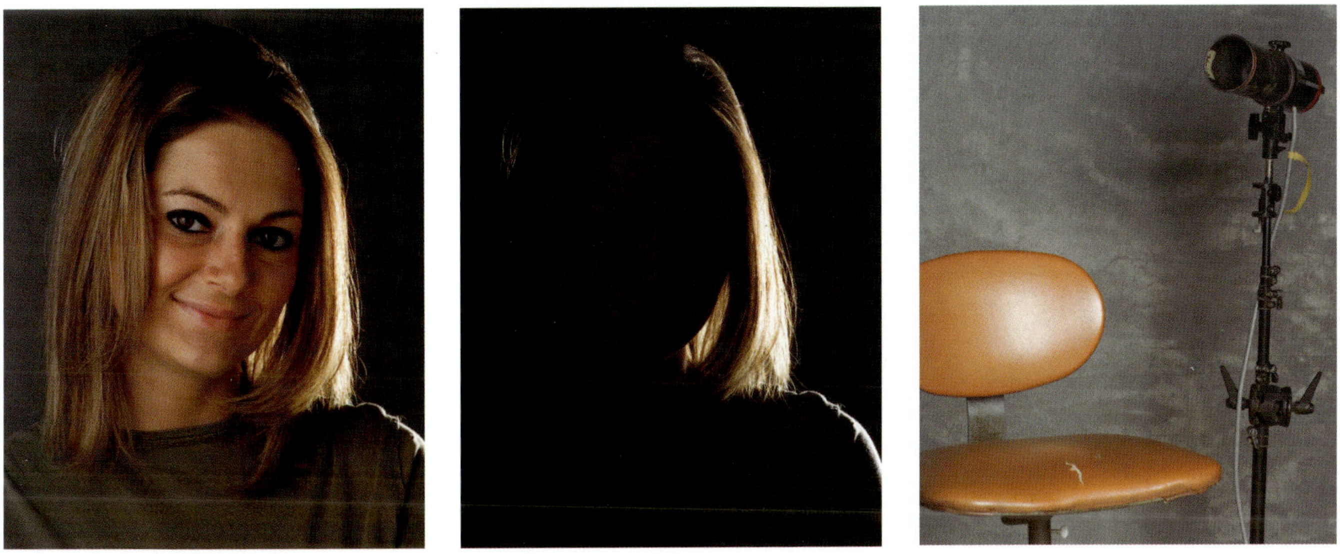

PORTRAIT 3. **Left**—For the third image, I used the stovepipe snoot to create a rim light on the subject's left side. This image shows the basic light with the rim light. **Center**—This shot shows the effect of the snoot alone. **Right**—This image shows the position of the snoot.

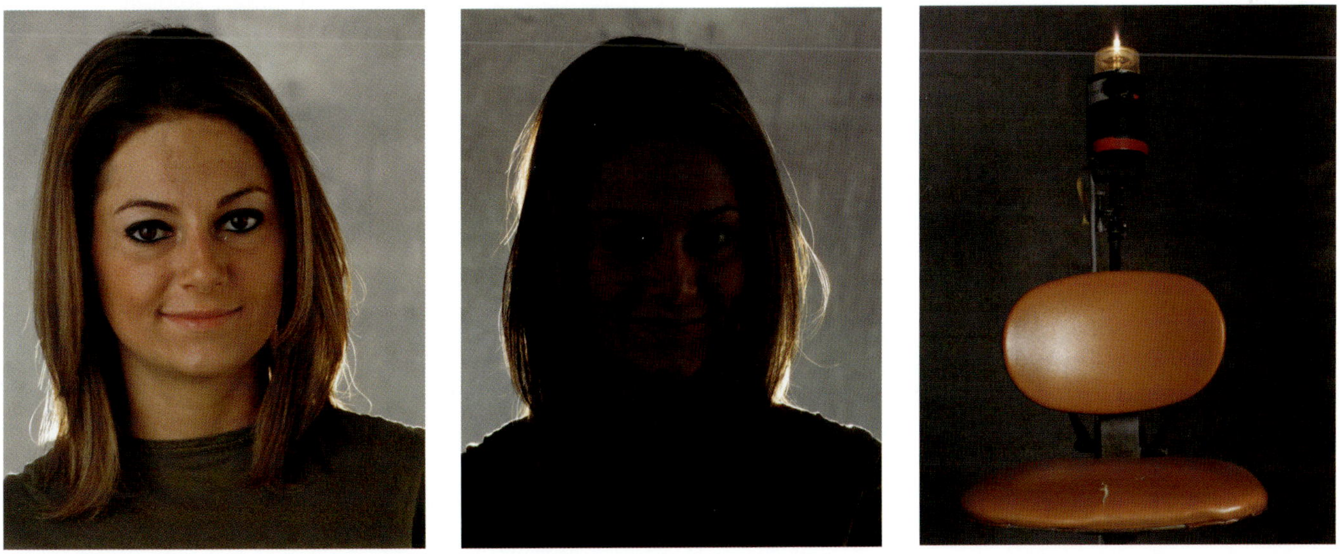

PORTRAIT 4. **Left**—A bare strobe tube placed behind the subject lit the background and created a rim light. **Center**—This image shows the bare bulb's effect on the model. **Right**—This image shows the position of the bare bulb behind the model's chair.

Portrait 5. For the fifth image, I used the snoot again to make a hair light. This is a hard light from above the subject that creates sparkle in the hair. For this shot, the strobe was positioned at camera right. Keep in mind that the position of the hair light is critical, so the subject has to stay in place.

Portrait 6. Finally, for the sixth image, I used a second light to add a catchlight to the eyes. You can see a small, hard catchlight in the eyes as well as more hard light on the subject. I used the shoe cover over the strobe to make this light. The cover has a nice oval shape and creates a good fill light.

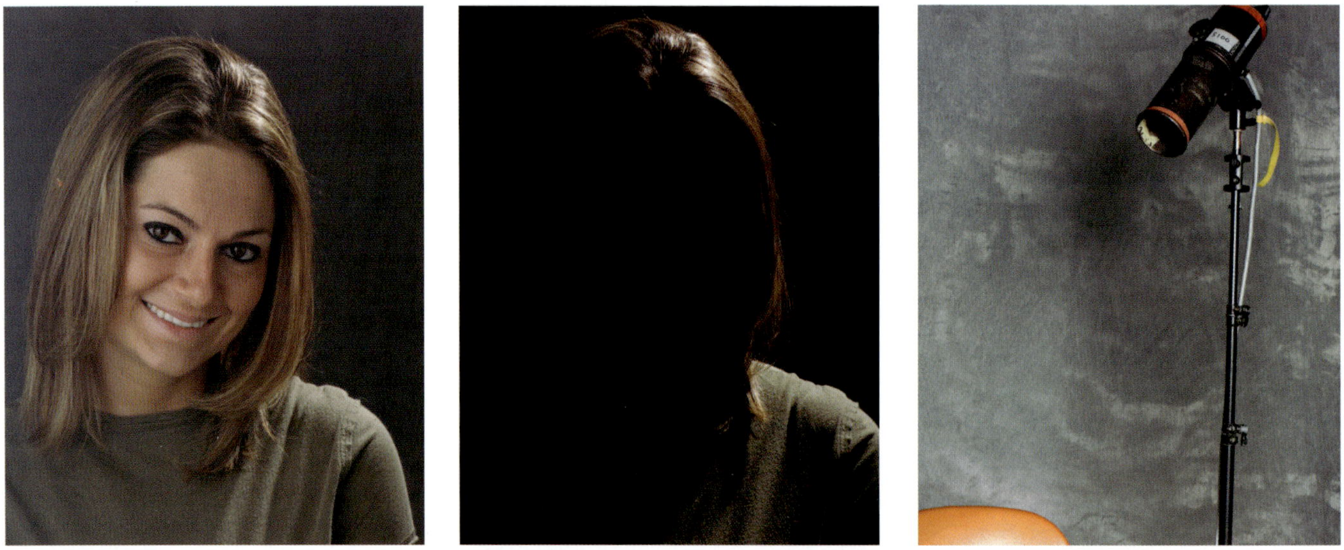

PORTRAIT 5. These images show how to use a hair light. **Left**—This shot shows the lighting effect produced with both lights. **Center**—I like the drama of just the hair light in shot. **Right**—Here you can see that the hair light was a lot higher than the subject.

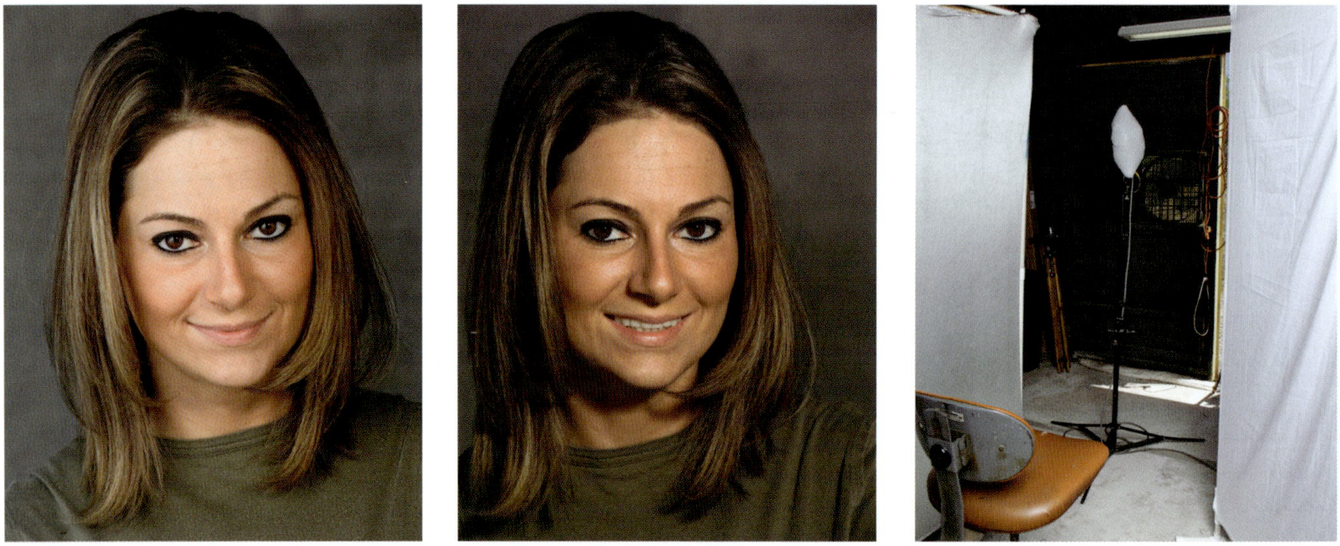

PORTRAIT 6. Left—Finally, I added a hard light in front of the subject to create a stronger catchlight and some sparkle. This image shows both lights. **Center**—In this image, you can see how much light I got from the strobe with the shoe cover. Of course, you could reduce the power to this strobe, but I liked the effect. **Right**—You can see the position of the light in front of the subject.

HARD VS. SOFT LIGHT

Earlier in the book, I described hard versus soft light. We'll take a close look at the topic here, but before we do, try a little test that will help you visualize the difference: At night, set yourself up in a dark room with a light with a large lampshade. Turn all of the other lights off. Note that objects near the lamp have soft shadows that slowly transition into lit areas. Objects farther from the lamp have shadows that go from dark to light quite quickly. This is soft light. Next, remove the lampshade and look at the way the light renders the objects in the room. Note that when light falls on objects that are not very close to the lamp, the highlights quickly transition to shadow. This is very hard light.

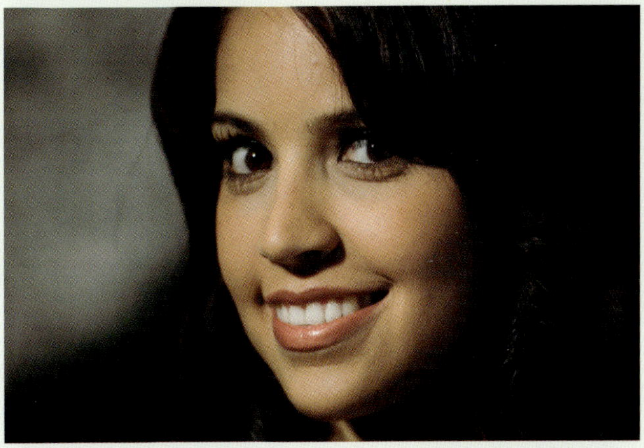

This shot was made with just one light with a reflector. The light shows detail and hard shadows on the face. This light is not very flattering for most people and is tricky to position. If you move the light very slightly, the shadows will move.

HARD OR SOFT LIGHT?

In the past, most portraits were made using hard light. Photographers worked with large format cameras and slow film and a lot of light. Without a lot of light, portrait subjects would have had to sit still for a very long time. Many fine portraits, for instance, the old Hollywood studio portraits, were made with lots of hot lights.

As we've learned, light sources that are large and close to the subject produce softer light than sources that are small and farther from the subject. As I discussed in chapter 3, there are many tools photographers can use to make a hard light source softer and more diffuse.

Ratio Lighting. A light ratio is the numeric description of the difference in intensity between the highlight side (illuminated by the main light) of the subject and the shadow side (illuminated by fill light). The fill light is placed more or less directly in front of the subject and thus provides light over the whole face. The main light is positioned between 1:30 and 3:00 and illuminates just one side of the face. The side of the face lit only by the fill light has a numeric value of 1 (e.g., one unit of light). If the main light provides the same amount of light as the fill, the bright side is said to have twice as much light as the fill side and has a numeric value of 2. The ratio in this setup, then, is 2:1. Notice the hard shadow under the chin and the shadow from the hair on the face in our first sample image (page 60). This is characteristic of hard light. If you increase the amount of light from the main light by one stop (a 2x increase), the light, the main light side of the face will have a numeric value of 3 and the fill side will have a value of 1, a 3:1 ratio. You can really see the difference in brightness between the two sides of the face. You can use stronger ratios, but they are usually considered better for black & white

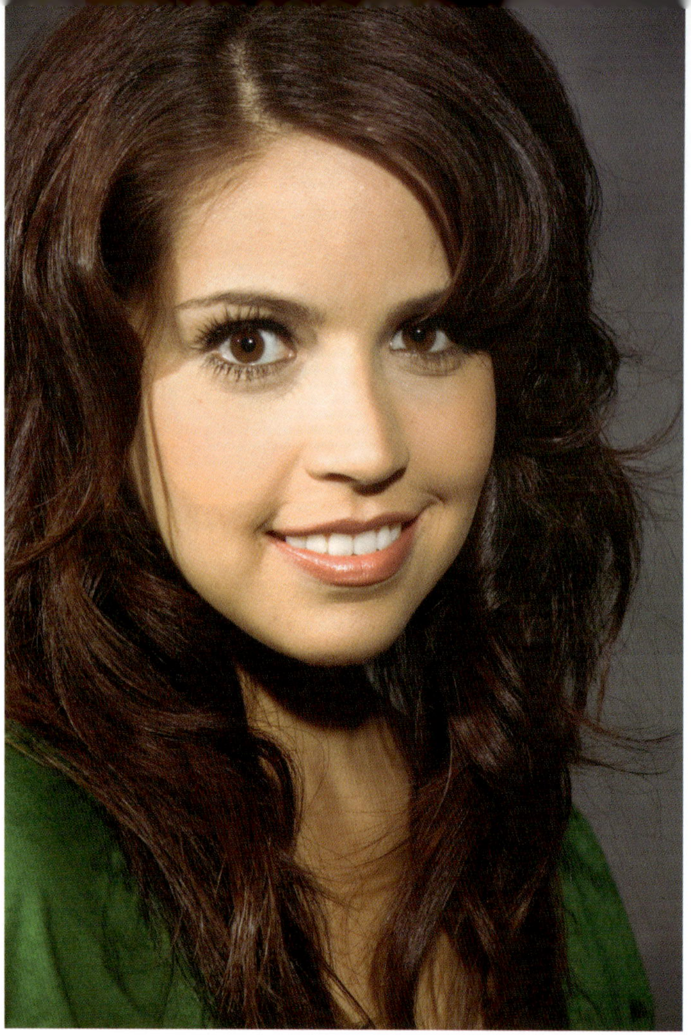
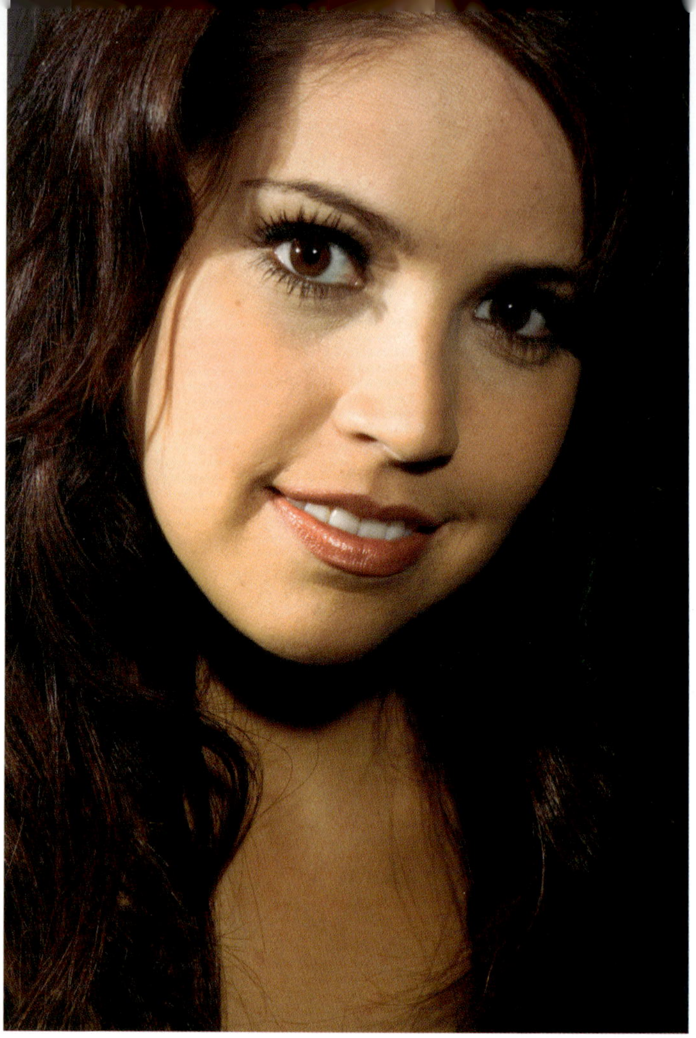
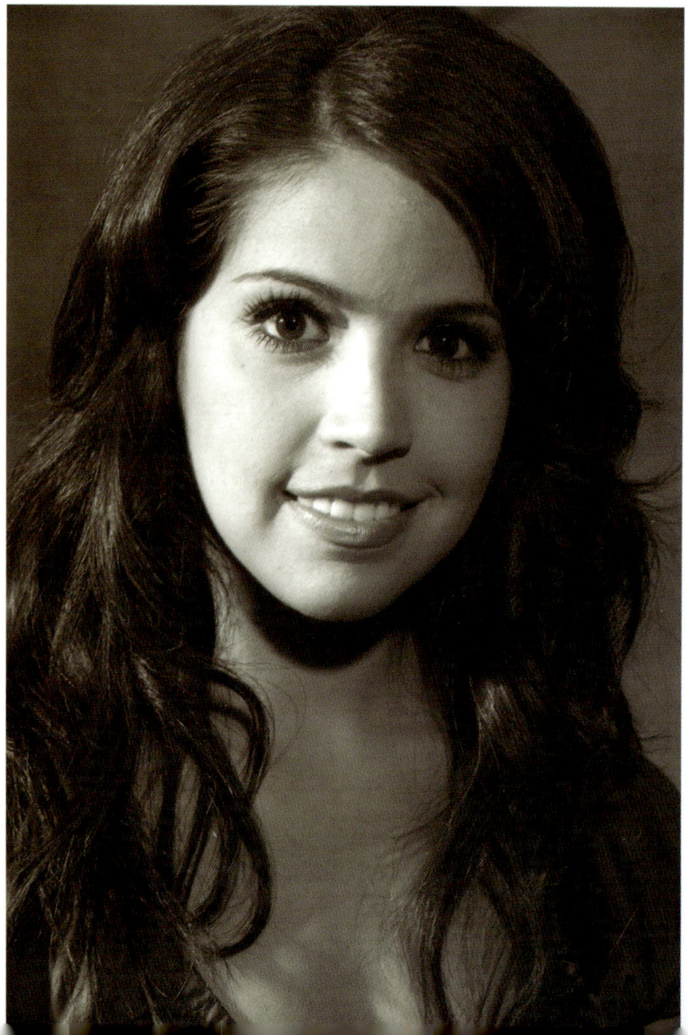
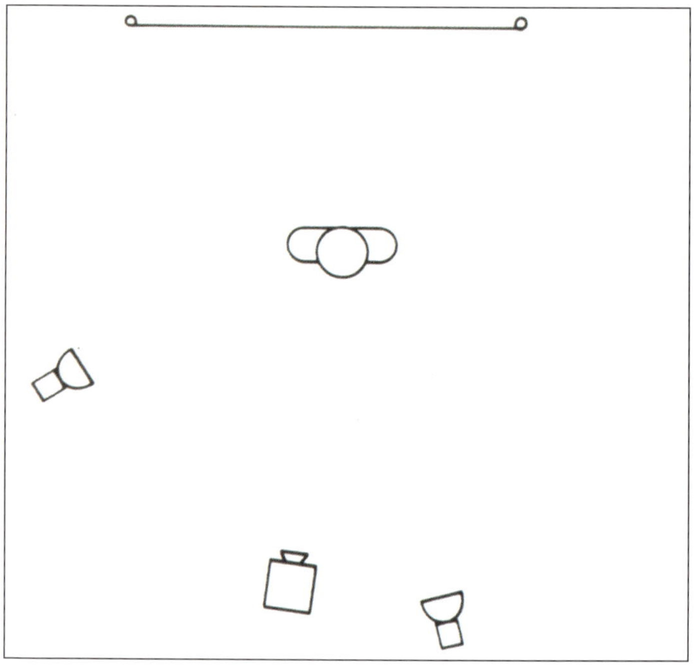

Top left—The light on the right side of her face is twice as bright as the light on the other side, so we have a 2:1 ratio. **Top right**—Here we have a 3:1 ratio. You can see that there is a little more contrast. **Bottom left**—A 5:1 ratio looks pretty good in black & white. **Bottom right**—As seen in the diagram, the camera and fill light were positioned at the 12:00 position, and the main light was positioned at 2:00. This is a standard way to set up ratio lights.

CHECK IT OUT

If you want control over your images, keep an eye on the effect your lighting is having on the scene. You can review your images on your camera's LCD screen if you're shooting portraits, but you may want to tether your computer to a laptop for other session types, as you'll be able to better gauge your results on your laptop.

images. In the final sample image (below), the main light is 2 stops (4x more powerful than the fill light). So the main light adds 4 units of light to the 1 unit of light thrown by the fill light, yielding a numeric value of 5. The fill provides one unit of light to the fill side. When you add it up, you have a 5:1 ratio.

Ratio lighting works with hard lights. In my career, I have witnessed other photographers trying to apply light ratios using soft lights. I try to discourage thinking in terms of ratios with large light sources, as the results don't show a characteristic difference between the two sides of the face. Of course, if you use more modestly sized light sources or position your lights farther from your subject, the light will exhibit more of the characteristics of hard light.

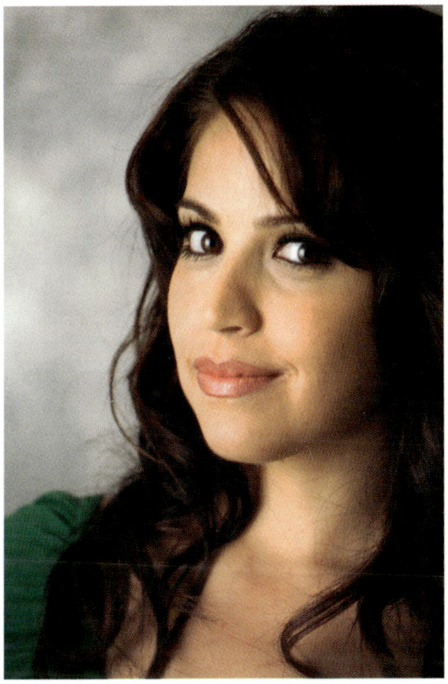

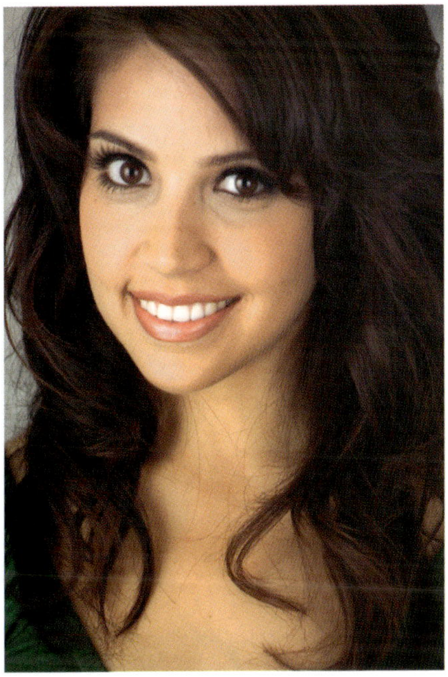

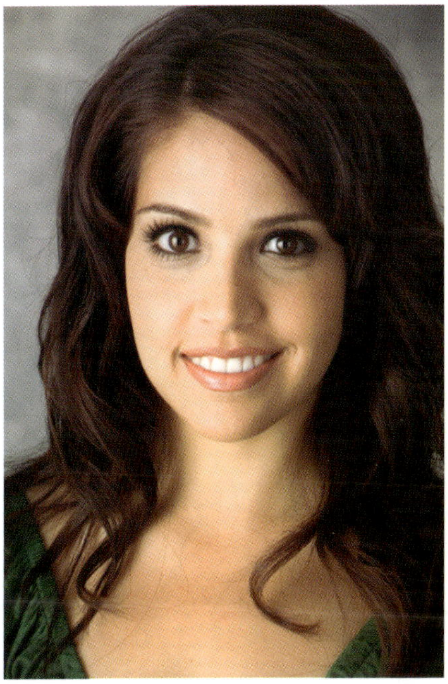

Left—This light produced by this single large light source is very soft. **Center**—The lights are set to a 2:1 ratio, but you can't see it in the face! **Right**—In this image, the lights are set for a 5:1 ratio, but the lighting is even. Ratios just don't mean much with large light sources. **Bottom**—This is the setup that I used for the shots with the large light sources. The lights were basically positioned like they were for the hard light setup, but the results are very different!

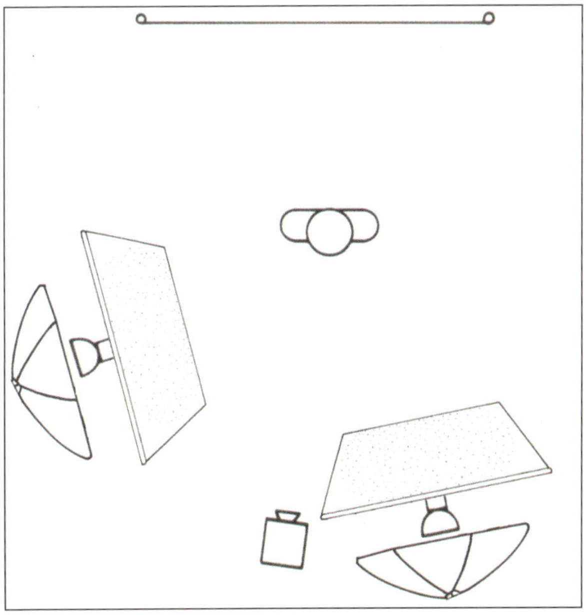

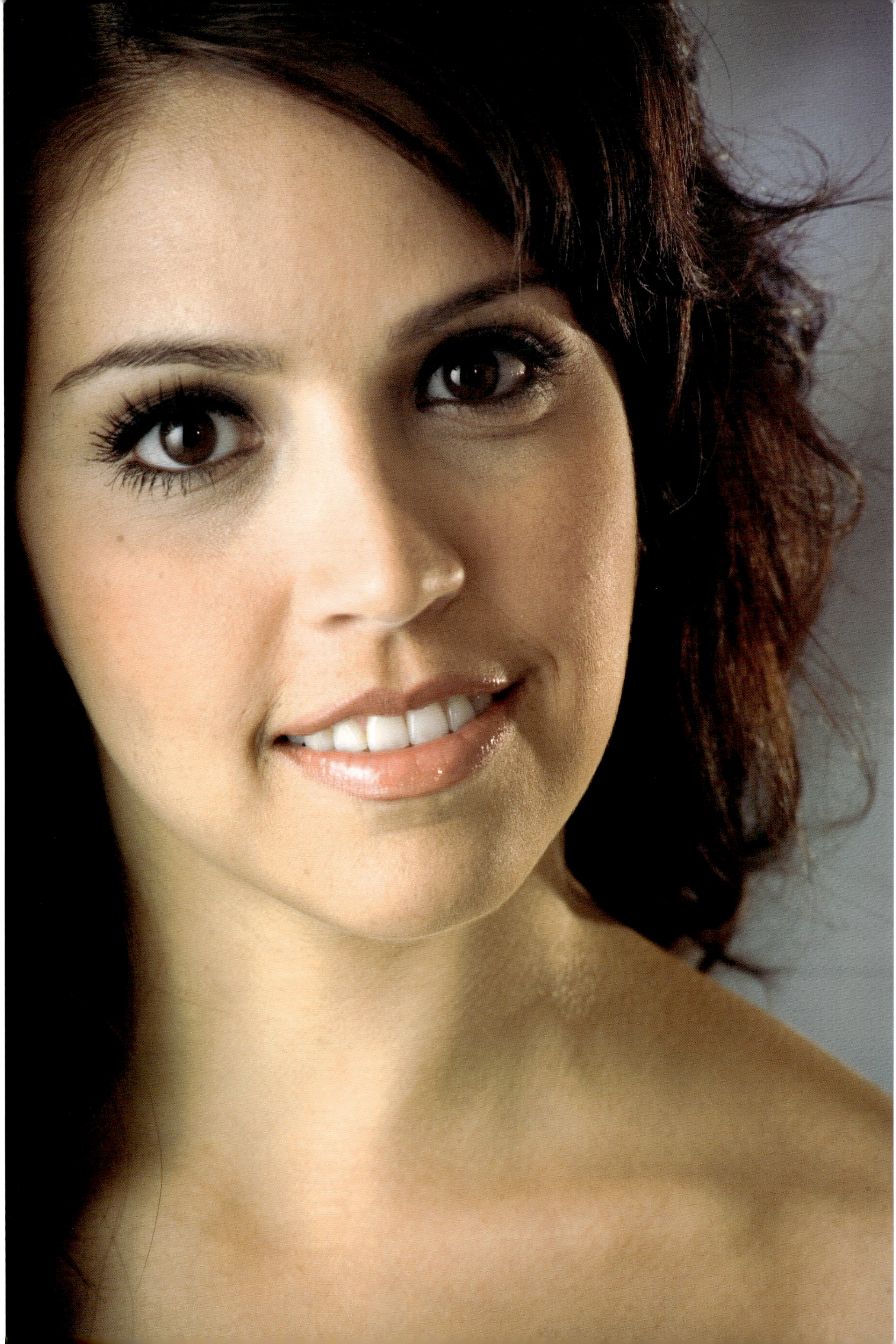

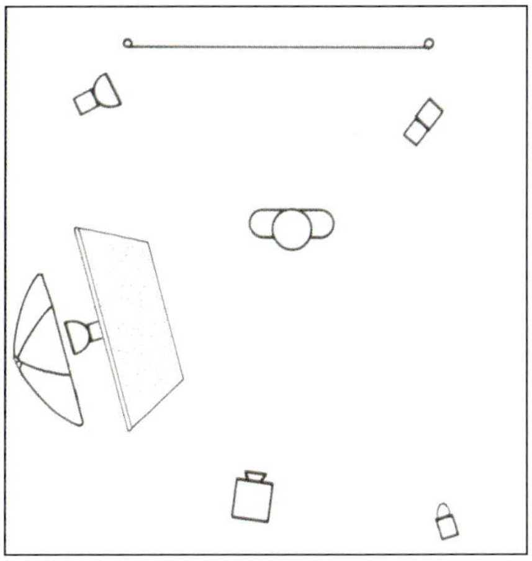

Facing page—To create this shot, I used four lights. By balancing the power, quality, and color of the lights, I was able to create a great image that presents a nice face shape and pleasing color. I didn't need a light meter; I was guided by experience and, of course, a review of the image on the laptop. **Above**—The diagram for the image. I used four light sources: an umbrella/light panel, reflector, snoot, and bare bulb.

Combining Hard and Soft Light. I think that the most expressive lighting for portraits—and many other subjects—is a mixture of hard and soft light and a mix of brightnesses. I used four lights—three hard and one soft—to create the image on the facing page. The soft light came from an umbrella/light panel set up just to the left of the camera. This provided the basic illumination for the shot. I set up a strobe with a snoot behind the subject. This lit the left side of her face and created highlights in her hair. The light produced a brighter area on the left side of the face, and I am particularly pleased with the way it defined her cheek and chin. I placed a warming filter on the light to add color. (In fact, I placed filters on all of the hard lights to put more color into the shot.) I put a much smaller strobe behind and to the right of the camera to add sparkle on her lips and in her eyes. Although I can find reflections from this light in the shot, this light had less effect than the other strobes. This light was also covered with a warming filter. You can also see the light I put on the background. Since this light had a blue filter on it, it added color to a normally gray background.

THE COLOR OF THE LIGHT

As you can see from the chart, different light sources have different color temperatures. You may choose to use a mixed lighting scenario to your advantage, as it can create a unique look with the right approach. Of course, you can also choose to modify one or more of the light sources by placing color-correction filters over some of the units.

Strobes and daylight (at midday) have the same color. Strobes can also be filtered to produce light that matches the color of natural light at other times of day, or to match the color temperature of another light source.

A small difference in the color temperature at the warm end of the scale is much more significant than the same difference on the cool side of the scale. Rosco and other manufacturers make filters designed to manipulate lights to match any color within this range. The great thing about filters is that they let you change the color of just one light in a shot rather than the whole shot. This enables you to have normal color on a subject and, for instance,

COLOR TEMPERATURE OF COMMON SOURCES

100-watt tungsten bulb: 2900°K
Sunrise or sunset (depends on circumstances): 3100°K
Tungsten designed for still or movie lighting: 3200°K
Golden hour (1 hour after sunrise or 1 hour before sunset): 3600°K
Sunny day: 5500°K
Strobes (depends on manufacturer): 5000°K to 6000°K
Overcast sky: 7000°K
Open shade: 9500°K

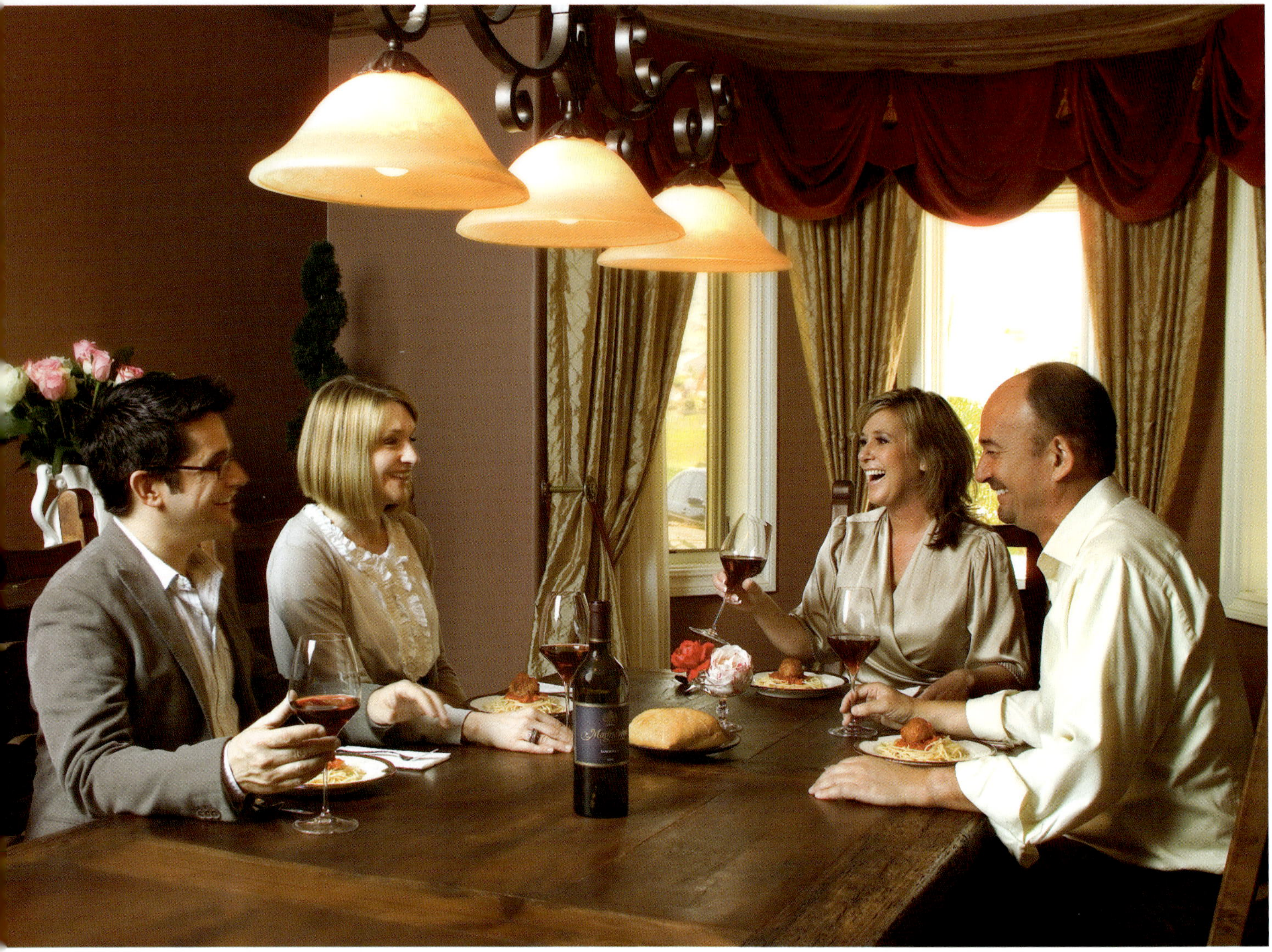

For this shot, I put blue color correction filters (Rosco 1/2 CTB) over my lights. When I filtered out the blue in Photoshop, I also warmed up the background.

a different color on the background. If you can't change the light on the background, you can change the color of your lights with filters, then pull the color out in Photoshop. For example, if you want to warm up the sunlight in the background of your image, you can add blue color correction filters to your lights, then make the whole shot warmer in Photoshop. Not only will you warm up your lights to normal, but you will also warm up the background at the same time.

There are a great many light sources that do not have a continuous spectrum. Sometimes these lights can create good overall color or can be filtered to do so. However, it is difficult to predict because the lights change over time and are not designed for precision photographic application. Whenever possible, I avoid working with fluorescent and mercury vapor or sodium vapor lights. Even with a digital camera and Photoshop, they can be difficult to control.

This next group of images shows the results of adding different filters to a light. The caption of each shot lists the filter and the approximate color

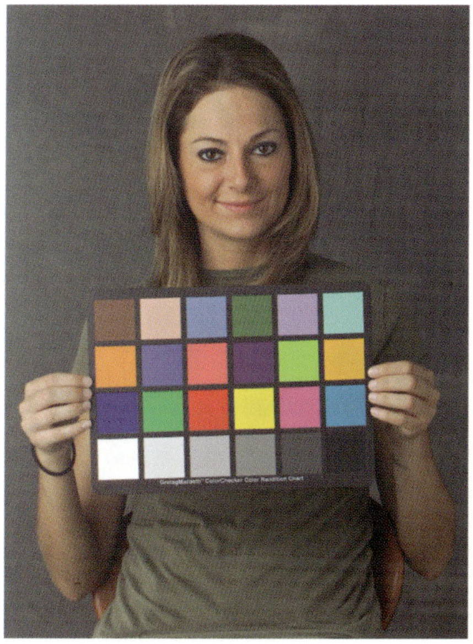

No filter. The shot was made with a 5500ºK light.

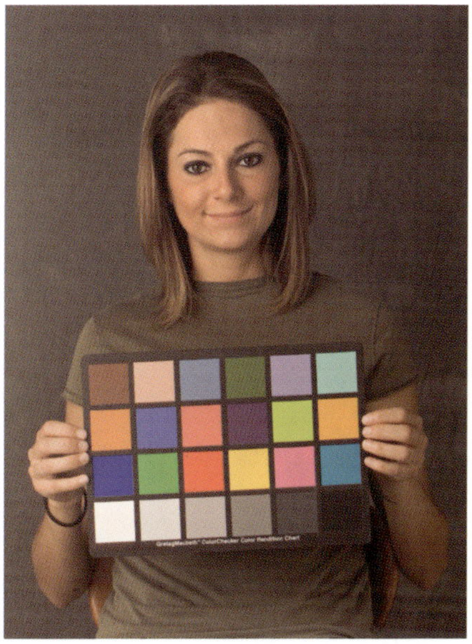

This was made with a 1/8 CTO. Color temperature is about 4900ºK.

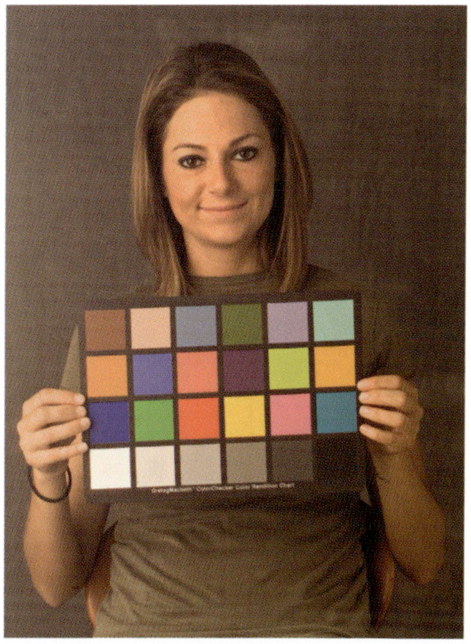

This was made with a 1/4 CTO. Color temperature is about 4500ºK.

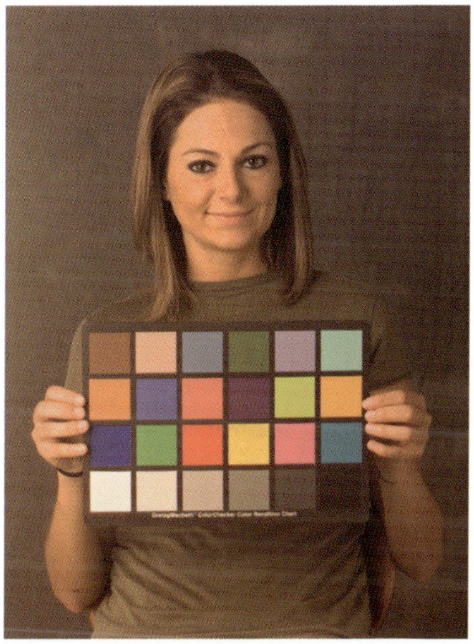

This was made with a 1/2 CTO. Color temperature is about 3800ºK.

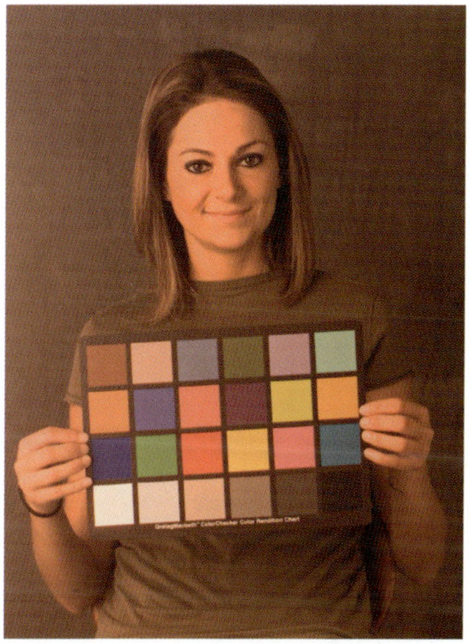

This was made with a full CTO. Color temperature is about 3000ºK.

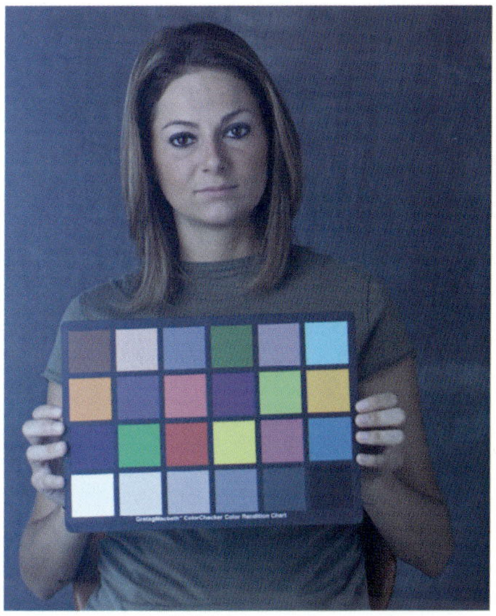

This was made with a 1/2 CTB. Color temperature is about 7500ºK.

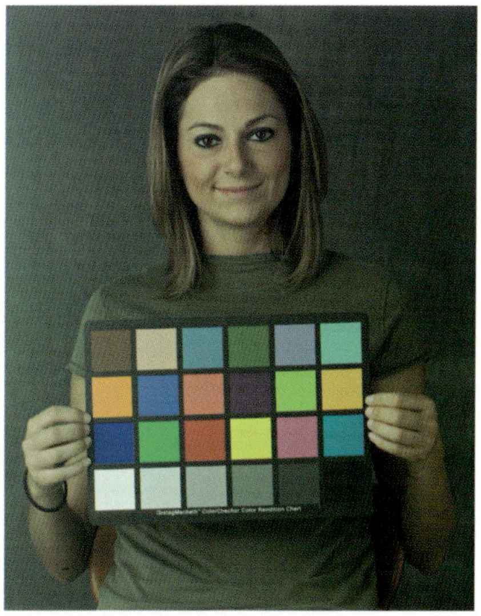

This was made with a full plus green. This filter is designed to make strobes look like fluorescent tubes.

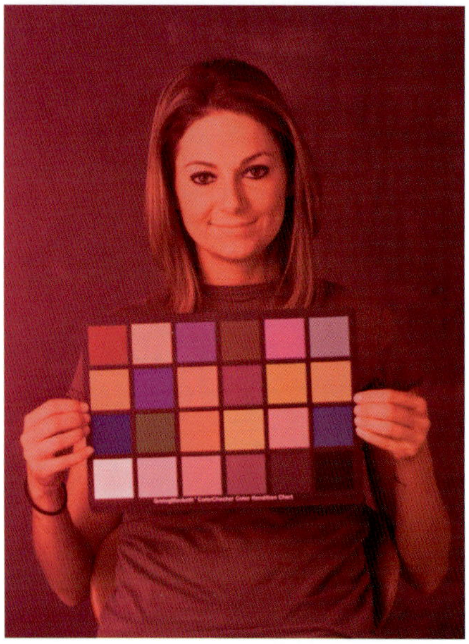

Red filter.

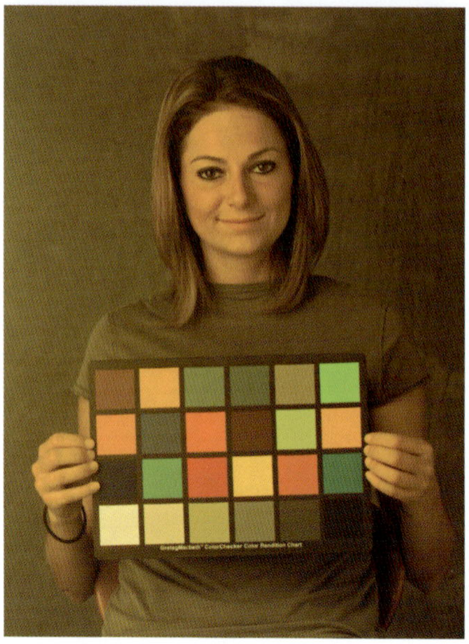

Yellow filter.

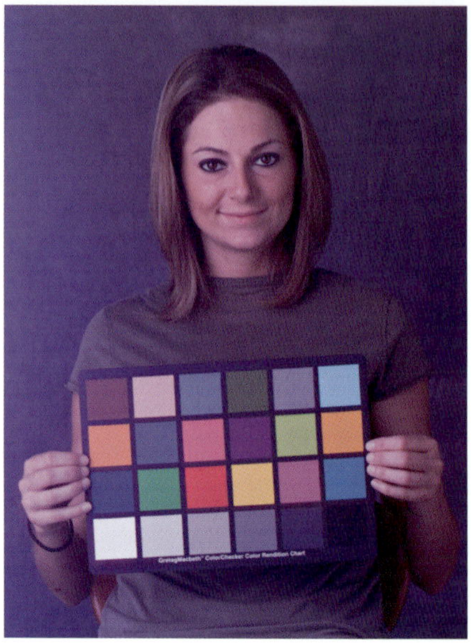

Blue filter.

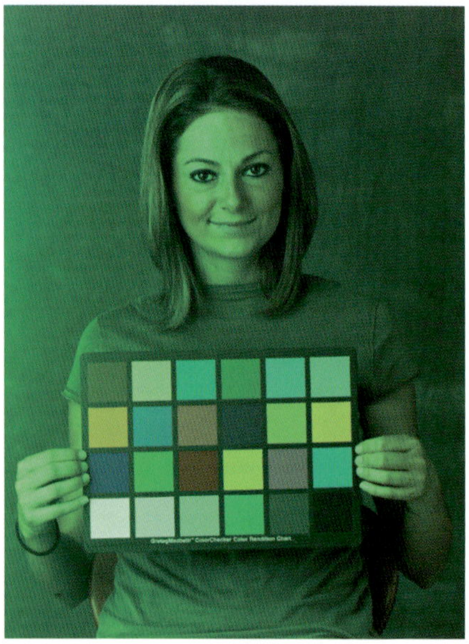

Green filter.

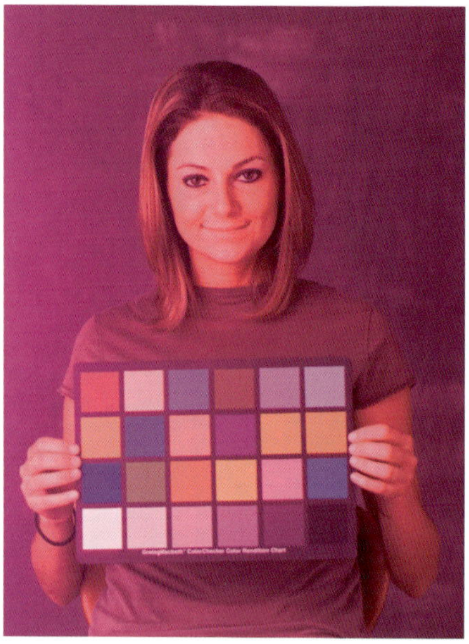

Magenta filter.

temperature of the light after the filter is used. These are color-balancing filters. CTO is a warm filter, CTB is a cooling filter, and plus green is supposed to convert a daylight source to a fluorescent color temperature.

In addition to color balancing filters, there is a whole rainbow of colored filters available to modify your light. There are sample books that will help you find any color that you need. I am including a few samples of shots made with colored filters. While I can't imagine any use for a shot using just these colored filters, I think they are great as accent lights.

CASE STUDY: BALANCING LIGHTS ON LOCATION

Balancing light in an architectural setting can be very difficult. You need to manage the light levels from your strobes and the ambient sources. The most important tool for striking a balance between strobe and ambient light is the shutter speed, because it only affects the ambient light. So, if you make the shutter speed longer, you'll record more ambient light. If you don't change the shutter speed, the amount of ambient light recorded will remain unchanged. If you make the shutter speed shorter, you can reduce the ambient light without affecting the strobe light. Of course, the aperture setting controls the effect of both ambient and strobe light.

When lighting an architectural subject, your first task is to establish where the camera will be placed. I chose this spot based on the windows and the light falling to the left of the camera. (I actually waited a while to bring that light more into the frame.) My other consideration was the placement of the front door. I liked this location, but I might have been a bit higher to separate the door from the banister.

I used five strobes plus some daylight to create this shot. This was a case in which I didn't need a lot of power, but I needed light in several places. Just as you wouldn't normally use one household light to illuminate your living room, you wouldn't use one strobe to light a room. The goal is to bring the contrast down in a shot like this. If you look at the original image, you will see that there is too much black, too much white, and not enough mid-tones. I usually use umbrellas for architectural work. They are easy to work with on location and create broad, even light. The first light I used was a 750

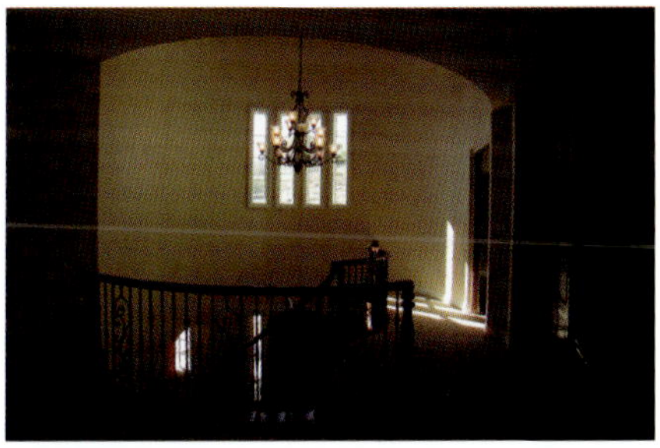

Above—Original shot, taken using auto exposure, before I did any lighting. There are no mid-tones, and there is way too much contrast. **Right**—Finished shot. I used five lights, and four of them were fitted with umbrellas.

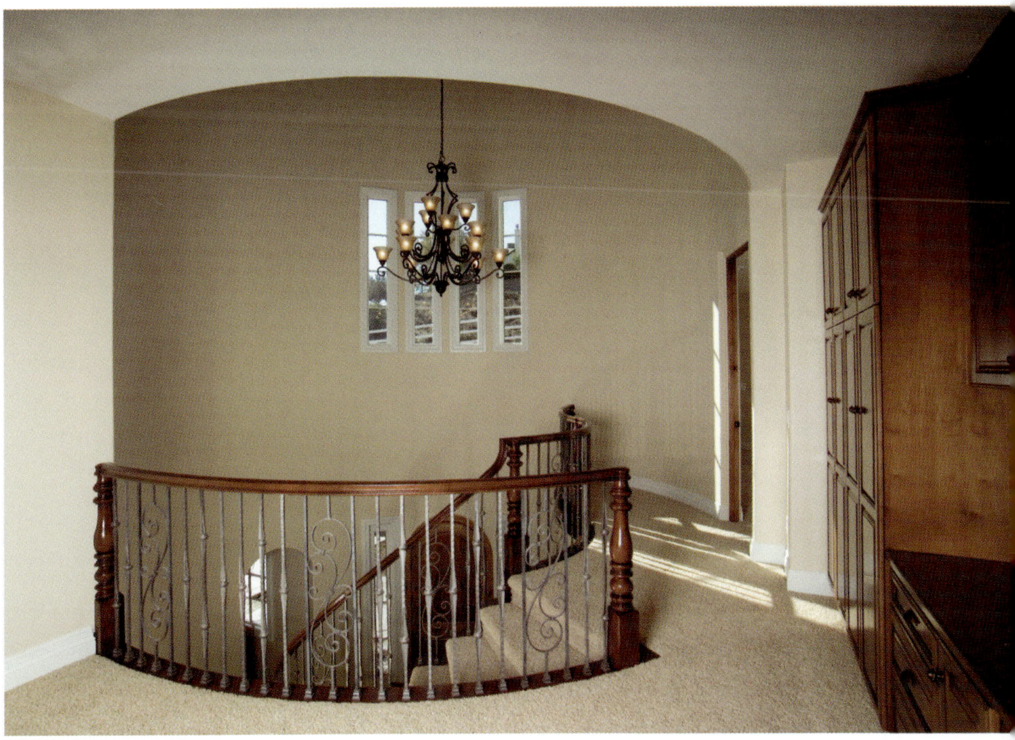

watt-second monolight (marked "D" in the diagram). I like to start with the biggest, broadest light, so I placed this combination near the camera. The reason for this placement is that the light here will cover most of what the camera sees, since they have a similar point of view. I used the monolight, which was the most powerful light I brought, because it has continuously variable power output. This makes it easier to bring the level of strobe and daylight into the right relationship. Since the light is near the camera and the computer, it is easy to make adjustments.

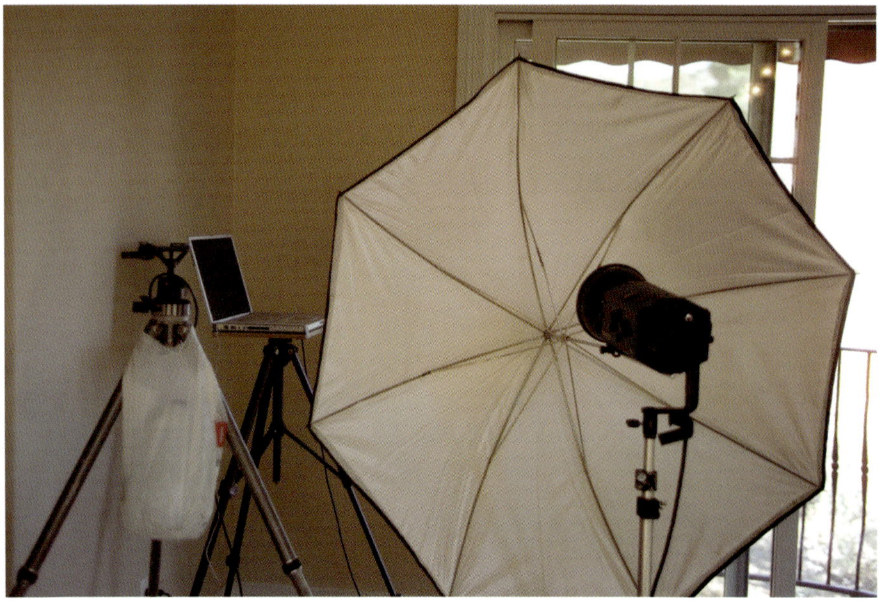

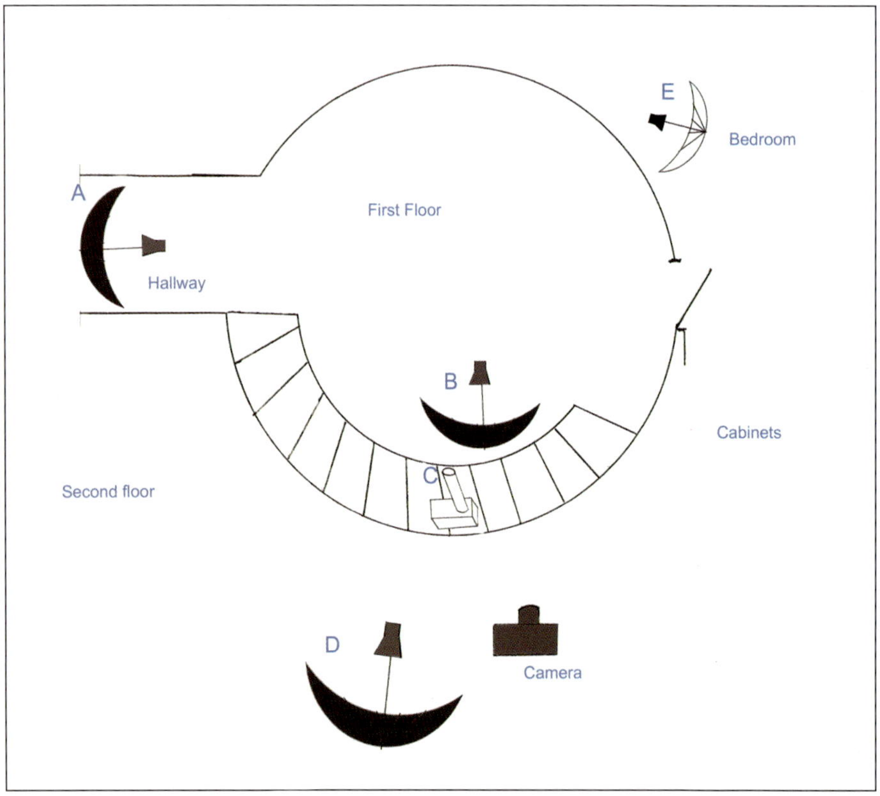

Top—In this shot, you can see the monolight and the umbrella. You can see the laptop in the background. The computer stand is a converted tripod. When the camera is tethered, I can fire the camera and change the aperture and shutter speed at the computer. This reduces the chance of moving the camera during long exposures. Note that the tripod isn't in the final position. **Bottom**—The diagram of the shot. Lights A, B, C, and E are 200 watt-second, battery-powered units. Light D is a 750 watt-second monolight.

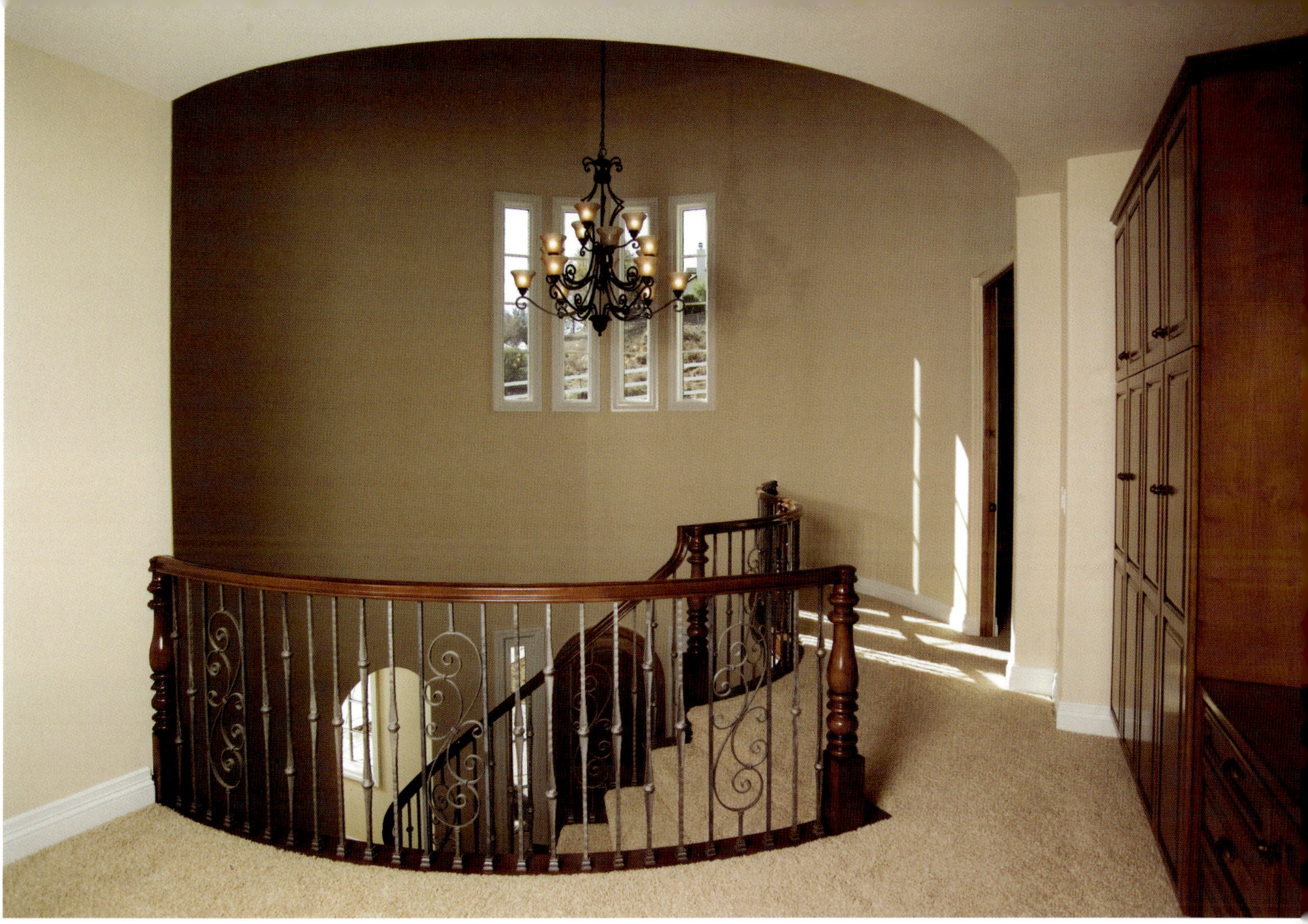

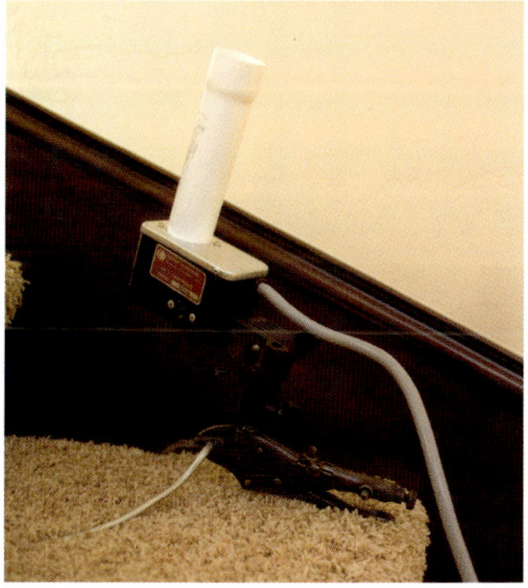

Above—The shot before the light was placed on the stair and across from the door. The extra lights gave the image more three-dimensionality. **Left**—The stair light. I used a piece of plumbing purchased from a hardware store as a snoot.

After I examined the first test, I added three more strobes. I needed to have light in the bottom of the cylindrical entry, opposite the front door, so I added a 200 watt-second, battery-powered strobe opposite the door (labeled "B" in the diagram). I spread this light with a 45-inch ribless umbrella. I also used the same type of strobe and umbrella in the ground floor hall to camera left (labeled "A" in the diagram). I used another 200 watt-second strobe in the bedroom on the right side of the camera on the second floor (labeled "E" in the diagram). I used a 30-inch white shoot-through umbrella with this light. The reason for a shoot-through umbrella is that it spreads light behind and in front of the strobe; consequently, I don't have to be critical with light placement. I only needed to be able to see into this room; I didn't need to see the details.

I like the battery-powered strobes for architectural work. The batteries do add some weight to the kit I use, but they save me from finding an outlet I can use and stringing power cords everywhere. These strobes offer a lot of power in a small package, can easily be hidden in a shot, and have enough power for a lot of lighting applications with a digital camera.

At this point, the image looked okay (see the previous page). It was not a bad start, but the left side of the cylinder was shadowed and the top was not light enough. This was a significant problem. This difficulty brings up one of the biggest problems with architectural lighting: you can't always put a light where you want, because it will be in the shot! When you look at the diagram, you can see the places I couldn't put a light. The stairs was my best choice, so I put one more 200B on a very small light stand, actually made from a vice grip (labeled "C" in the diagram). I put a piece of white plastic plumbing pipe on the Norman 200B, something I found at Home Depot. This homemade snoot puts a lot of light out the front and some light out the side. This tool performed very well here, better than I expected. You can see what happened in the final shot, shown below. I was pleased with what had happened to the side and top of the cylinder.

A Checklist. When you are shooting an interior space, it is a good idea to start with all the strobes at ½ power and take a test shot. This will allow you to see if your framing is good, where the reflections are, and what your depth of field is. It should also give you information about the light balance. Next, ask yourself the following questions:

The final shot.

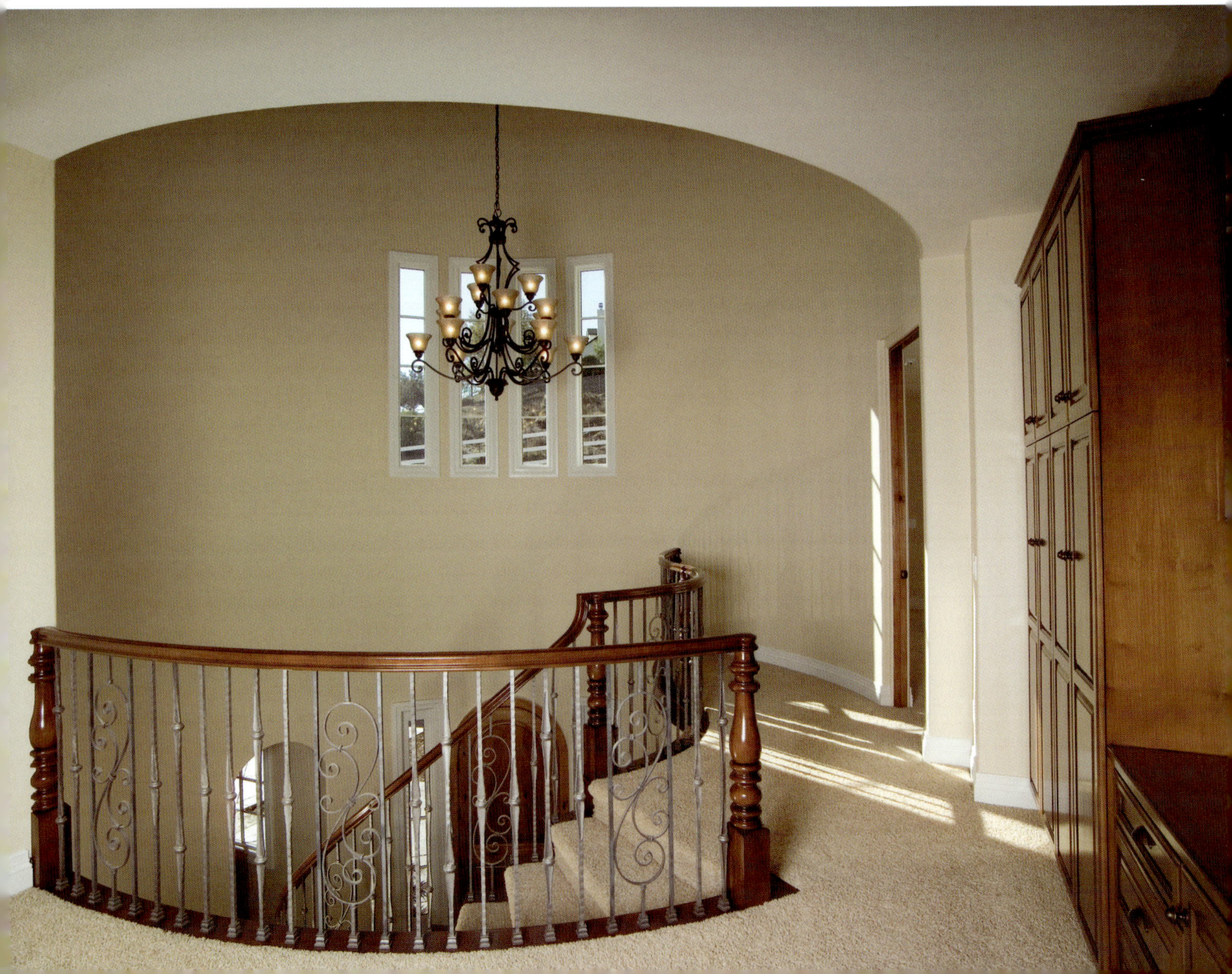

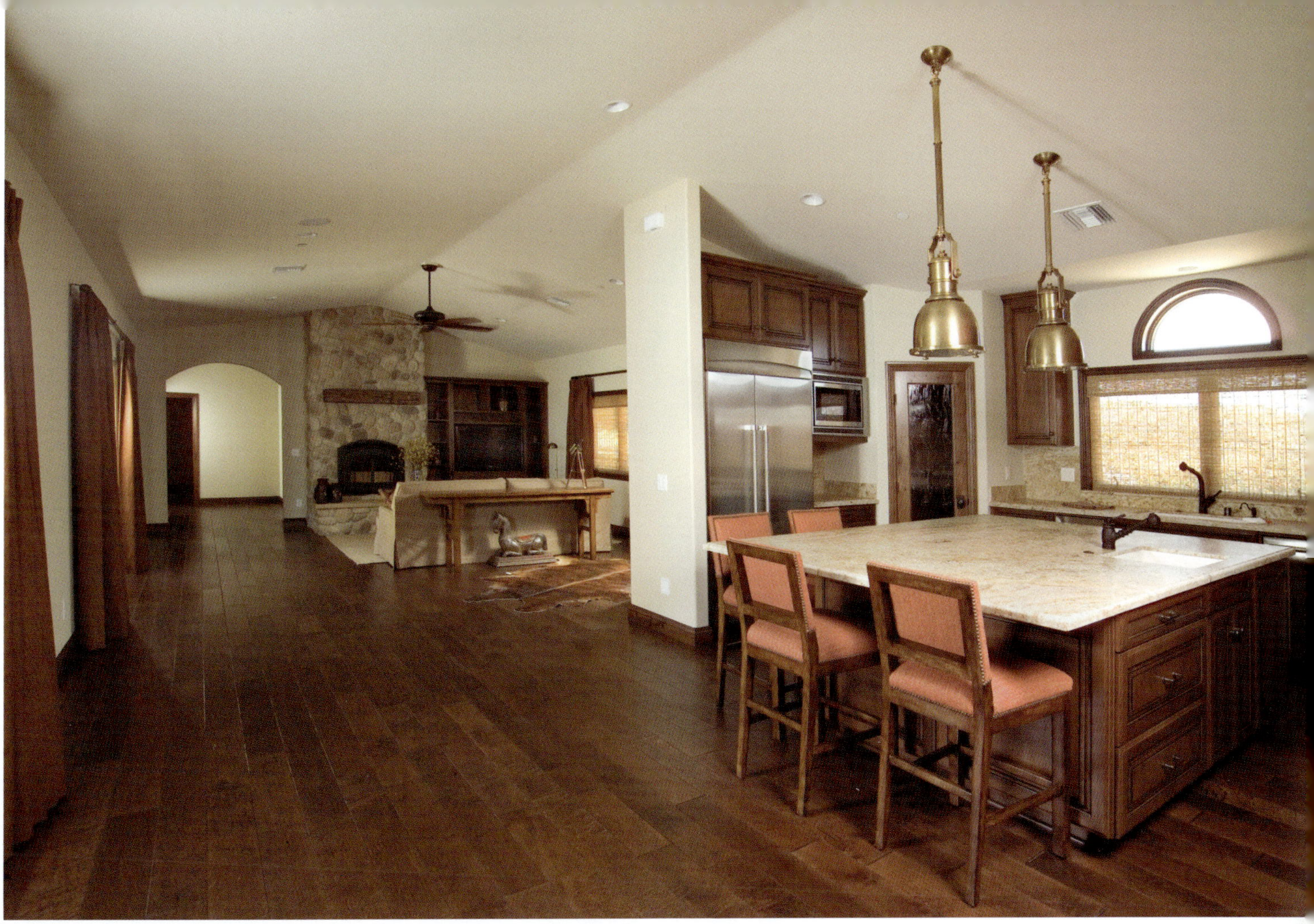

There are five lights in this shot. My favorite placement is outside the window on the left side of the shot.

- Is my first guess at exposure any good? If not, take another trial shot using another aperture.
- Are any of my lights set too bright or not bright enough? Change the appropriate lights.
- Are there any problematic reflections? Find out which light caused the problem (you can turn off each light individually to find where the problem comes from). You may be able to remove or reduce the problem by changing the position of the light. (For more suggestions, see the chapter on architectural lighting.)
- Do I have the right level of ambient light? If you have too much, increase the shutter speed—but don't exceed the sync speed. If you don't have enough, make your shutter speed longer.
- Do I need to filter any lights to correct color?

Now repeat the process, looking for the right balance. Your ability to balance light will improve as you exercise these skills.

To create the image above, I used five light sources. I placed a strobe on either side of the camera, both with large umbrellas. A third strobe was hidden by the short wall behind the refrigerator, also with an umbrella. There is a strobe outside the room; its light came through the windows on camera left. Finally, I placed a strobe in the hallway at the end of the shot. While I might have liked to have more light, there was no place to hide it. As you can see from the shadows in the living room, the light from the strobe out the window on the left side of the shot was significant. I had the bamboo shades pulled down for two reasons: the landscaping wasn't finished and it reduced the light coming in the windows. Because the light coming from the windows at camera right was decreased, I could get a little more ambient light from the windows on camera left, in addition to the light from the strobe.

As you can see, your first task when placing strobes for interior shoots is to put them where you can hide them. With this done, you can use the light sources available. Remember to pay attention to the color of the light sources.
Watch what you are doing so that you create balanced light.

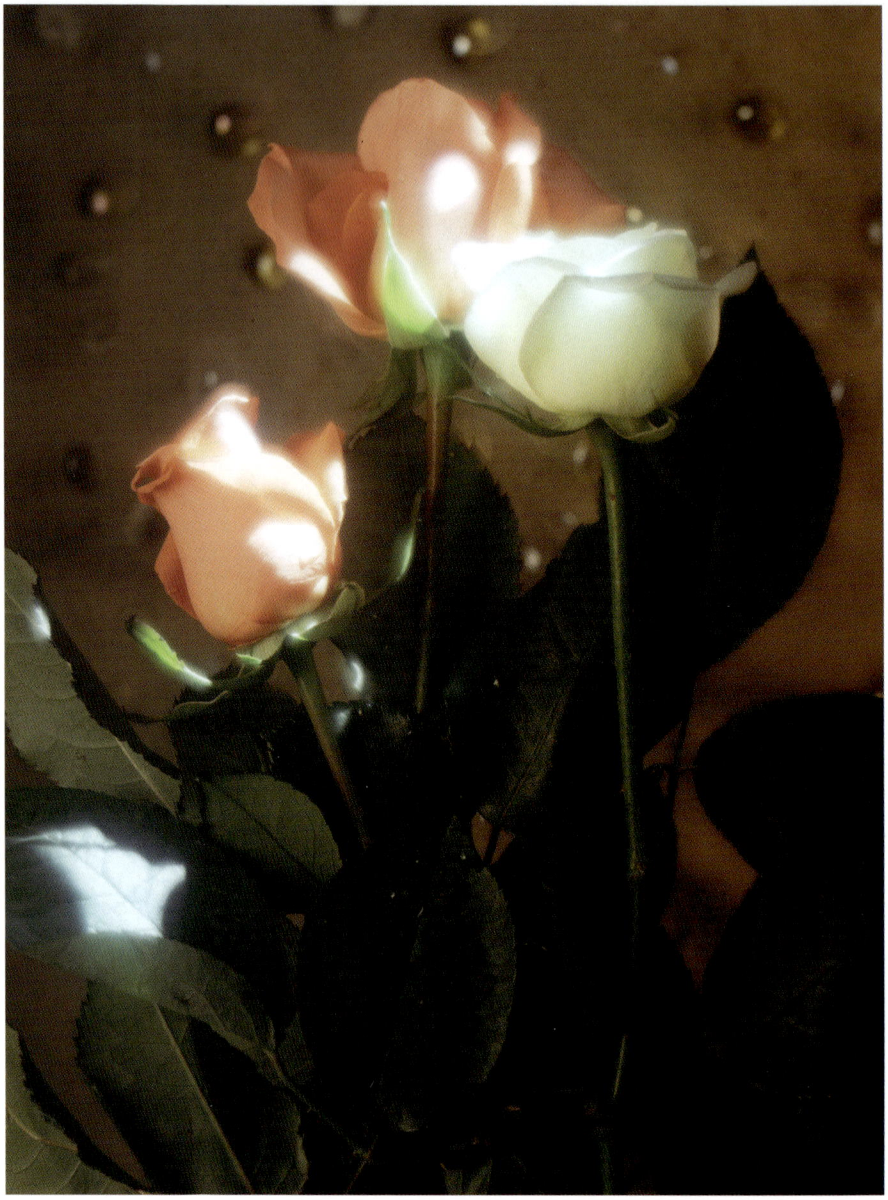

This shot was a lot of fun to light. The hard light comes from a slide projector at the top of the shot. This allowed me to make a very tight spot. Another large light was used to create overall light on the subject. Soft focus effects were created in Photoshop. I used a duplicated layer with Gaussian Blur.

8. TAKING GEAR ON LOCATION

For photographers who do most of their work on location, the information in this chapter won't likely come as a surprise. If you seldom shoot on location or are preparing for your first location shot, however, you'll find that the information that follows can streamline the process.

PREPARING FOR THE SHOOT

One thing is for sure: nothing can make your heart flutter like realizing that you've made it to your location session only to find that you've forgotten a piece of equipment you need for the shoot. To avoid this, make a list of all of the equipment you'll need (camera, computer, lights, stands, tripod, sync wires, grip gear, light modifiers, etc). If you're a more visual type, take a photo of all of the equipment you've packed and save it so you can more quickly prepare for your next location shoot. If you're shooting on location often, it might be easier to keep a bag packed and at the ready.

You'll want to be sure that you consider the weight of your bag when you're shooting on location. If you'll need to carry your equipment up a couple of flights of stairs or down a long, winding footpath, you'll be glad you packed light.

YOU'LL WANT TO BE SURE THAT YOU CONSIDER THE WEIGHT OF YOUR BAG WHEN YOU'RE SHOOTING ON LOCATION.

PACKING FOR THE JOB

When I work locally, I take a couple of cases. I have my battery-powered strobes in two cases, along with accessories and equipment to modify the light. I have it set up so that I can take just one of these cases on a simple shoot. When I'm not going by air, I like to pack so that the lights and tools are together. It makes it easier to find the tools I need.

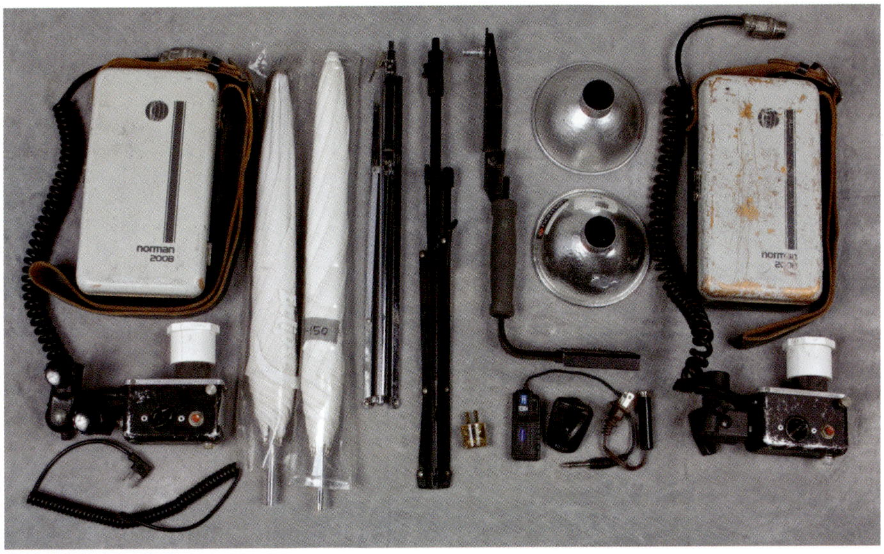

I use pictures of my gear to remind me what to pack.

When I finish a location shoot, I put everything back as if I was packing for the next shoot. This keeps me prepared, but it also makes it easier to be sure I packed everything. It is easy to leave a slave or a flash card behind if you don't do some kind of inventory.

When I get back to the office, I immediately back up the files from the shoot, recharge all the batteries, and check my gear. You should always be ready for your next shoot.

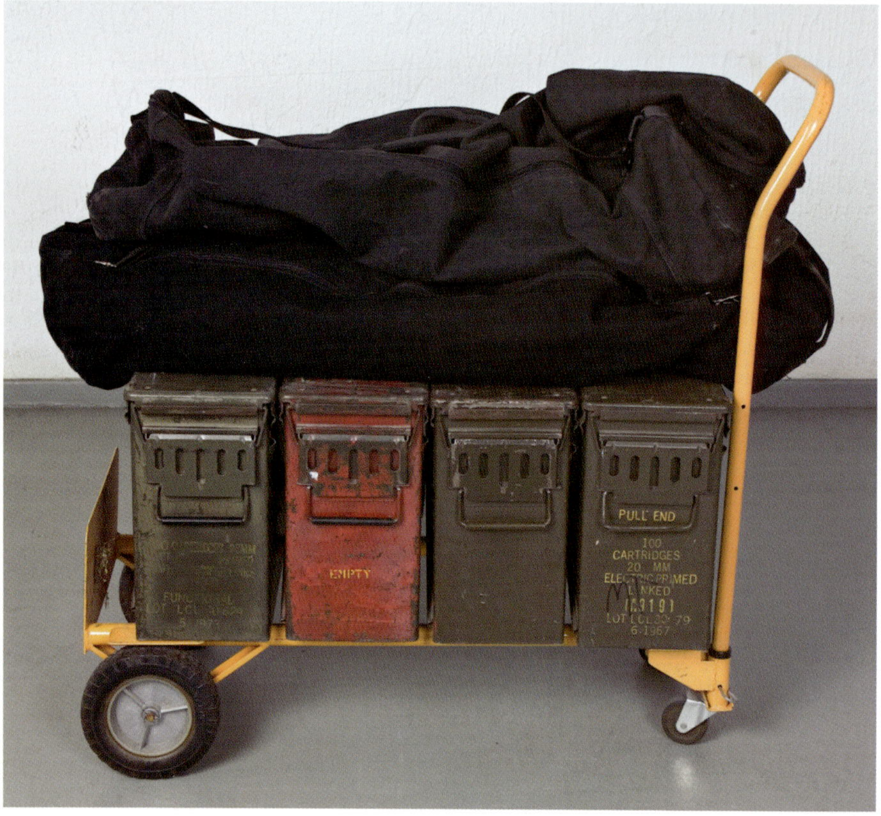

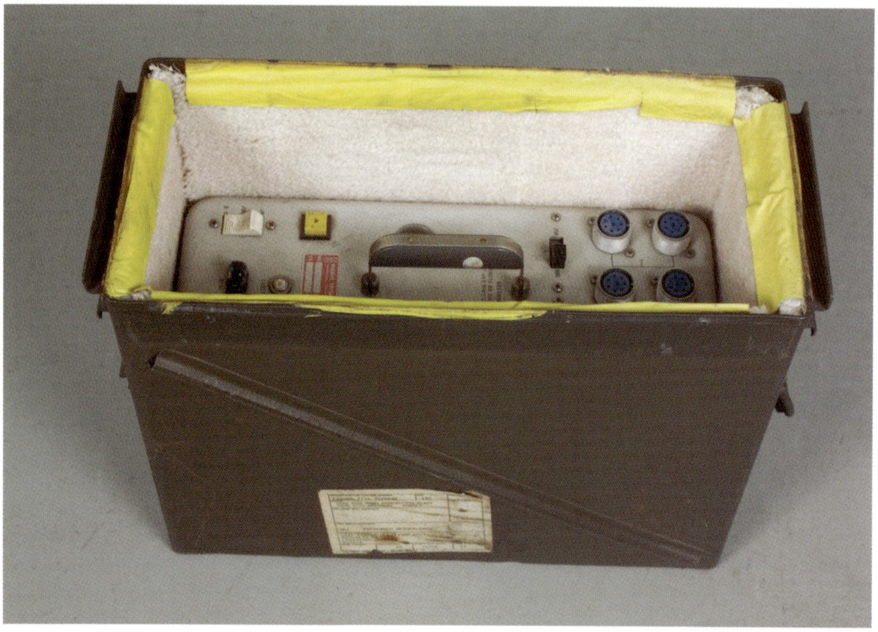

Top—This is my cart loaded with the military case and a couple of duffel bags for umbrellas and stands. The cart really saves my back! **Bottom**—My lighting equipment fits well into the military cases, with a little room for padding.

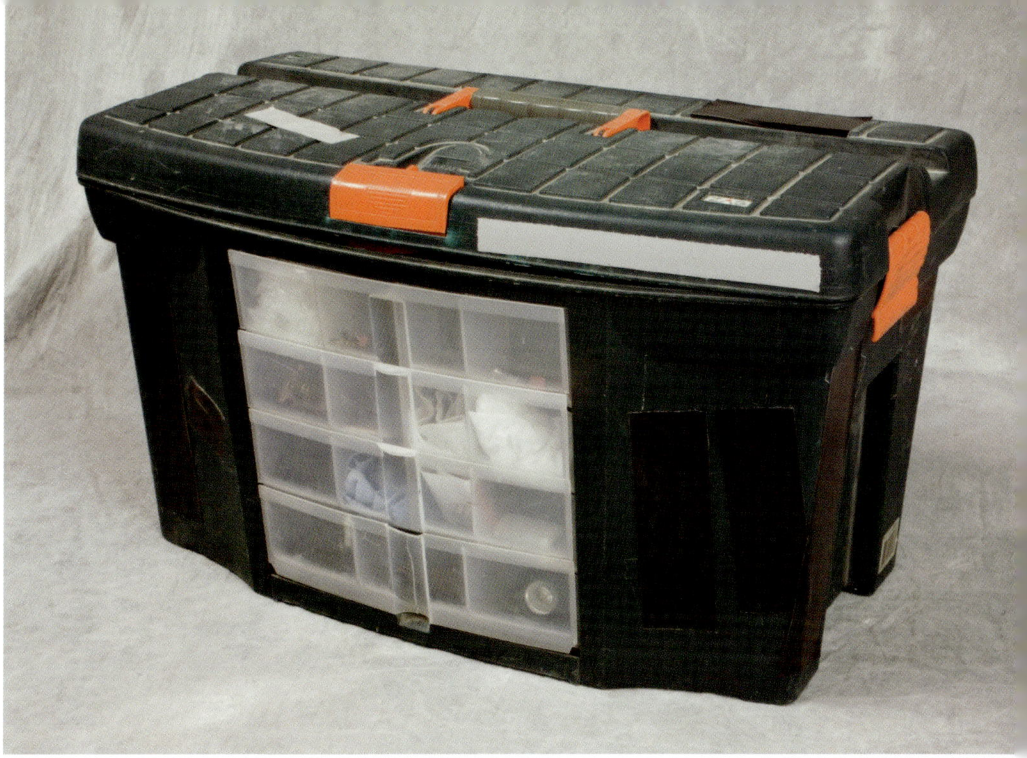

I keep tape on my cases, so I always have some at hand. Doing so also makes my cases less attractive to thieves.

Here are some practical ideas that will help you when you're taking your equipment on the road:

IF YOU WANT TO WORK WITH BATTERIES, BE AWARE THAT YOUR RECYCLE TIMES CAN BE LONG ENOUGH TO INTERFERE WITH SHOOTING.

- Don't draw attention to your gear with fancy cases. I like cases from the home improvement stores and military surplus. The surplus cases are really heavy duty.
- You should be able to stand on some of your cases. It's easier than bringing a stepladder.
- Get a wheeled cart. It's more useful than wheeled luggage.
- Bring as much backup equipment as you can.
- When you fly, you can lose some of your luggage. Each bag should have some lighting gear, some camera gear, and some grip gear in it. Your preferred camera and laptop should go in your carry-on luggage. That way, if you and your baggage part ways, you can still shoot the job.
- Put tape on the outside of your cases. It is easy to forget gaffer's tape, but if it is on your cases, you won't leave without it.

BATTERY-POWERED STROBES

Several strobe systems and the dedicated strobes for your camera are designed for battery power. If you want to work with batteries, you should be aware that your recycle times can be long enough to interfere with shooting. This is particularly true with dedicated strobes running on just a few AA batteries. Also, there is a limit to how many flashes you can get from batteries. There are battery packs for Canon and Nikon strobes, but these only hold eight batteries. Quantum, Norman, and Lumidyne all make battery-powered gear that is powerful and fast. Of course, a dedicated strobe will be the most

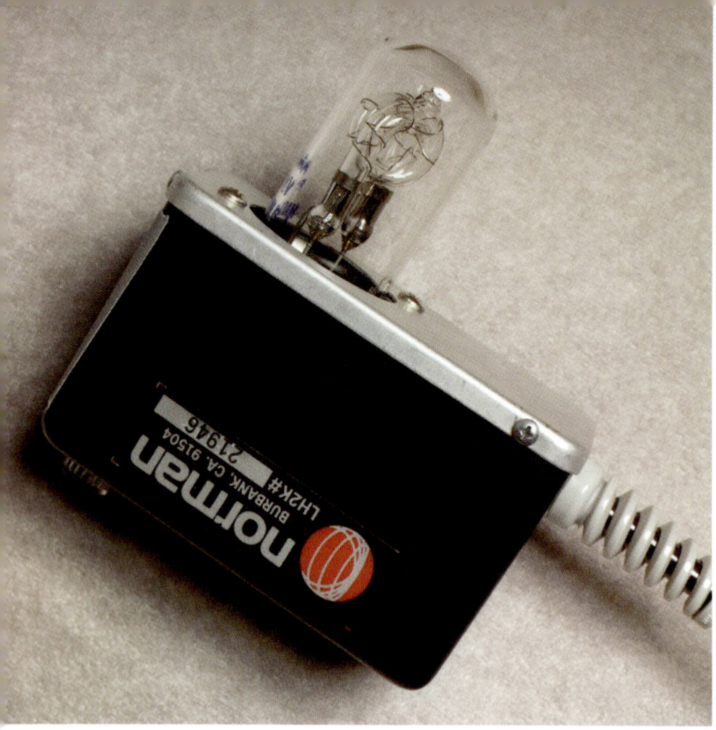

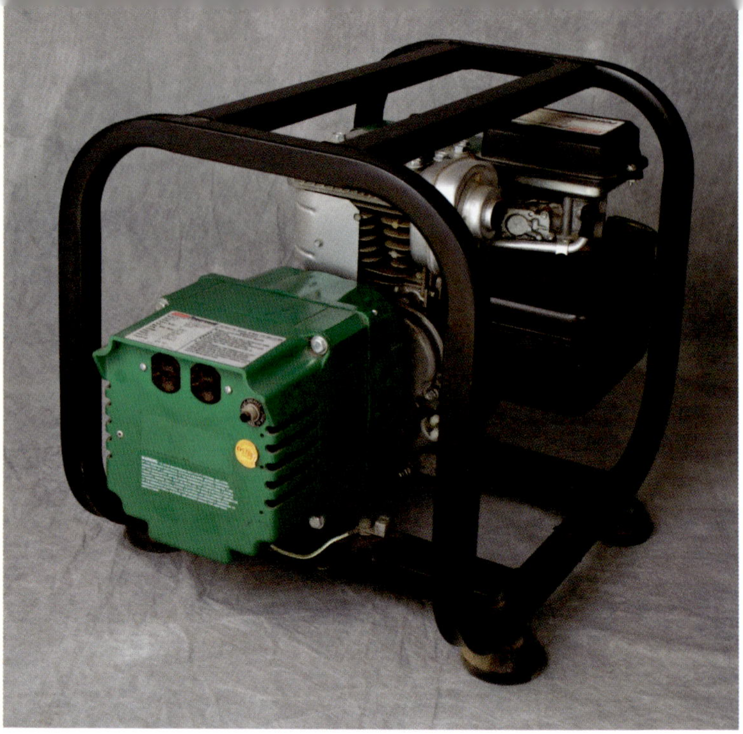

Left—This is a Norman 200B strobe. The head fits on a stand or bracket, and you can carry the battery pack. These make good location lights. **Right**—Gas-powered generators can be very effective on location.

effective light for shooting flash fill and events because of the automated exposure controls.

AC STROBES ON LOCATION

If you are working inside a building, you can expect AC power, and your only concern should be having a bunch of quality extension cords on hand. If you are outside or somewhere you don't have AC power, you have several options.

Many strobe manufacturers make dedicated batteries for them. These batteries weigh about twenty pounds and offer hundreds of flashes, but your recycle time may be longer than with AC power. You can also use a generator; I do. Although it is heavy, about fifty pounds, it gives an unlimited number of flashes. Generators can run several monolights and maintain quick recycle times, plus they can be useful if your power goes out at home. Do not run a generator for more than a few minutes in an enclosed space. New generators are available for a couple of hundred dollars. Finally, you can use an inverter. These devices convert the 12-volt DC power from your car to 110-volt AC. There are many small, inexpensive inverters available. These can be very useful for running battery chargers, but you do have to check that they don't overheat. You need a much larger inverter to run strobes, say about 2000 watts. These cost about as much as a generator. They don't weigh much, but they don't go anywhere your car doesn't go.

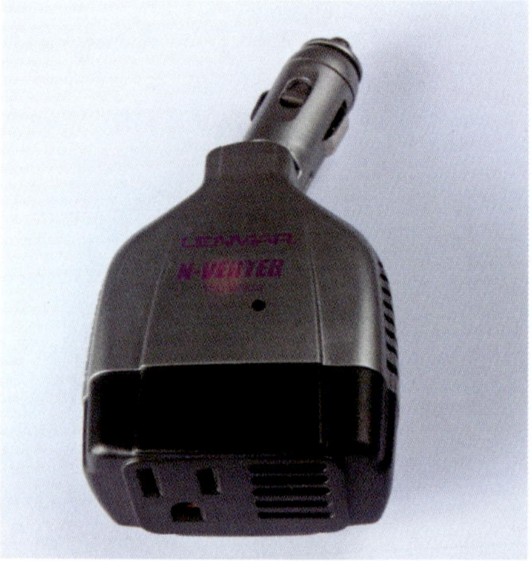

This little inverter will slip into a cigarette lighter socket. It can charge most batteries, but it can't power a strobe.

9. PORTRAITURE

CONSULTING WITH THE SUBJECT

A great portrait depends on more than just light—certainly, the pose and the mood created in the image are also important. If you define the subject's face well and create lighting that is appropriate for your subject, you will make more successful portraits.

This is one of my favorite portraits. I call the shot *What?*

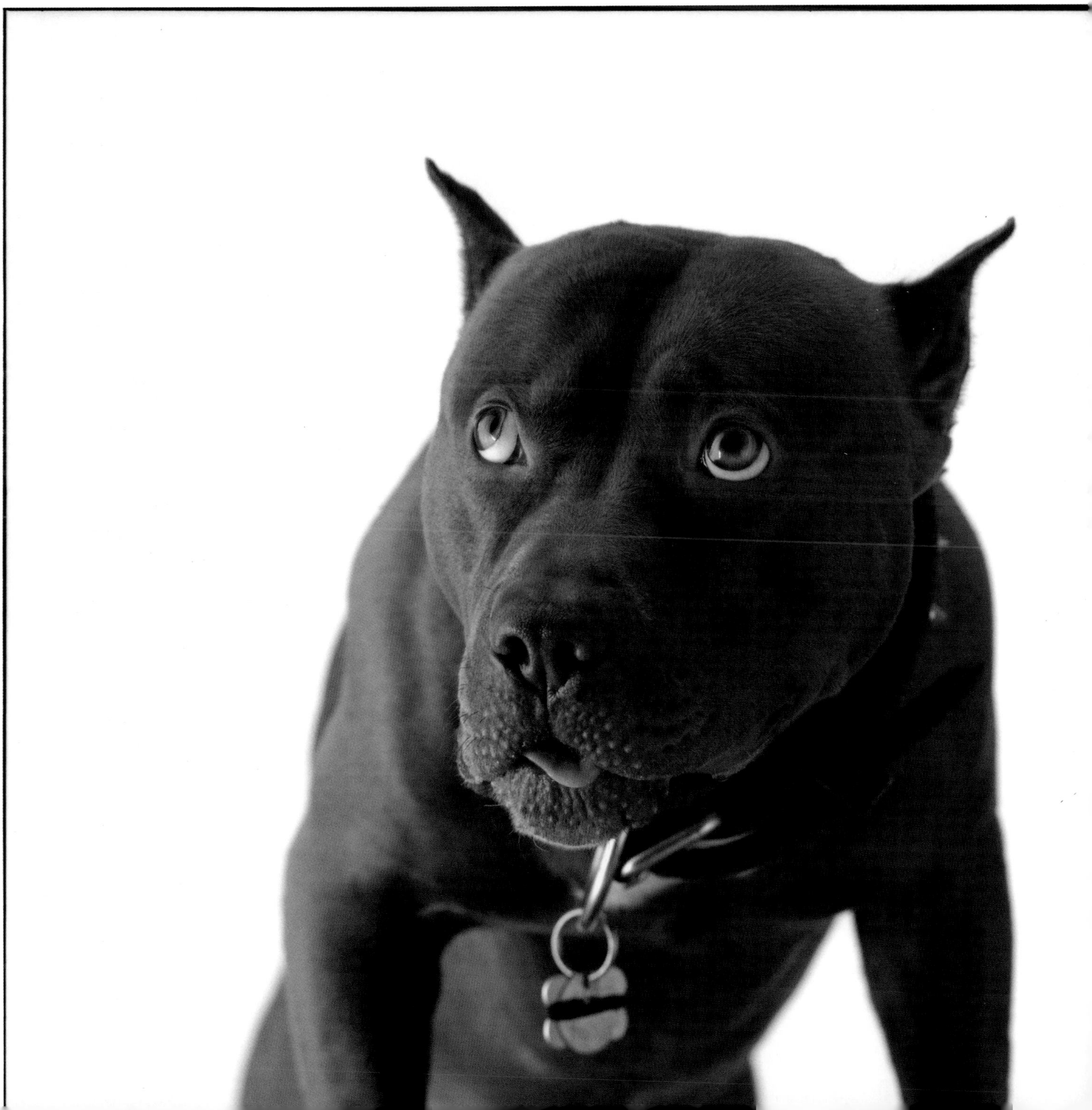

Before I take a single shot, I talk to the subject about how they want to appear. Listening to the client voice their expectations gives me time to study their face and decide whether I want to work with hard or soft light. I also try to identify features I want to highlight or hide and consider what background might complement the clothes. I make it a point to ask the client how the image will be used. A shot that will be in an annual report should be carried out differently than a portrait made for a loved one.

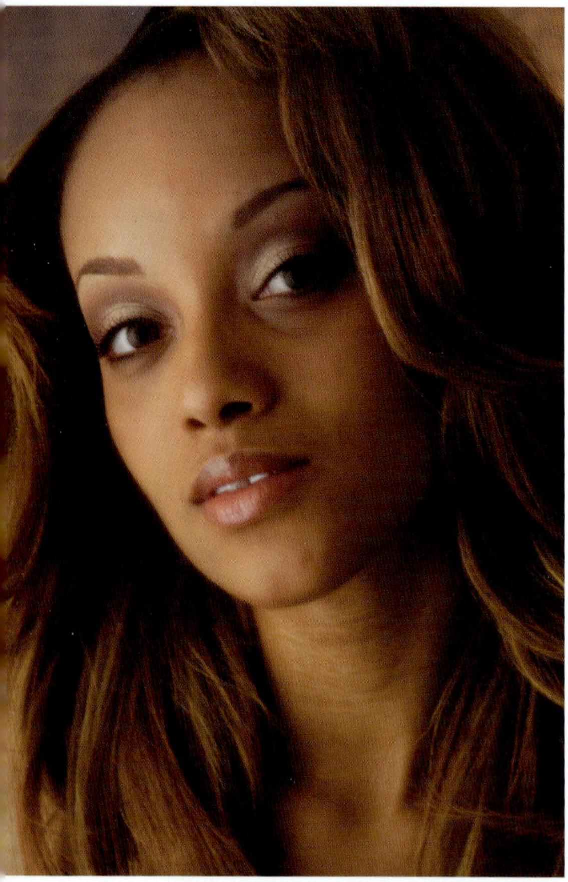

Since all people do not look alike or want to be shown in the same way, lighting should be customized for each subject. While department store studios don't do this, it is one of the ways an independent photographer can add value to their services.

All people have different facial features and skin tones, which depend on their ancestors' origins. I use a longer tonal scale with pictures

Top left—Light creates definition, shape, and color to any shot. Each portrait should be lit to suit the subject. **Bottom**—Sometimes character is what makes a shot compelling. **Facing page**—Not all portraits are about the face.

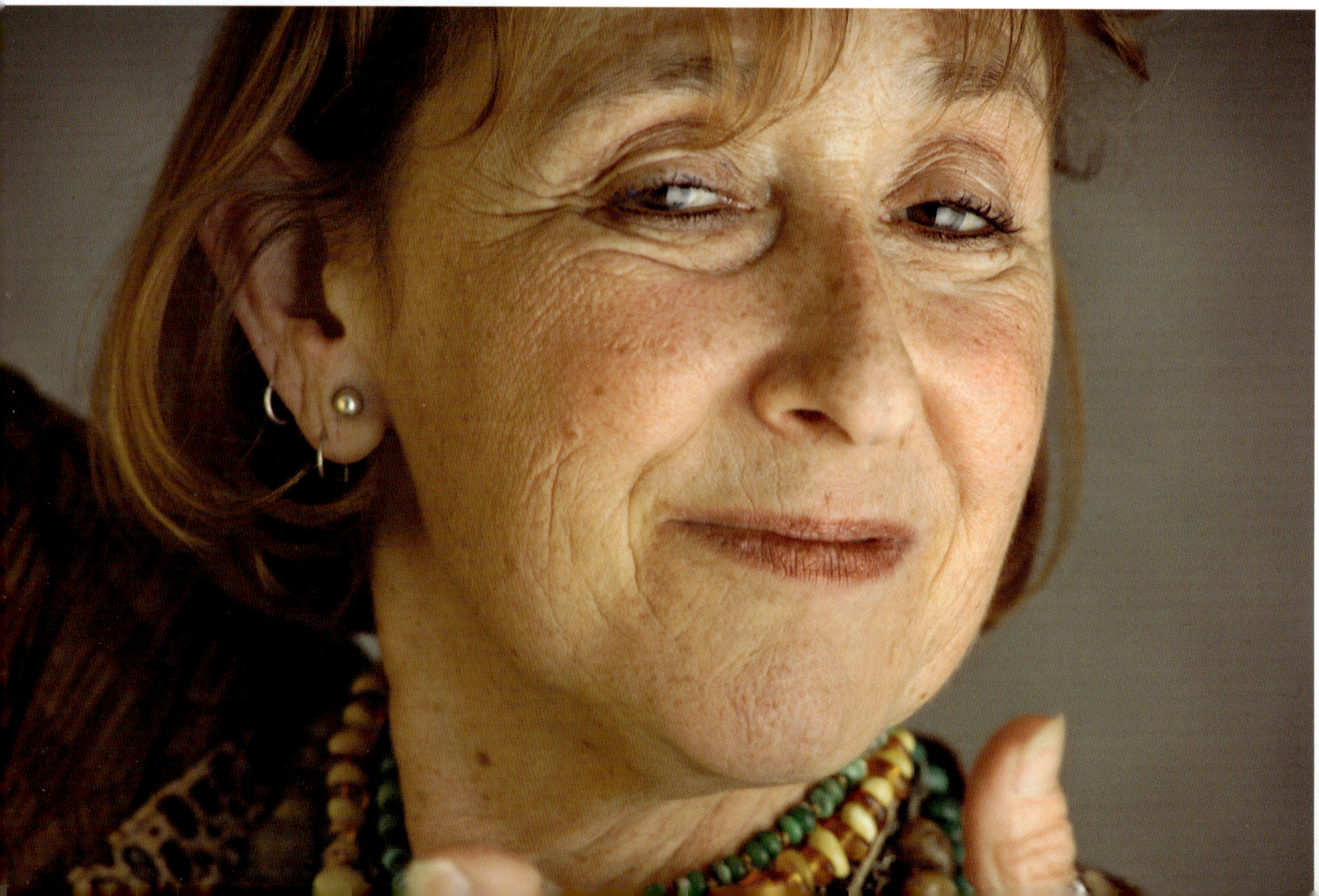

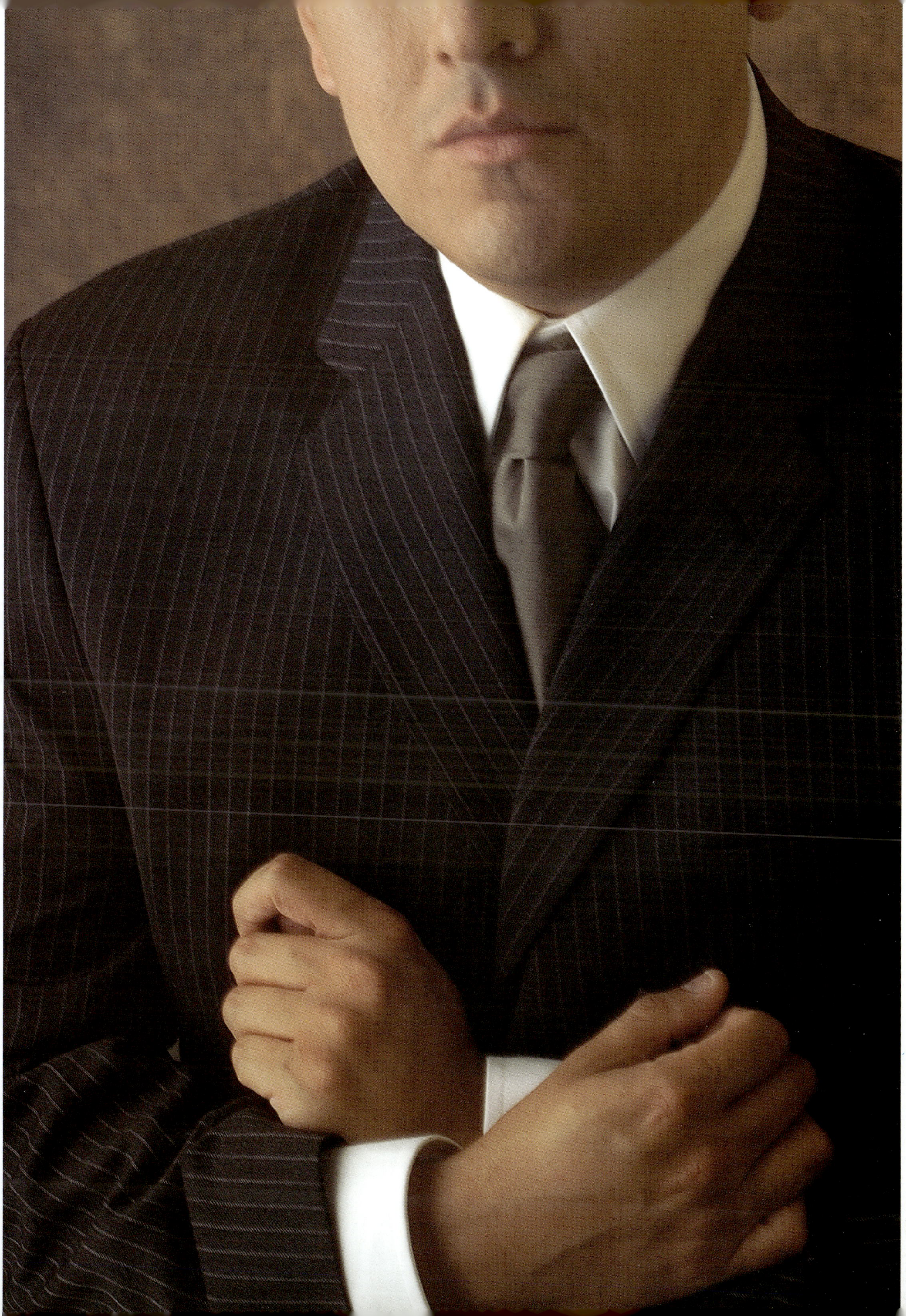

of people of African origin than persons of European origin. For persons with Asian ancestry, I build more contrast into the face to make the image more three-dimensional.

Finally, when you are making decisions about how to light your subject, you should consider his age. We might create character lighting for a man using a small light source, say just an umbrella. For someone who wants to appear more youthful, I would use a large light source and a reflector, just as a start.

LIGHTING IDEAS

There are a few things that I do for most portraits. I start with a large light source (usually the umbrella/light panel combination) placed to one side of the face to accentuate the shape of the face. Sometimes this is the only light, but I typically add a smaller, harder light near the camera. This gives me catchlights in the eyes and changes the contrast in the face. I might use a warm filter on this light. I may even mount this on a camera bracket rather than a light stand, so the light travels with me. The third tool I have is a reflector, usually a light panel. I have a silver cover on one side and gold on the other. I don't use this setup constantly. Nothing works for everyone. I would set this

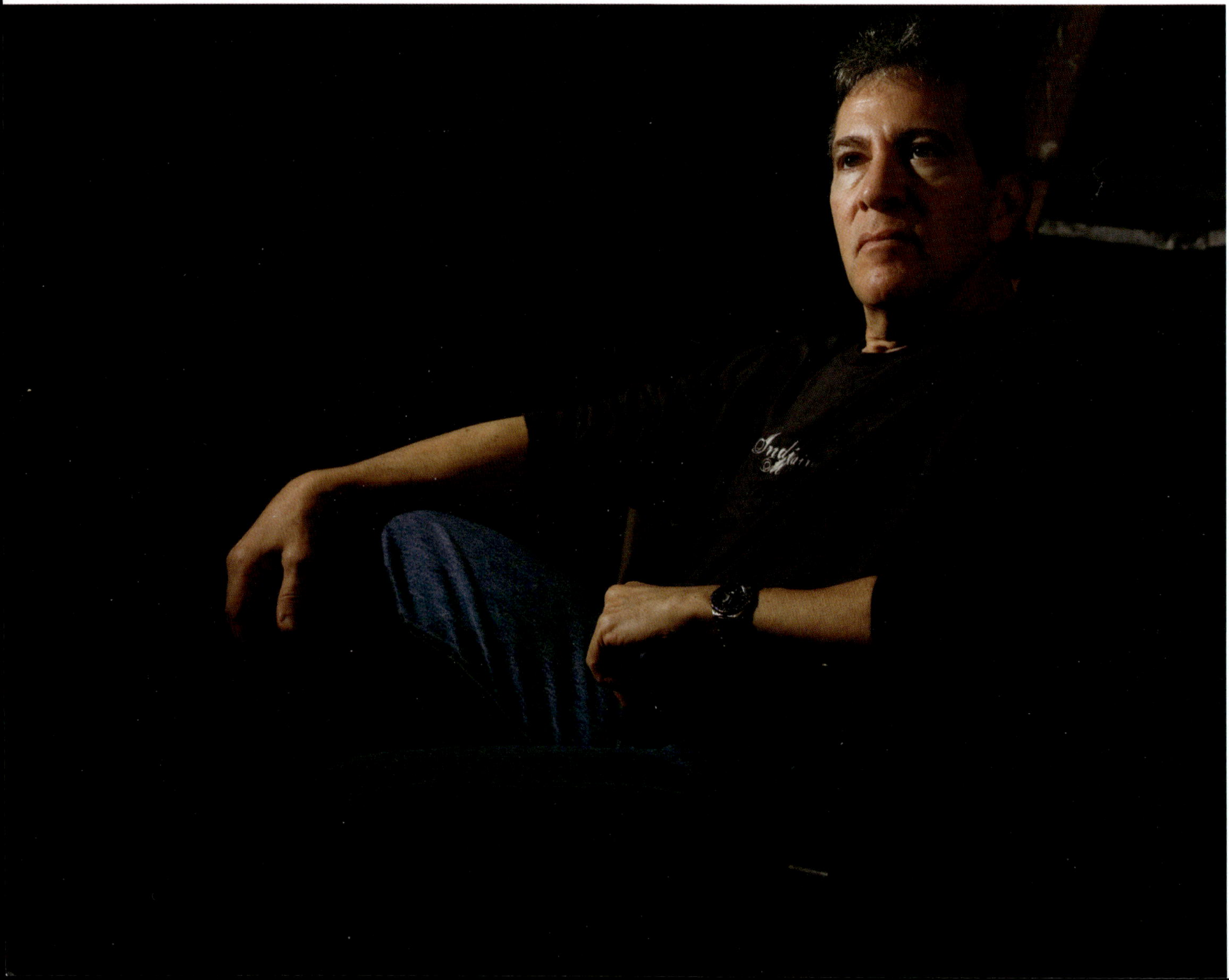

For this shot, the only light was a snoot. I used a large reflector for fill.

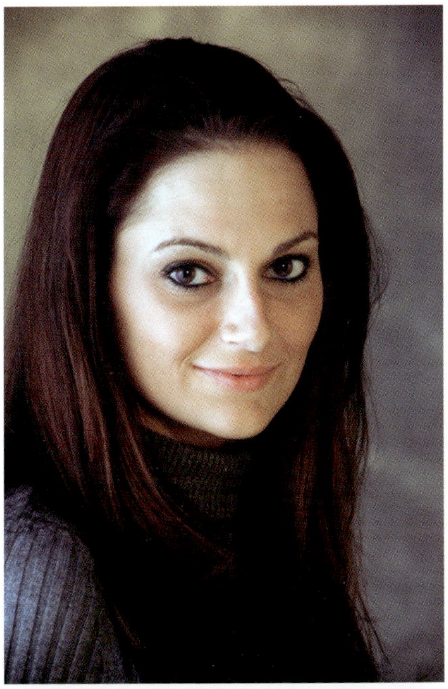

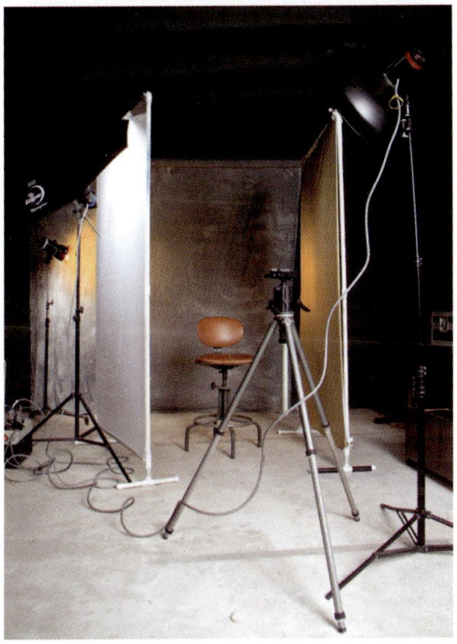

Top and bottom left—A simple setup was used to create this soft and delicate image. There are three lights: an umbrella/light panel (large light), a beauty dish (this smaller light was used for the catchlight), and a reflector (background light). **Right**—In this shot, the hair light was important. It added definition and sparkle to the hair.

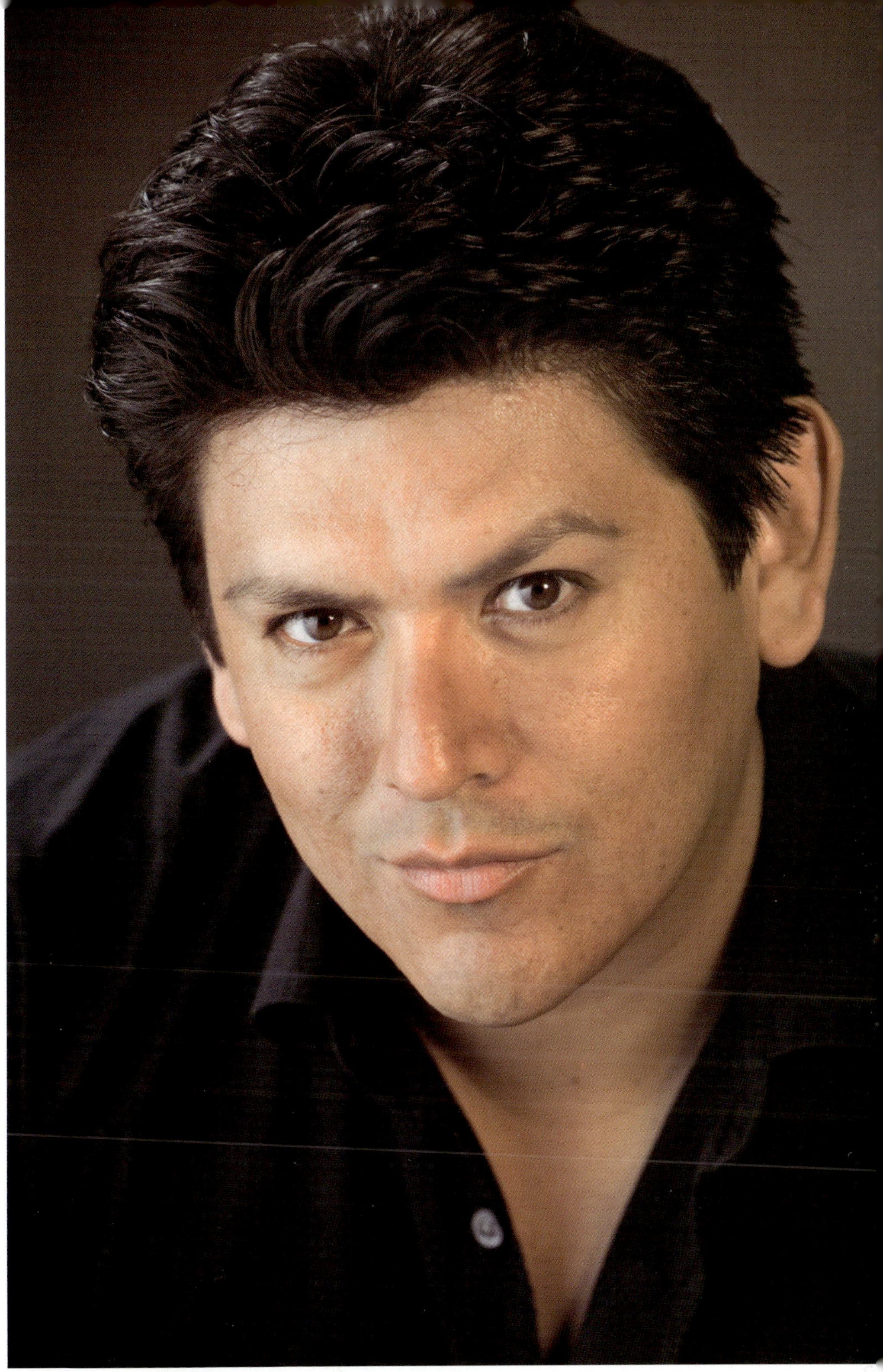

up if I didn't know anything about whom I would be shooting. Since I do commercial shooting, this happens pretty frequently.

There are many special-purpose tools for portraiture, and there are other ways to use the more typical tools. The basic tools I use are the large light source, a hard light for contrast, and a reflector. I may use a hair light on a boom or a rim light positioned behind the subject. However, I start with a simple setup.

USING STROBES OUTDOORS

This is probably the best use for a dedicated strobe. This is an easy way to control the light your camera will photograph and create better outdoor portraits. The object of this lighting, called flash fill, is to add light that will primarily affect the shadows in your shot, while leaving the highlights unchanged. I should point out that I almost always use flash fill when shooting outdoors. It is better to ask yourself why you shouldn't use flash than to wonder why you should.

Most cameras on the market have a flash compensation dial that enables you to balance the flash with daylight. While some cameras will make good decisions about flash fill automatically, it is often useful to set the compensation to a negative setting. This will mean that the sun, not the flash, will be the dominant light source for your shot. If you are shooting in open shade or on an overcast day, the compensation should be set to a negative value so the contrasty lighting from your flash doesn't overwhelm the soft light from the sky. Of course, you can and should check the lighting effect on the camera's LCD screen.

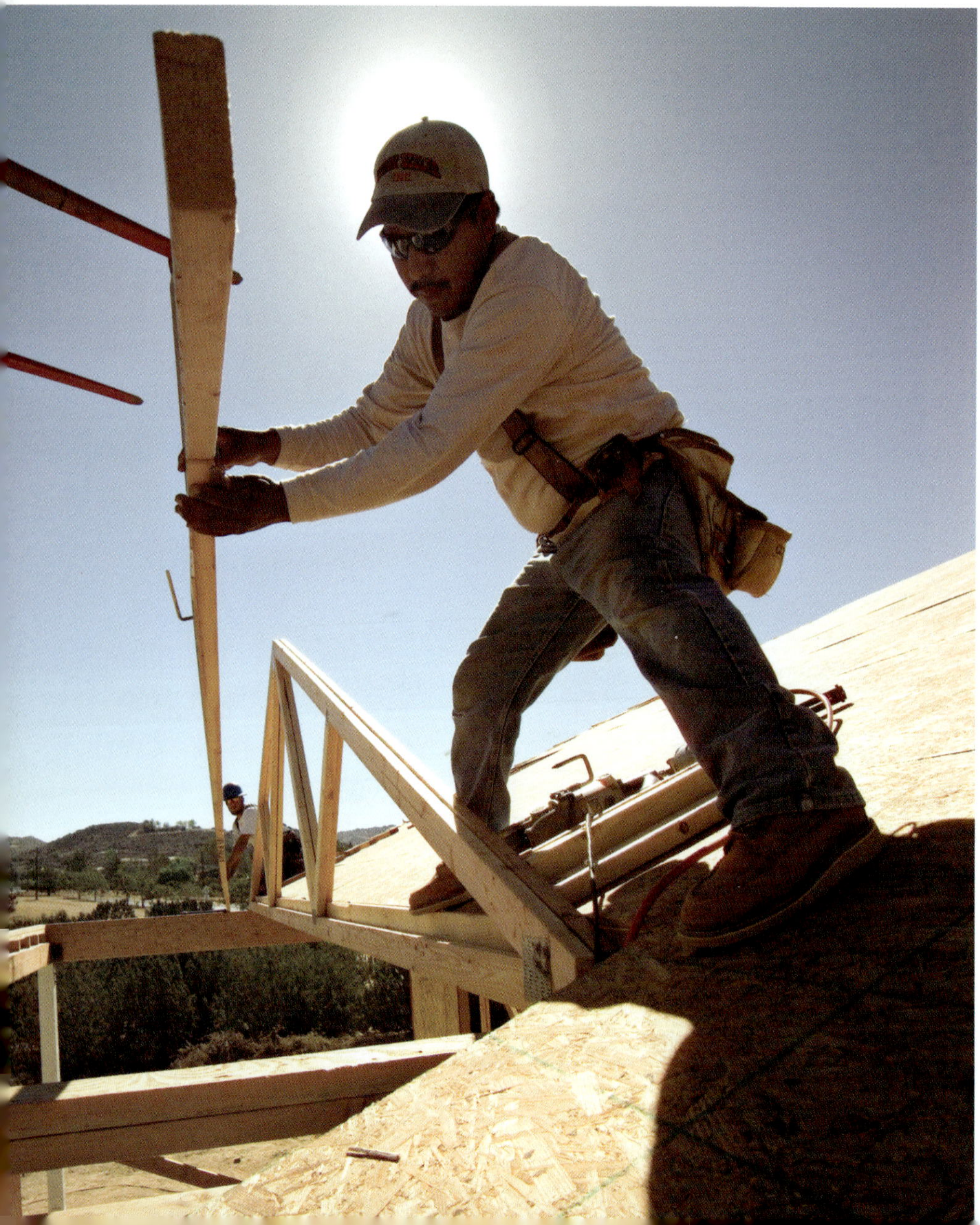

The sun is behind the subject. Without flash fill, the subject would have been just a silhouette.

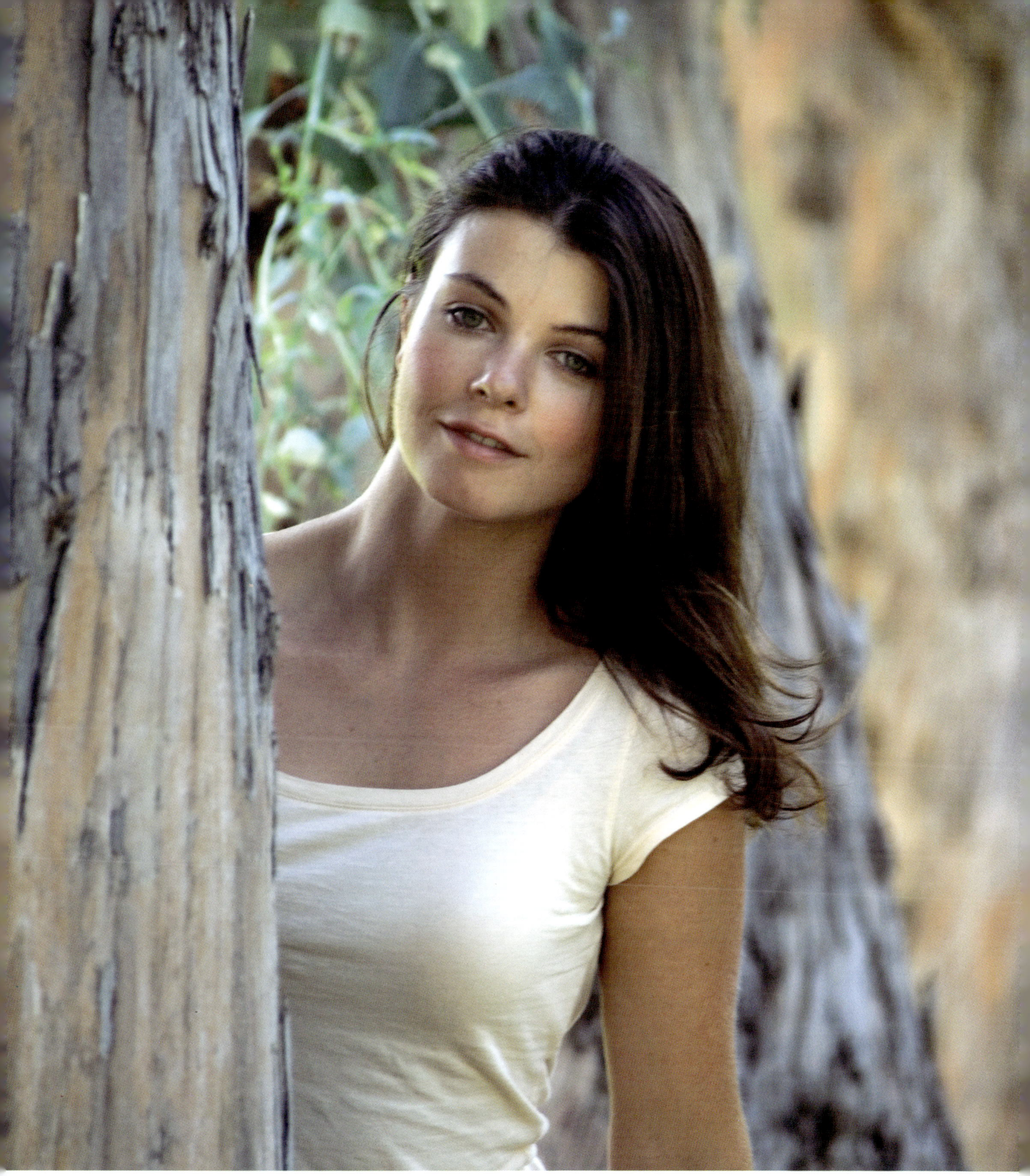

One of my favorite flash fill shots. I only used a little light from the strobe. If I had added more, I would have ruined the delicate feel of the shot.

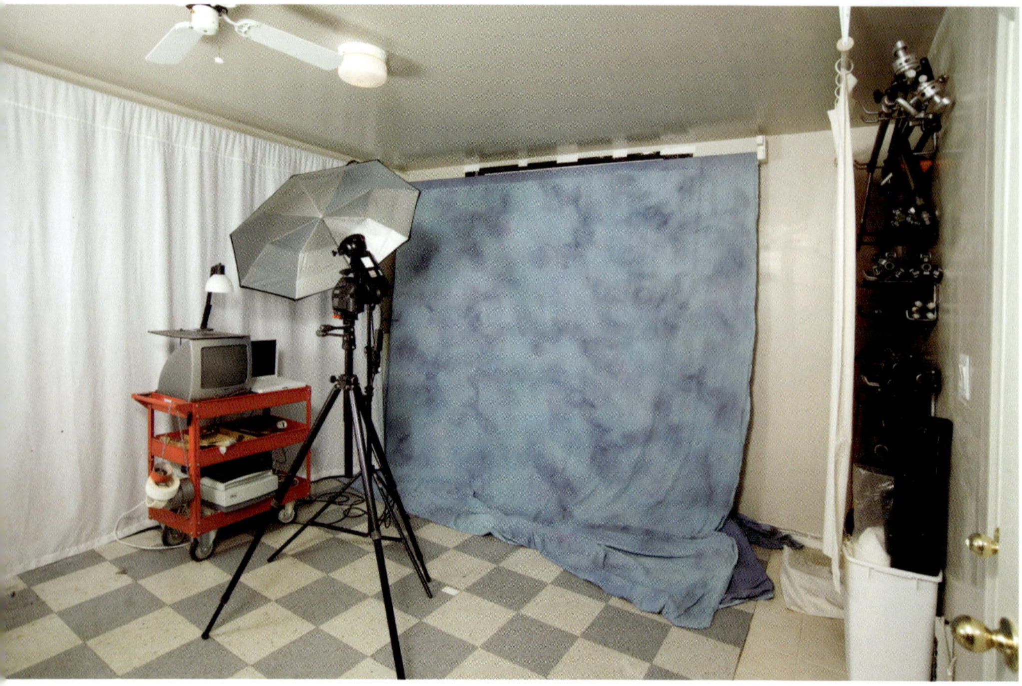

A friend made a small studio space very useful. Notice how curtains have been used to block windows and the equipment storage. In a small space, you need to be very careful about what can be reflected back into the subject.

You can also do this with a strobe that is not dedicated to your camera, checking your exposure with the histogram and the proofing image. Changing the aperture will affect both the light from the strobe and the ambient light, while the shutter speed will affect only the ambient light unless you go over the sync speed. I use manual strobe frequently for flash fill. I find that changing the power of the strobe, rather than changing the camera settings, is the quickest way for me to work with a manual strobe for flash fill. In fact, I can leave the camera on auto and have my strobe set to ½ or ¼ power for many shots.

INTO THE STUDIO

A studio is a place where the photographer controls the light. You don't need a huge space to run an efficient studio. If you're using strobes, you can control all the light almost anywhere, as your strobes can overpower almost any other light source.

CHANGING A LOOK

You can use lighting to create different moods in your images. By changing the placement of your strobes or the way the light is modified, you can create numerous portrait looks, suited for different viewers or recipients. Let's take a look at some examples.

The first shot (facing page) was created by a big light source (an umbrella) and a large reflector (a light panel). Since the light sources are so large, the light is very soft and the transition from light to shadow is gradual. This type of lighting tends to make a subject appear younger, and it did so in this shot.

SCULPTING THE FACE

Your lighting can help you sculpt the shape of your subject's face. If there is a shadow side of the face, the face will appear thinner. If you light both sides of the face evenly, the face will appear broader.

Next, I decided to create a setup that would render my subject a little more mature and elegant. To do this, I used a harsher light. I put a Norman 200B on the camera as a second light. This gave me a hard light, which I set at very low power. In addition to this, I used the light with the large umbrella that was used in the last shot, and I removed the light panel reflector. Most of the light comes from the light with the large umbrella, but you can see the effect of the 200B when you look at the catchlight in the eye and the shadow under the chin.

These are the easiest to see differences, but you can also see differences in the area around the eye and the eyebrow. If you changed the power levels of these two lights, you could make additional changes in the face. I will be

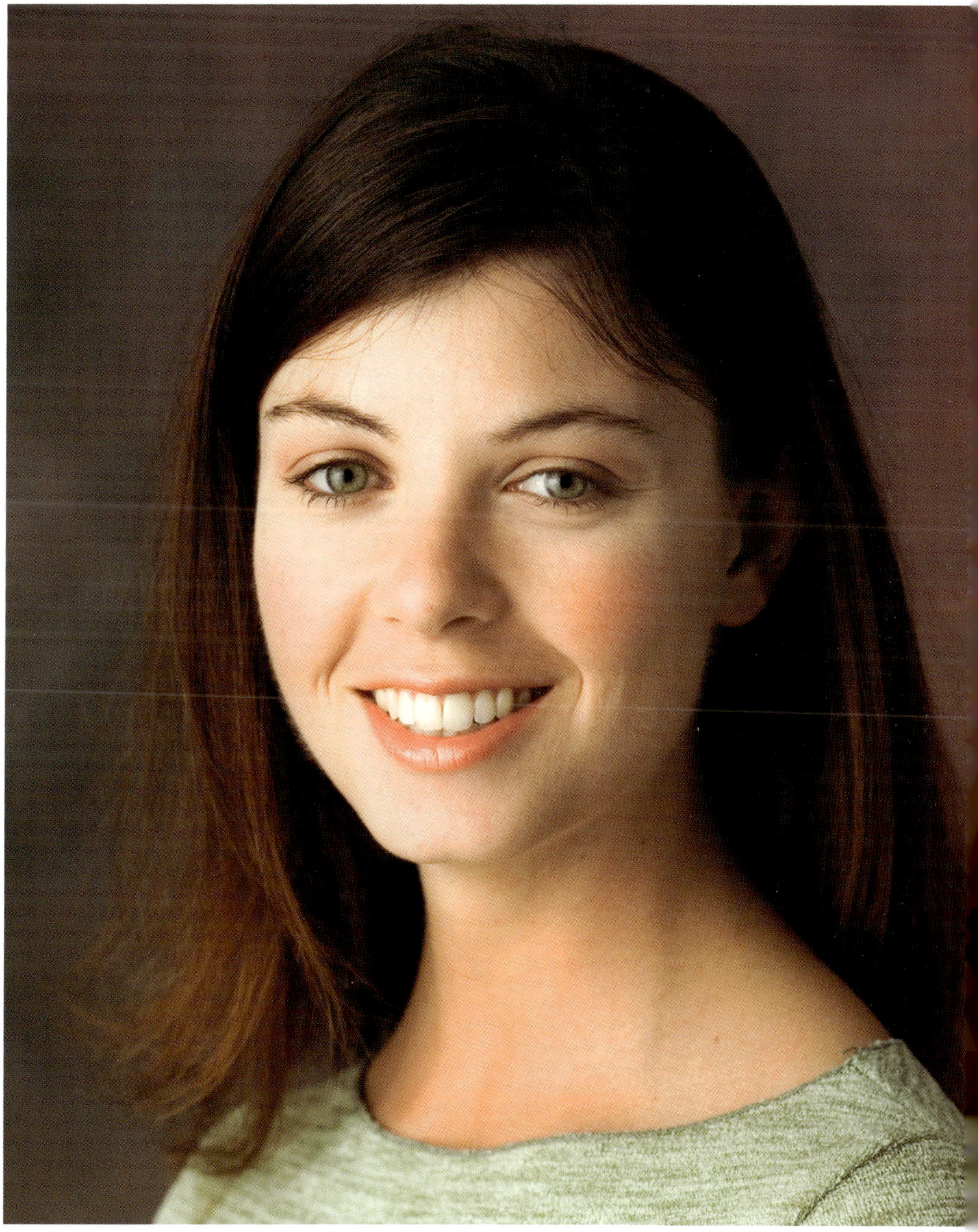

To create this shot, I used a big light source and a reflector. The light softens the details of the subject's face.

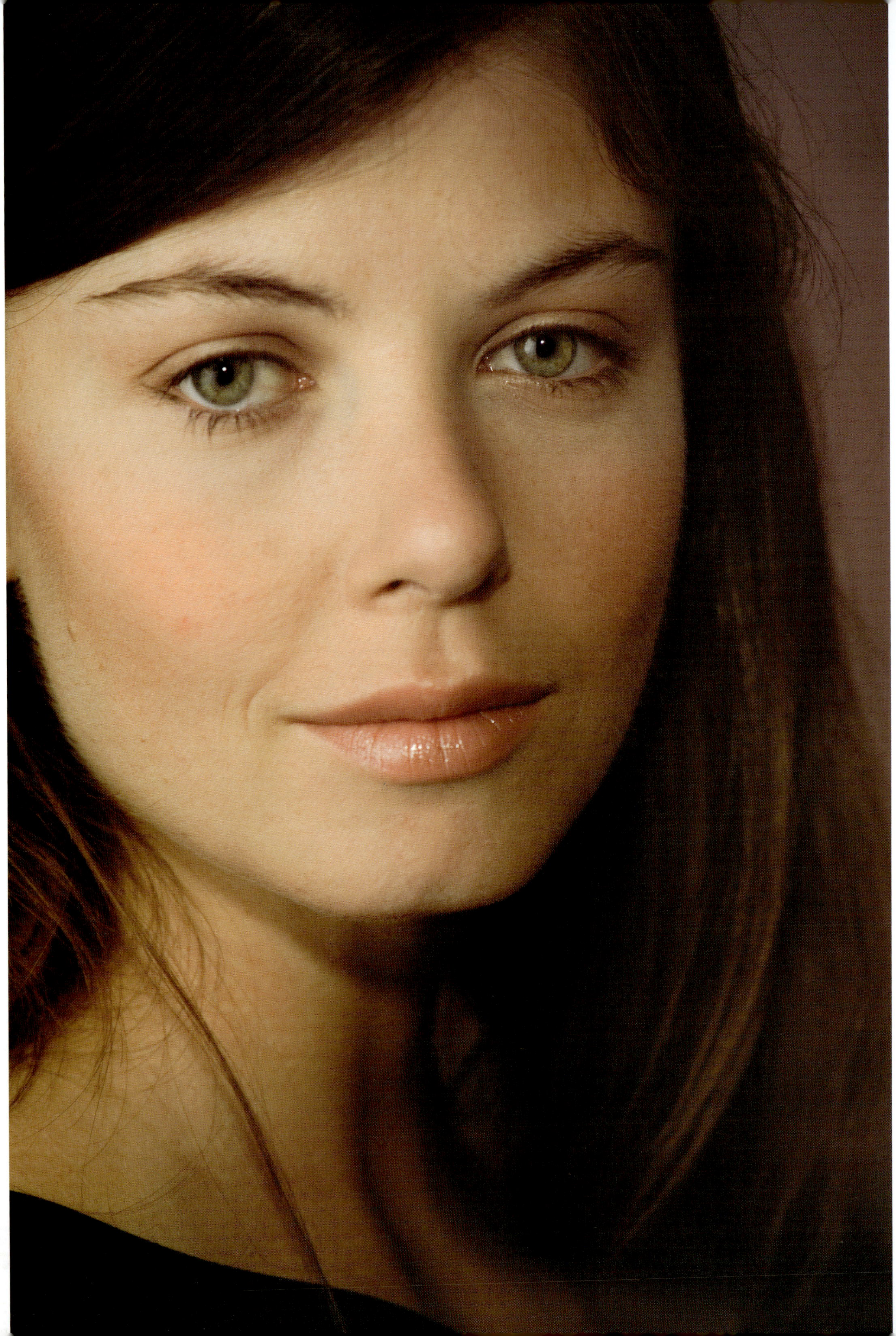

talking about changing the power levels between lights a little later in this chapter. This small change in light, coupled with a change in the model's expression, creates a big difference between these two images.

One thing I want to point out about these images: the lights are close to the subject. This enables me to control what they do and assures me that my big light sources will act like big light sources.

Facing page—I added a small strobe to the large light source and removed the reflector. The strobe and the increase in shadow give more definition to the shape and detail of the face. **Below**—I used just a single umbrella to light this subject. I wanted to maintain the detail and texture in the face.

CHARACTER LIGHTING

Charlie has a great face for photographs. He looks like he just walked out of the Dust Bowl. When somebody has a great face, they are generally easy to light. You want to put contrast and detail into the face. Consequently, you

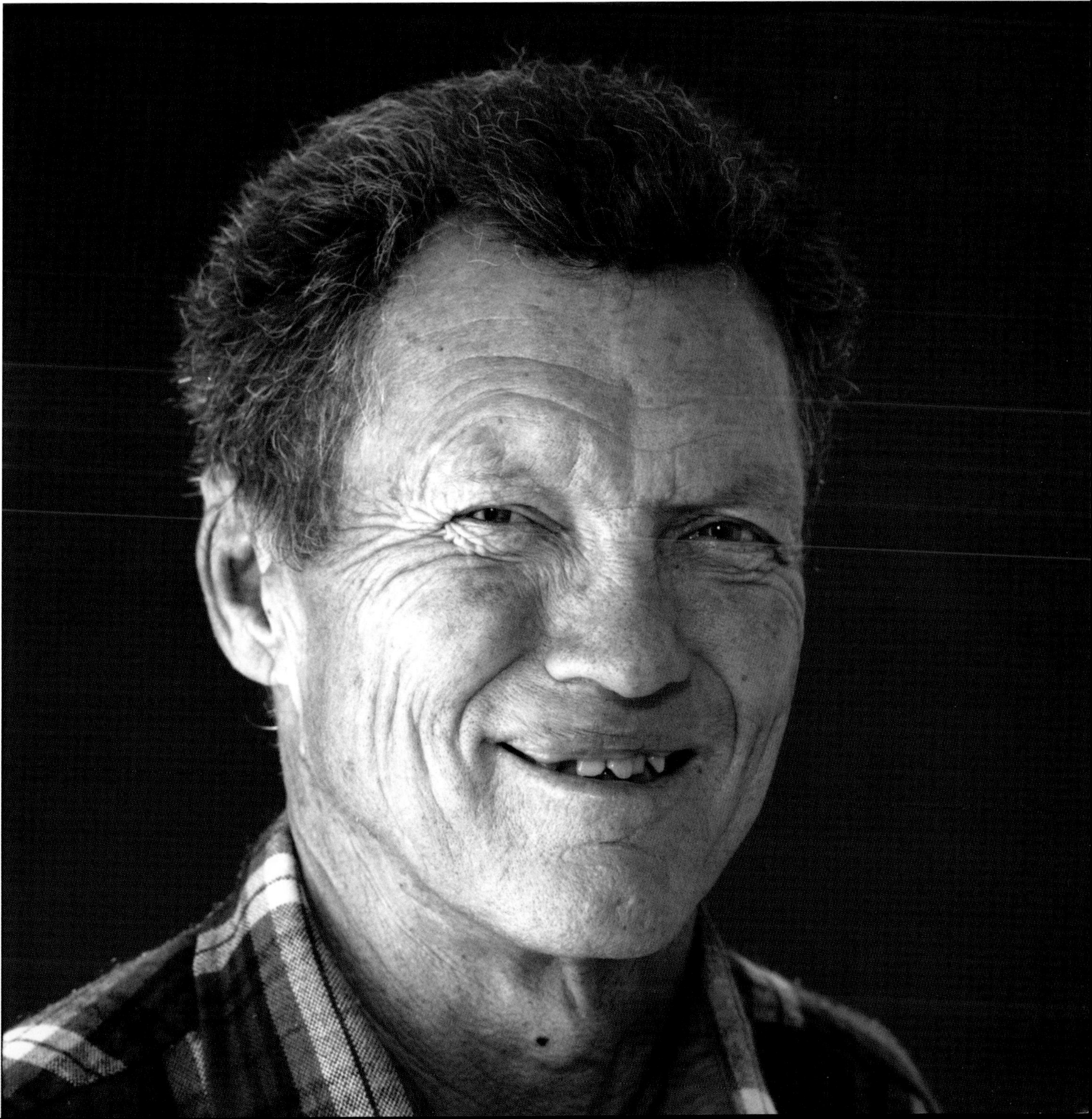

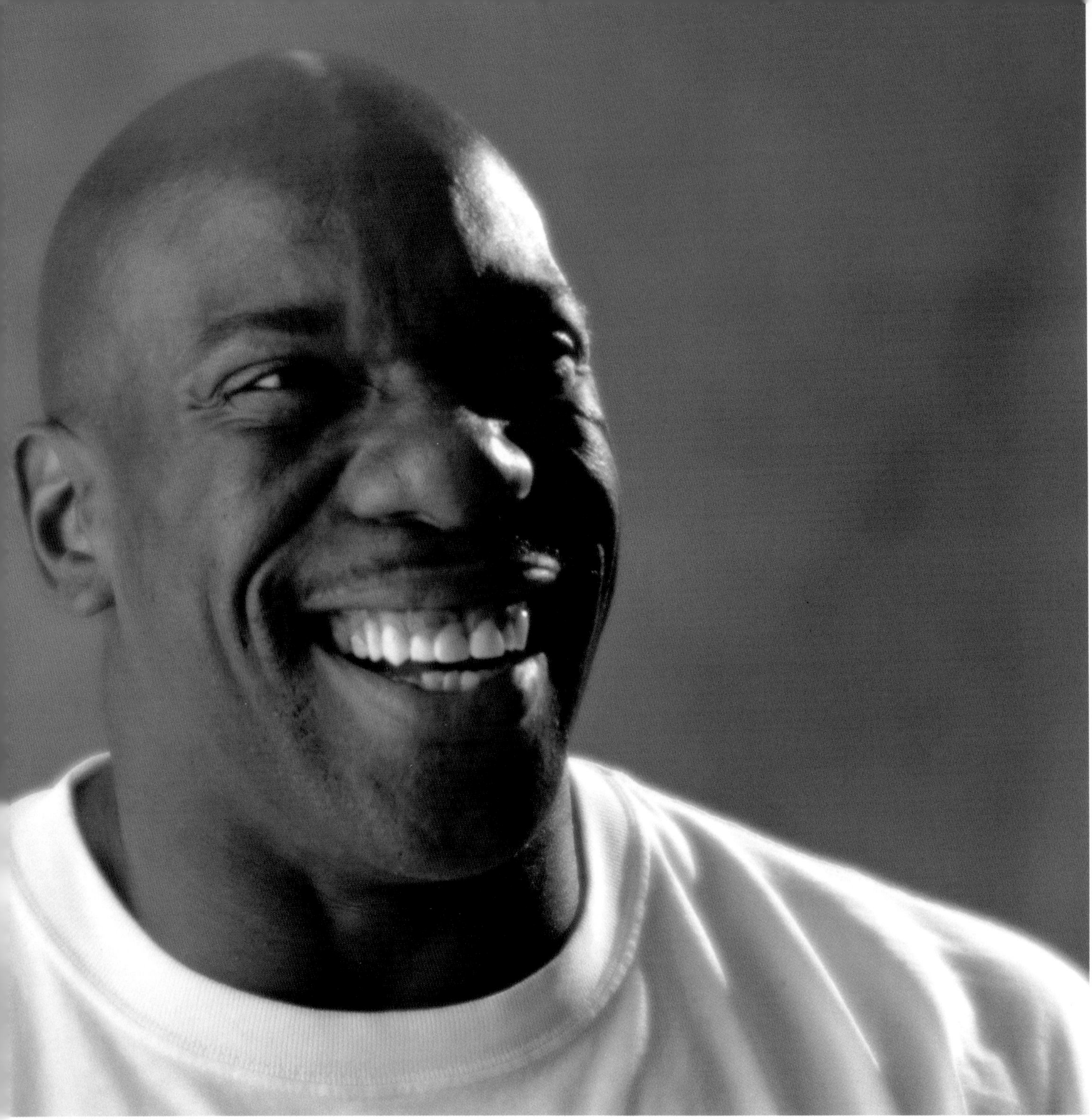

are going to use a smaller light source. In this case, I used one 42-inch ribless umbrella. This gave me everything I could want from the face. The umbrella is about 60 degrees to the left of the camera. The fill comes from the light scattered by the umbrella. The background is black seamless. While I often don't like a black background, I think it works well in this shot. Although I made several shots of Charlie, this is the only time he smiled.

Randy also has a great face, but this shot has a lot more going on in it. First, the light is soft because I used a large light source again. I also used a Hoya

I used a large light and a light with a snoot for this shot. The snoot was placed behind the subject, on the right side. This produced the highlight on the right side of the image. I used a soft focus filter to create a glowing effect.

Softener A filter, which further softened the shot. These are the best soft focus filters. In portraiture, hard light is often used to create highlights in the hair (a snoot is a great tool for this) and to create a rim light around the subject (the light is placed behind the subject and creates a glowing outline around him or her). The rim light on Randy came around to the front a little bit and added light on the side of his head. That area of brightness draws the eye away from his shirt, which would otherwise be the brightest part of the shot.

SPECIAL LIGHT

I wanted to do a shot that could only be done when the photographer has control of all light, in the studio. To create this image, I positioned an umbrella/light panel at camera left. This was the main light. I introduced a hard light, my Kodak slide projector, as a second light source, positioned at camera right. To modify the light from the projector, I slid a piece of Cinefoil with cutout crescent shapes and a red gel where the slide would typically be

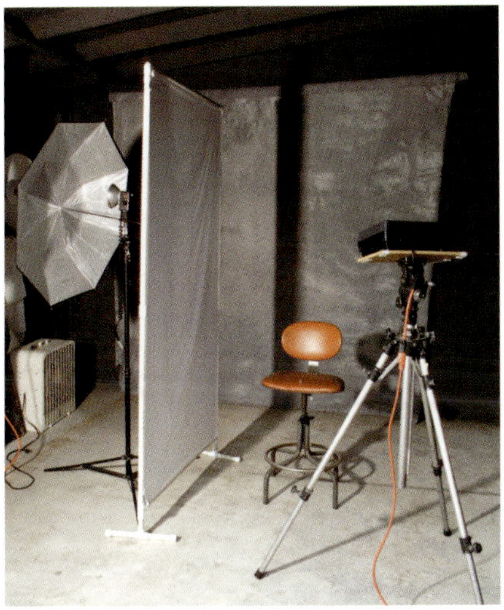

Above—The slide projector is a great special purpose light. You can see the projector mounted on a tripod in the setup shot. This requires a heavy-duty tripod. **Right**—A slide projector, a red gel, and a piece of Cinefoil with cutout shapes allowed me to create this dramatic image.

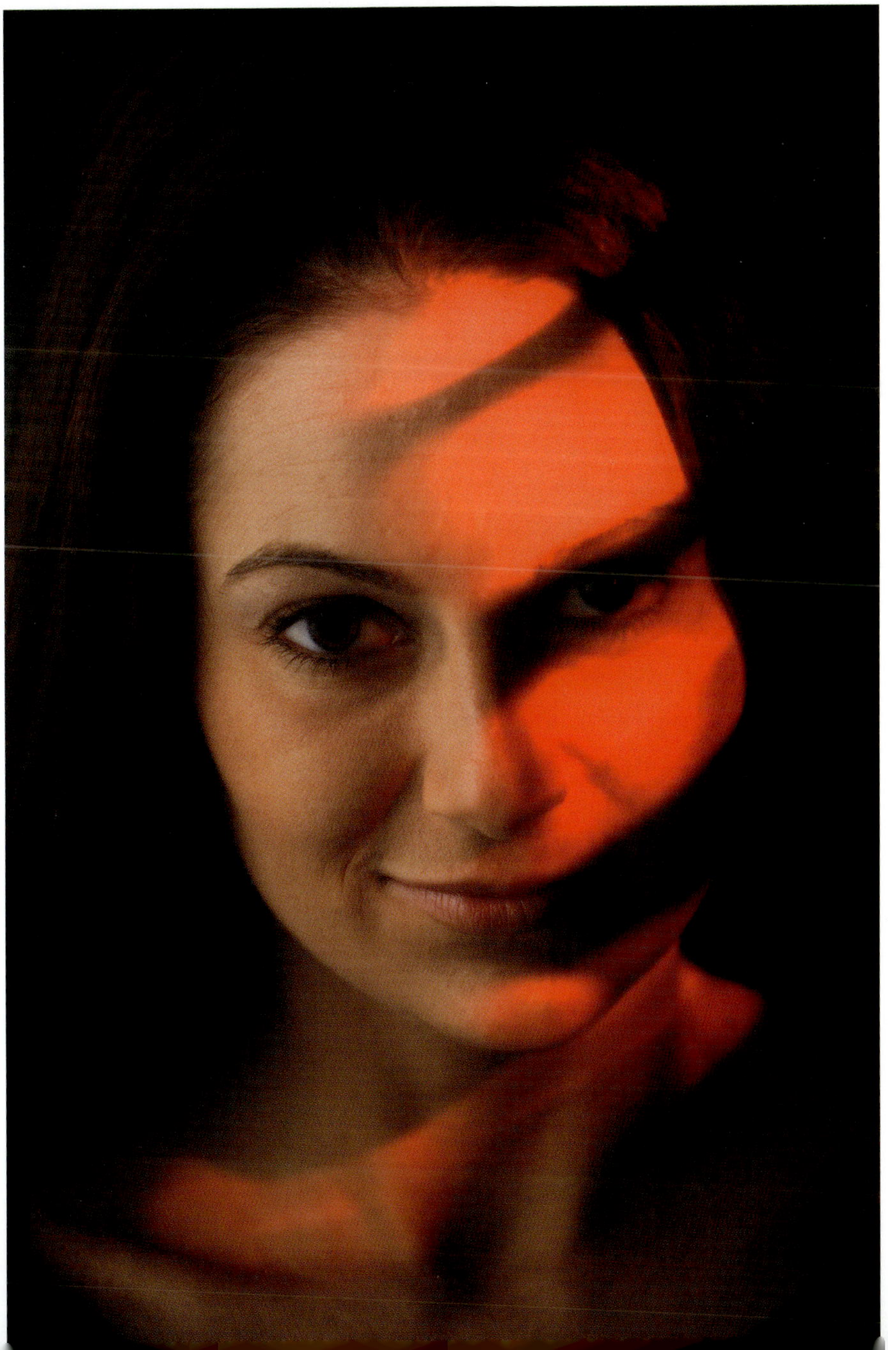

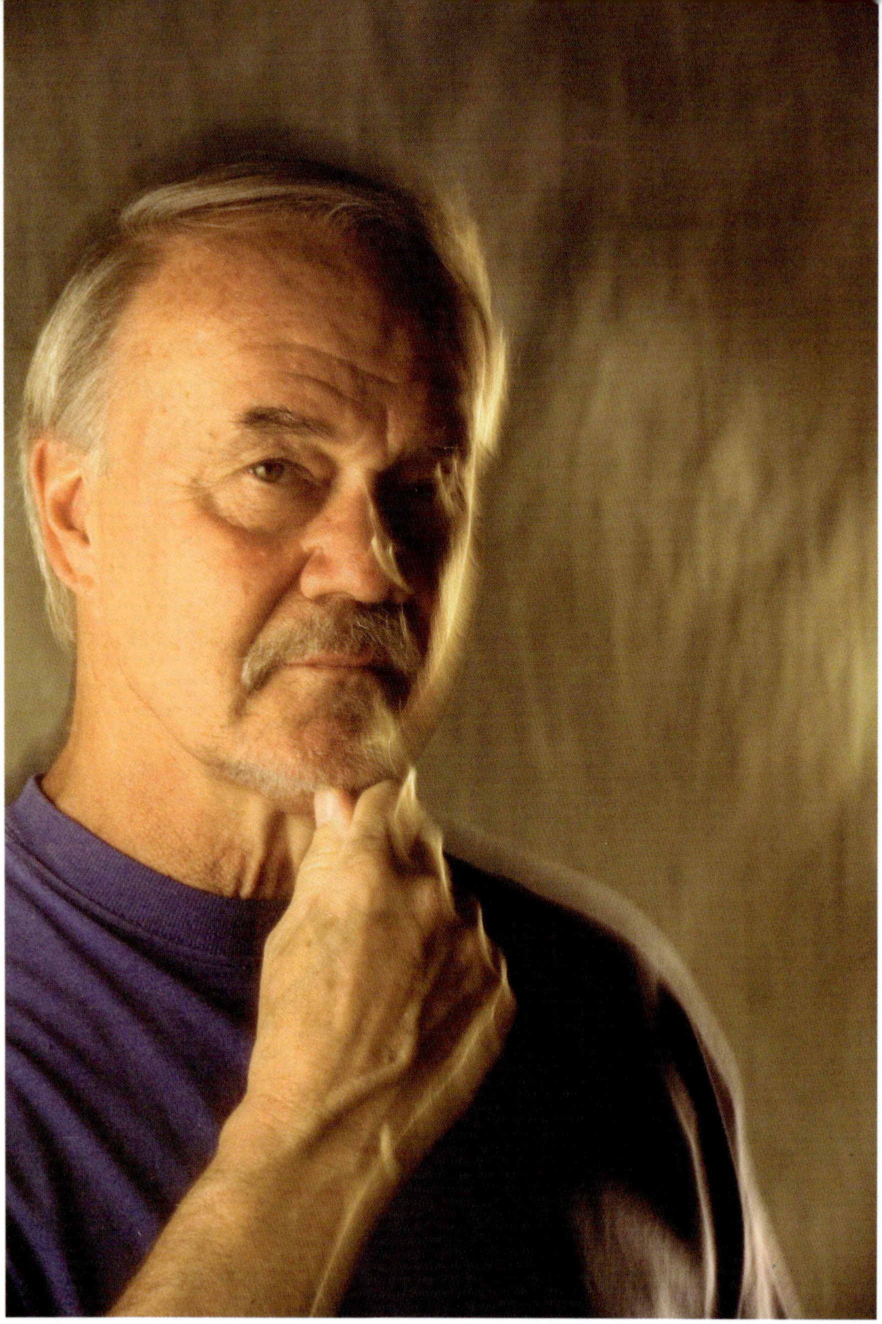

A large light source, the umbrella/light panel, was used to light the subject. I used continuous lights on the background. This created the blur.

inserted. By changing the position and the focus of the projector, you can control the pattern on the face.

The trick in doing this kind of thing is that you have to focus when the room lights are on and then lock the focus on the camera by setting it to manual focus. Be sure to turn all the room lights and the modeling lights off when you shoot; otherwise, they will affect the light on the face. You should also use rear-curtain sync, as the subject may move or blink when the strobe goes off. If you use rear-curtain sync, the movement will occur after the shutter closes.

The exposure on this shot was ⅔ second at f/5.6. The strobe was at just 100 watt-seconds. If you try something like this, shoot a lot of images, as many will not work. This is because it can be difficult to see your subject's expression using just the light of the slide projector.

You can also make use of existing or continuous light sources in your portraits. In this shot, I used a few continuous lights on the background and had the subject move while the shutter was open. This can add a very interesting look! The great thing is that the movement creates additional separation, which can make the face pop out of the image. This works well with a window for a background. I shoot a lot of frames when I do this; a good image requires some luck!

LIGHTING THE BACKGROUND

Most of the time, we need a background that will support the image of a person without competing with the subject. I have several backgrounds that I use for portraits made in the studio, some of which I also use on location.

I think that 9x20 feet is the minimum. Why so big? Well, you can do a full-length shot on this size backdrop and have the subject standing on the background. Another important aspect of a big background is that you don't

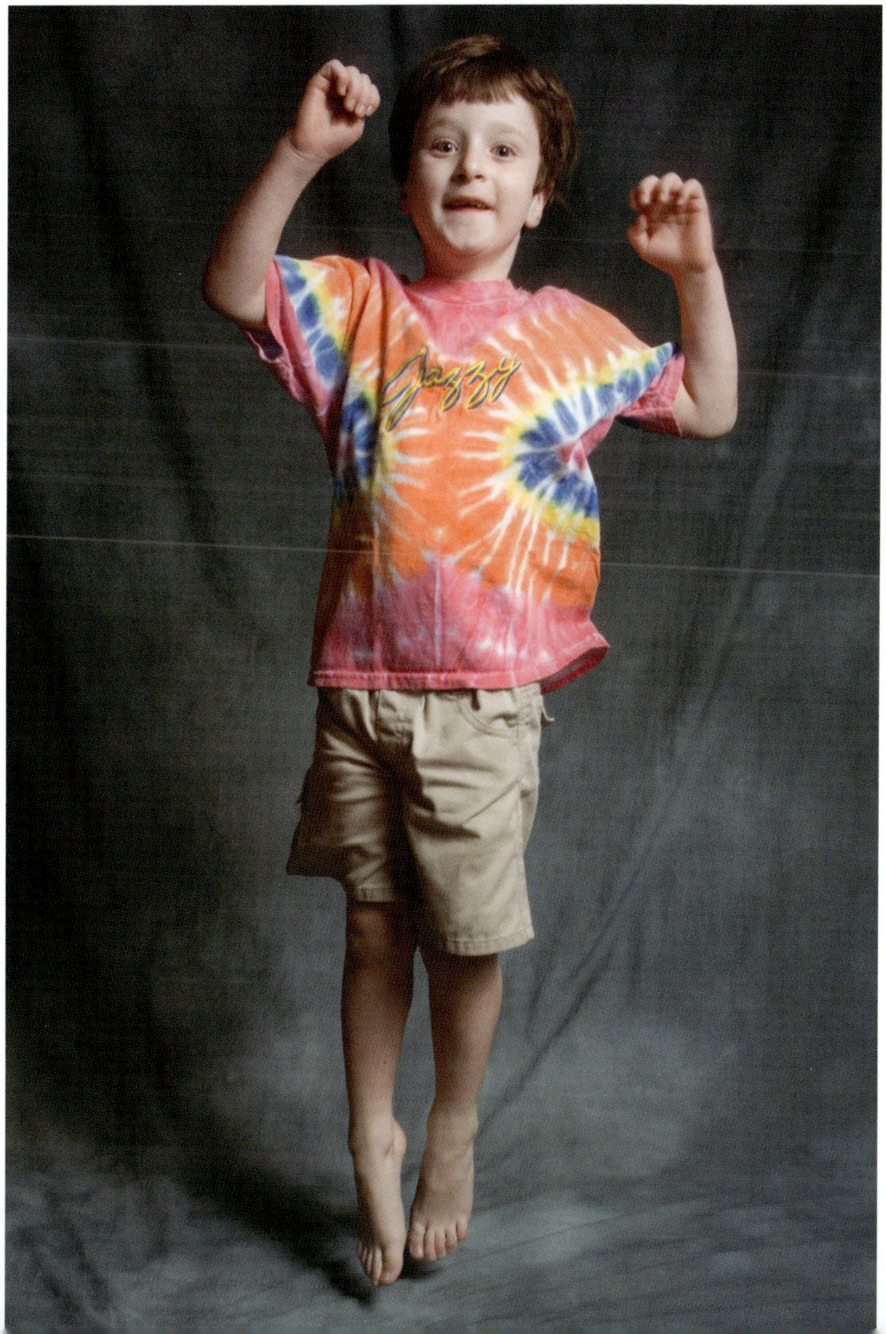

You need a large background because some subjects just can't stay still!

have to worry about whether you have enough on the sides. This frees you up to move around in front of the subject. The other thing a big drop provides is the ability to move the subject away from the background light separately from the light on the subject. This allows you to manipulate the color and density of the background without changing the light on the subject. The extra distance between the subject and the background means that you can solve the problem of the subject's shadow falling on the background. I generally want at least 5 feet between the subject and the background, and I often use even more.

I GENERALLY WANT AT LEAST 5 FEET BETWEEN THE SUBJECT AND THE BACKGROUND, AND I OFTEN USE EVEN MORE.

I set up a series of shots of a male subject to show you how changing the light on the background can change its appearance. I used a mottled gray background. I think this is the most useful background to have, particularly if you are changing the color of the background with lights. To light the subject, I used a single strobe with a small, shoot-through umbrella positioned close to the subject. The light defines his features, creates a sense of three-dimensionality in his face, and adds some definition to his hair. Next, I placed a light panel with a black cover between the light and the background to reduce the light falling on the background. *(Note:* When the subject's light strikes the background and you add the background light, the background will be rendered a more pastel shade, which can be useful for some shots.)

To create the second image, I added a blue gel. The background light and the subject light are at the same power. Pretty vivid blue, huh? I wanted to make a point with this; in an actual portrait, I would make the background darker (this would require a simple adjustment of strobe power).

For the third image in the series, I reduced power to the background light and used an orange gel. I think this is a very usable background.

For the final image, I lit the background from behind. This brought out the different densities in the fabric. It also created a more interesting falloff. I also used a red filter on the light. I like this look. It seems more three-dimensional.

Below—The setup. The light on the left is for the background. For the last shot in this series, I put it behind the background and lit through the muslin. **Right**—The background isn't lit. There is some spill light from the light on the subject. Notice the subject's distance from the background.

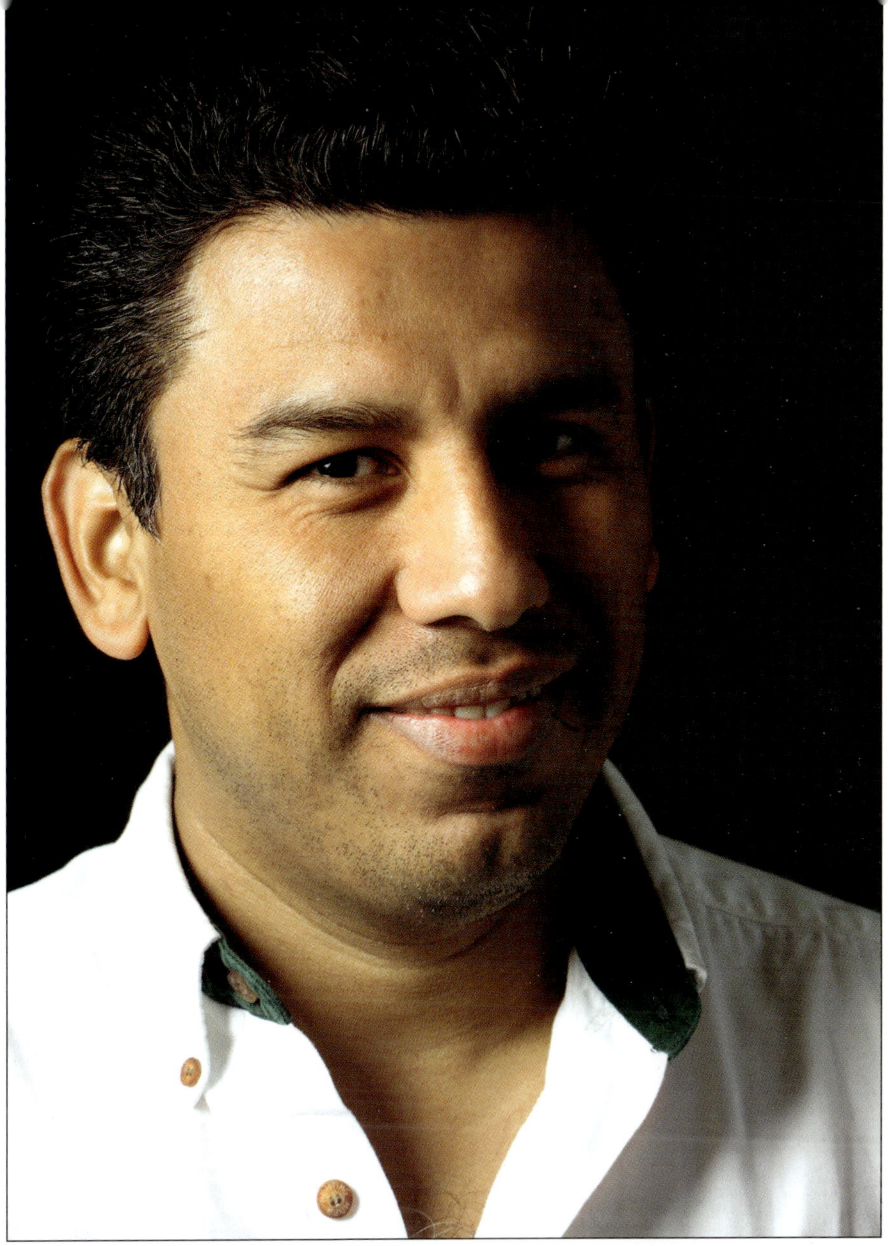

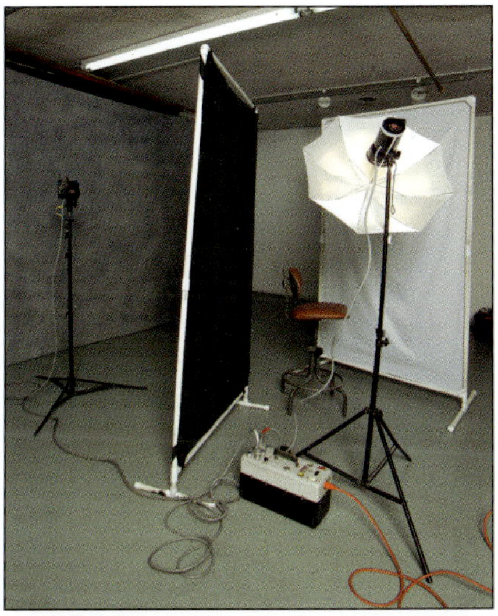

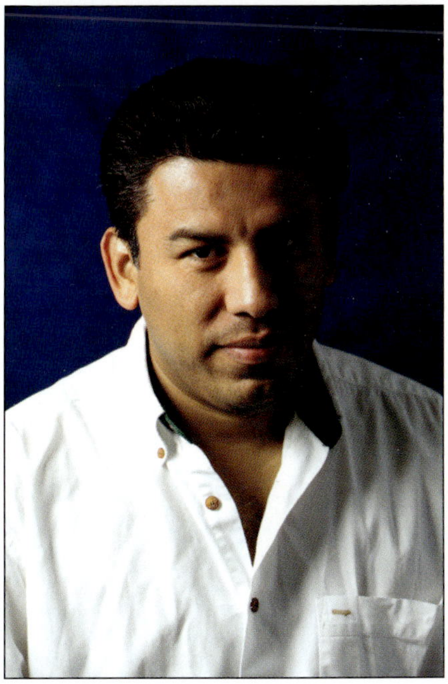

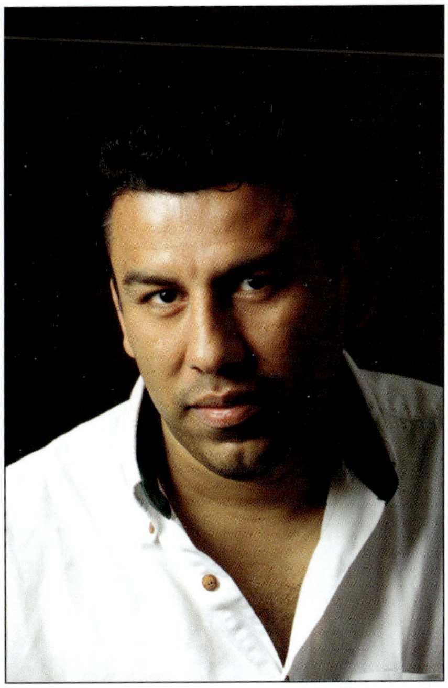

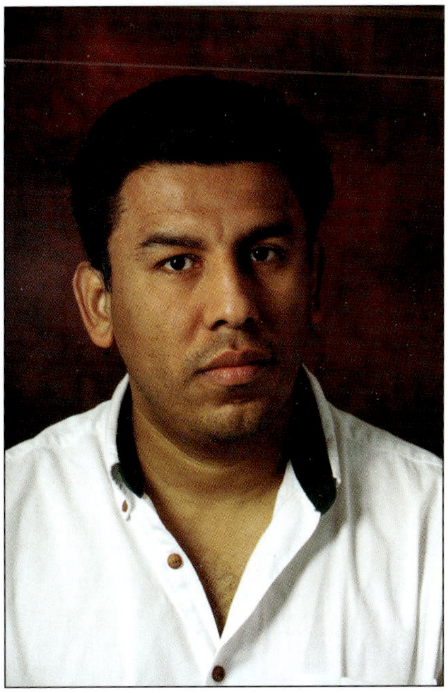

Left—A blue filter on the background light. **Center**—I used an orange filter here, and I reduced the power of the background light. **Right**—For this image, I placed a red filter on the light and positioned it behind the muslin background.

10. PRODUCT AND TABLETOP PHOTOGRAPHY

Product photography used to be one of the most lucrative areas of commercial photography. Unfortunately, as many jobs require making a record of the product using a cut-and-dried lighting setup (these images are referred to as "drop and pop" shots), digital capture and Photoshop have allowed skilled nonprofessionals to do the job. There are other product jobs, of course, that require a creative lighting approach—and these require special lighting skills.

Whether you are shooting products for major companies, generating good shots for a web site, or photographing still-life subjects, this chapter will give you the skills you need to handle the job.

Musical instruments make wonderful subjects for still-life images. Here, most of the light comes from a large light source above the sax.

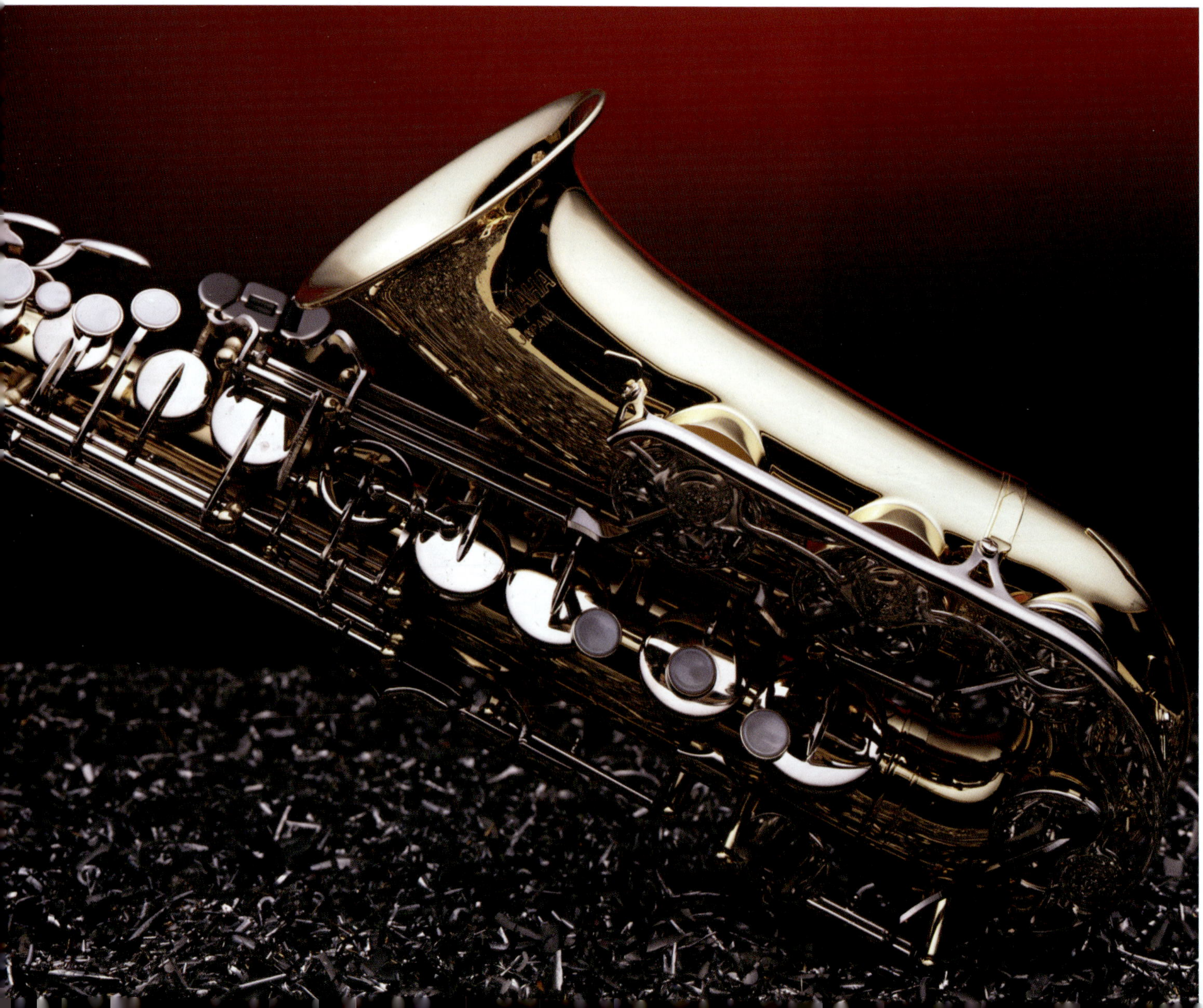

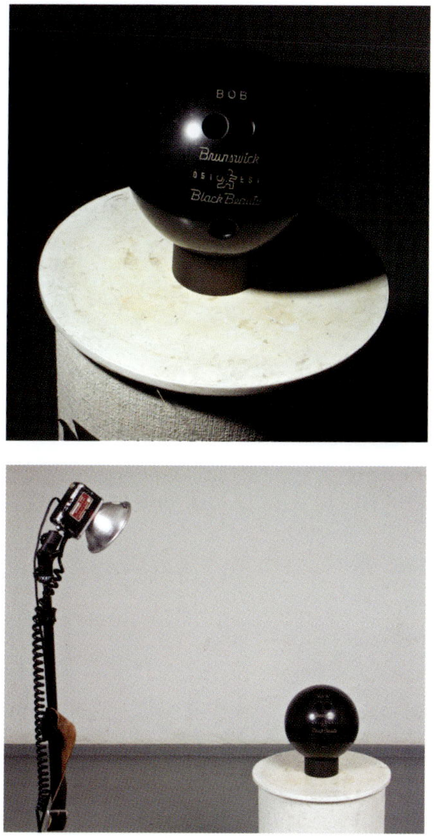

Here, Bob the bowling ball is lit with only a reflector. Because the clip-on reflector was the only light used, the room behind Bob appears dark. Notice how quick the transition from light to dark is.

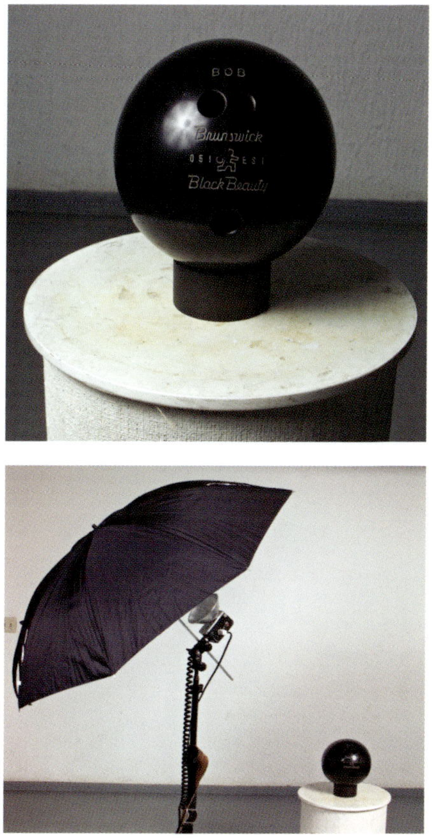

The umbrella spreads light to the room, so Bob is easier to see. The transition from highlight to shadow is much softer. Note that you can see the umbrella in the reflection.

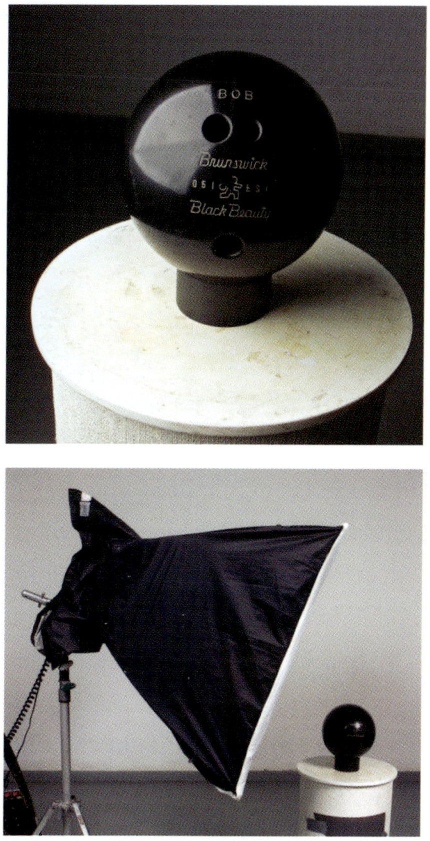

You can see the softbox reflected in Bob, but it is less annoying than the reflection from the umbrella. The front of the softbox is much closer to Bob than the umbrella, so the light is softer.

REFLECTIONS AND SHADOWS

Reflections and shadows are very important in product images. Properly placed light and shadow give the subject shape and a sense of three-dimensionality. Poorly placed light and shadow can detract from the impact of the image. Although you can remove reflections in Photoshop, it is more efficient to control them in the shot.

LIGHTING FOR SHAPE

To create these images, I used a Norman 200B, which is a small light source. Let's examine how we can use light modifiers to shade a sample product. We have Bob to help us with this. Bob is very patient. Bob is unchanging. Bob is very difficult to light well.

The first shot finds Bob on top of a white column (actually all the shots will find Bob in the same place, Bob is unchanging). Notice the reflections and the shadows on Bob. The small, bright reflection is called a specular highlight. With a small light source, the specular highlight is always very intense. The area of Bob that is lit but not reflecting light is called the diffused highlight.

The difference in brightness between the diffused highlight and the specular highlight is greatest with a small light source. Note that the diffused highlight abruptly transitions into shadow. The strobe also created a lot of tiny highlights on Bob, which add sparkle. The small light source produced a lighting effect that revealed the texture of the subject but did not define the shape of the bowling ball.

My first light modifier was an umbrella. I still think that umbrellas are the best all-around lighting tool available. They are inexpensive and easy to set up. They have only two drawbacks: they light everything and they leave telltale reflections all over the shiny stuff in your shot.

THE FIRST LIGHTING TOOL I GOT WAS AN UMBRELLA. I STILL THINK THAT UMBRELLAS ARE THE BEST ALL-AROUND LIGHTING TOOL AVAILABLE.

Let's move on to the second shot. When you look at Bob, you can see that the specular highlight is now shaped like an umbrella. (Keep this in mind. You can often determine how a shot was lit by "reading" the reflections and highlights.) The specular highlight isn't as bright relative to the diffused highlight as it was in the previous image, so there is less contrast in this shot. The transition between light and shadow is much smoother, and the shadow is smaller and less intense.

I used a softbox to light the third image. Softboxes give us a little more control than umbrellas do because they have a flat face. As with the umbrellas, the softbox is better if it is big, as it gives you a larger area of very smooth light. Softboxes also create a characteristic specular highlight, but it is square and even, making it less objectionable than the one produced by an umbrella. The relationship between the values in the specular highlight and the diffused highlight are similar to those produced by an umbrella if the size is the same. However, a softbox is generally placed closer to the subject than an umbrella, as the umbrella is placed away from the light and the subject, while the softbox is between the light and the subject. This can make an umbrella's light a little softer. It is a good idea to get a softbox with different covers so you can change the shape of the light, at least between a rectangle and an oval. This will allow you to change the shape of your specular highlights.

I find a very small softbox (12x18 inches) particularly useful for product photography. I know that this is a contradiction to what I said above, but this is a beautiful size for shooting bottles and glasses; it allows you to control the reflection in the bottle. When you see a shot with a long, thin reflection on a bottle of wine, a small softbox is often the light source. A lot of people like to use a softbox on a boom overhead for lighting products. The overhead angle seems natural, since light comes from above in so many situations.

Light panels are very effective at making soft light. They are easy to set up and manipulate in the studio. Keep in mind that you can use several together to light very large products. Of course, the fabric you use affects the shot. I generally use cotton broadcloth, but nylon works well for product

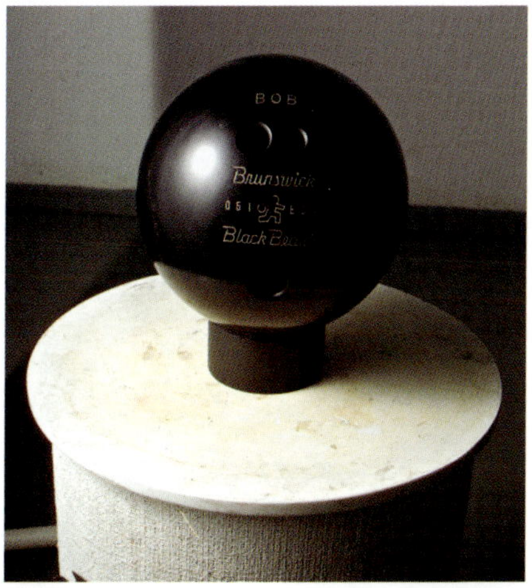

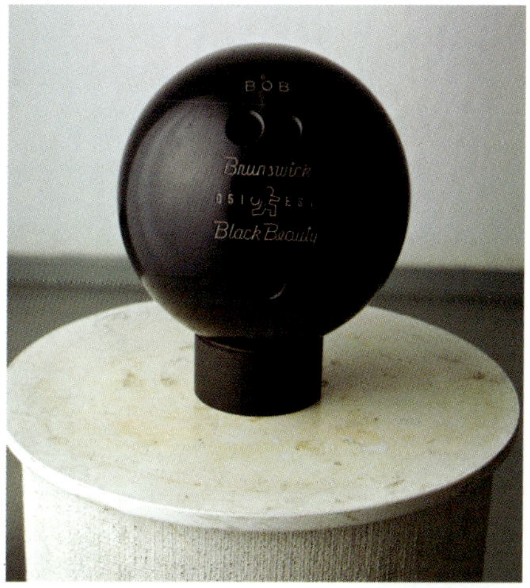

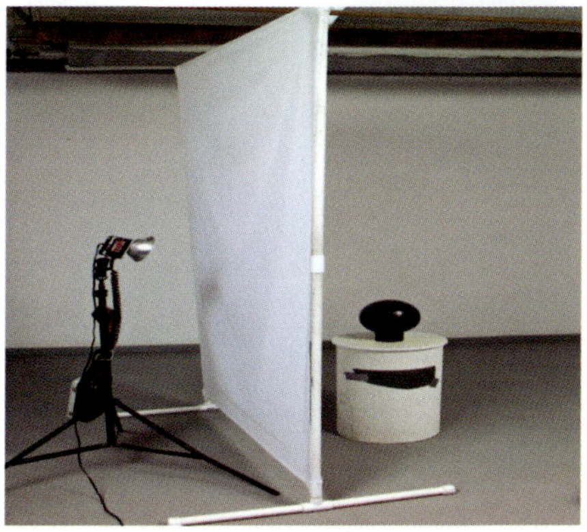

The light from the light panel looks good on Bob. The gradation works well on a spherical subject.

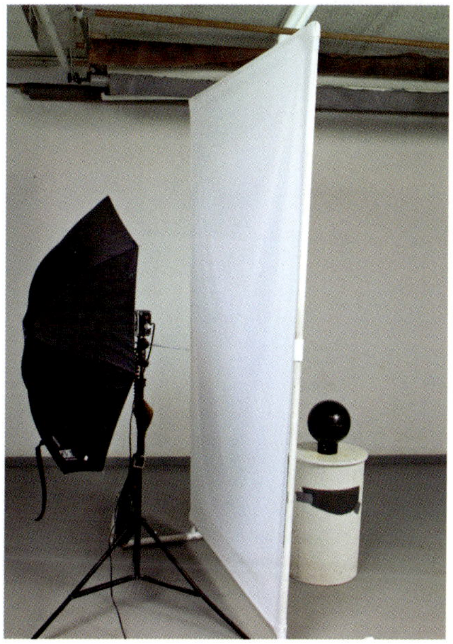

This is a very soft look. There is hardly any shadowing here. You can create a good light for many subjects with this setup.

photography too. It makes a very smooth surface. I also like silver lamé for product shots. You will also want to purchase or make black covers for your light panels, as controlling the light spilled from the sides of the frame can be very important with product photography.

CONTROLLING THE LIGHT SPILLED FROM THE SIDES OF THE FRAME CAN BE VERY IMPORTANT WITH PRODUCT PHOTOGRAPHY.

In the fourth image (above left), I pointed the strobe, with a clip-on reflector, directly at the light panel. This made the light on the panel brighter in the center and darker on the sides. Still, this photo looks pretty good. The light is bright in the center and falls off, sort of like a fireball, creating a good sense of Bob's shape.

For the final image, the light was bounced off of an umbrella and through the light panel, creating smooth, even light on the panel's surface. The gradation from diffuse highlight to shadow is remarkable. The shadow from Bob is a slight darkening, not the pool of inky blackness that we saw in the first shot. Note how smooth the light is on the column and how it falls off smoothly across the bottom. As you can see, the specular highlight is very close in value

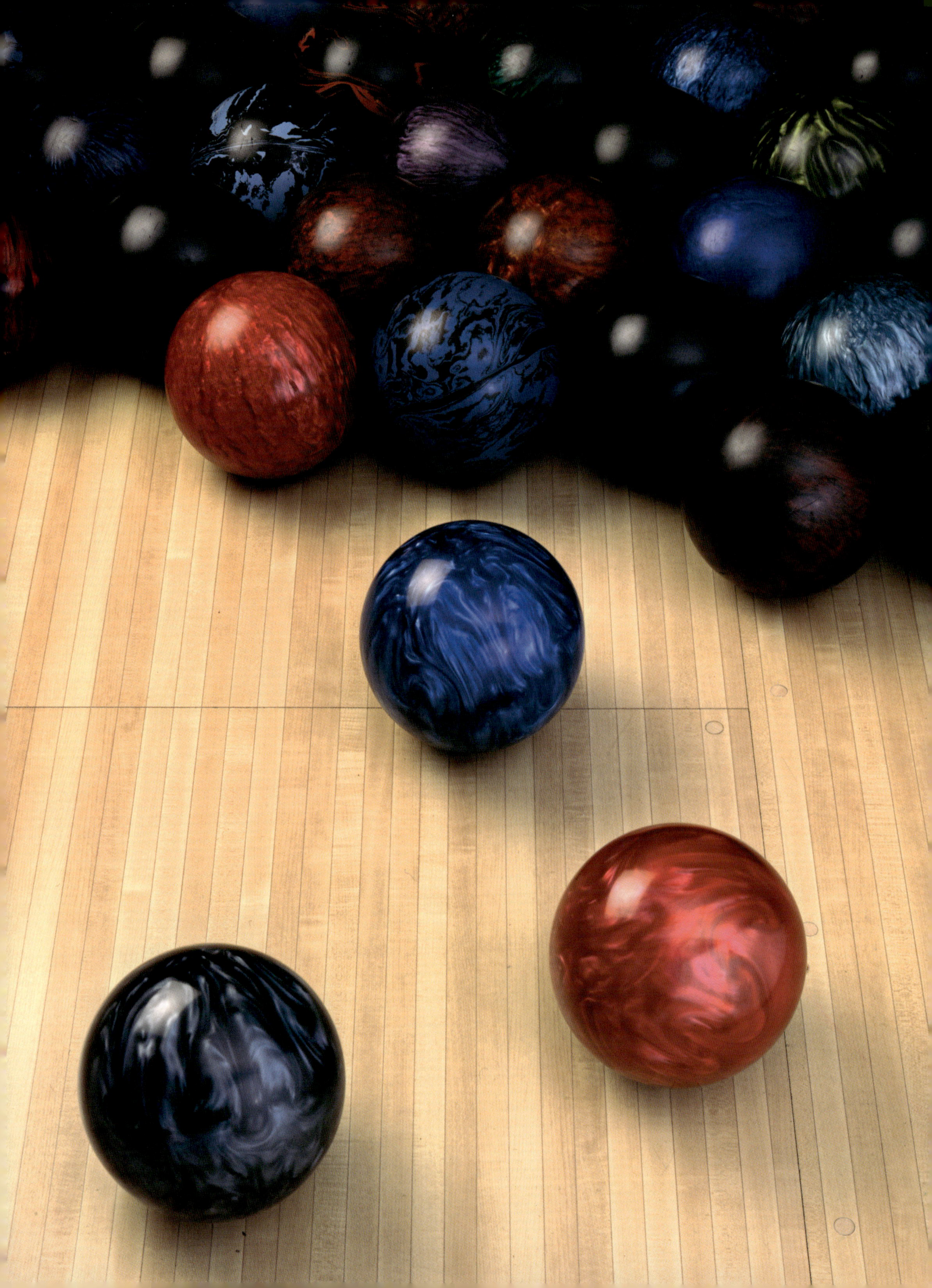

to the diffused highlight. This is because a very large light source was used. As you can see, the highlight doesn't have the telltale image of an umbrella in it.

Also note that the light has now spread to the background. This did not happen in any of the other shots. This is due to the spill from the umbrella. One more thing I should point out is that by repositioning the light with respect to the panel, you can make useful changes in the light. For instance, if you raise the umbrella and light, the panel will darken as it goes to the floor. This will be reflected in the specular highlight. A difficulty with this light is that you need a considerable amount of power from your strobe to get a usable f-stop. Because the light spills out the sides, I often use another panel covered with black fabric to control the light.

Thanks, Bob!

Facing page—This was the first magazine cover I shot. I used a large softbox and a reflector to light Bob and friends. **Below**—I really enjoyed replacing the bow with flowers. The combination of hard and soft light make this shot work.

The image of the violin is a simple shot with just two light sources—a soft light positioned above the instrument and a harder light at camera right. I placed a warm gel on the harder light. The short depth of field in the image and the warm color of the light help to make it an effective shot.

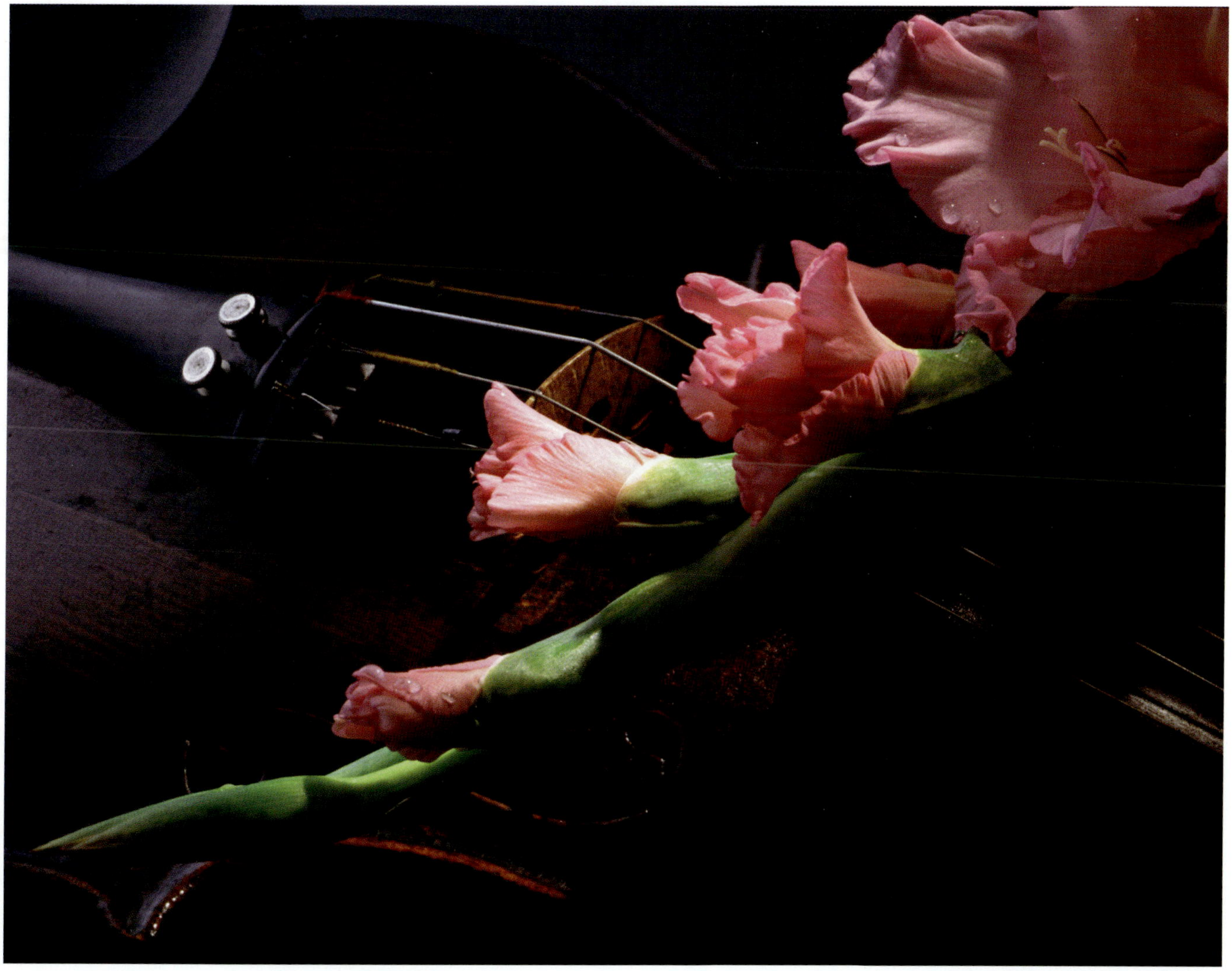

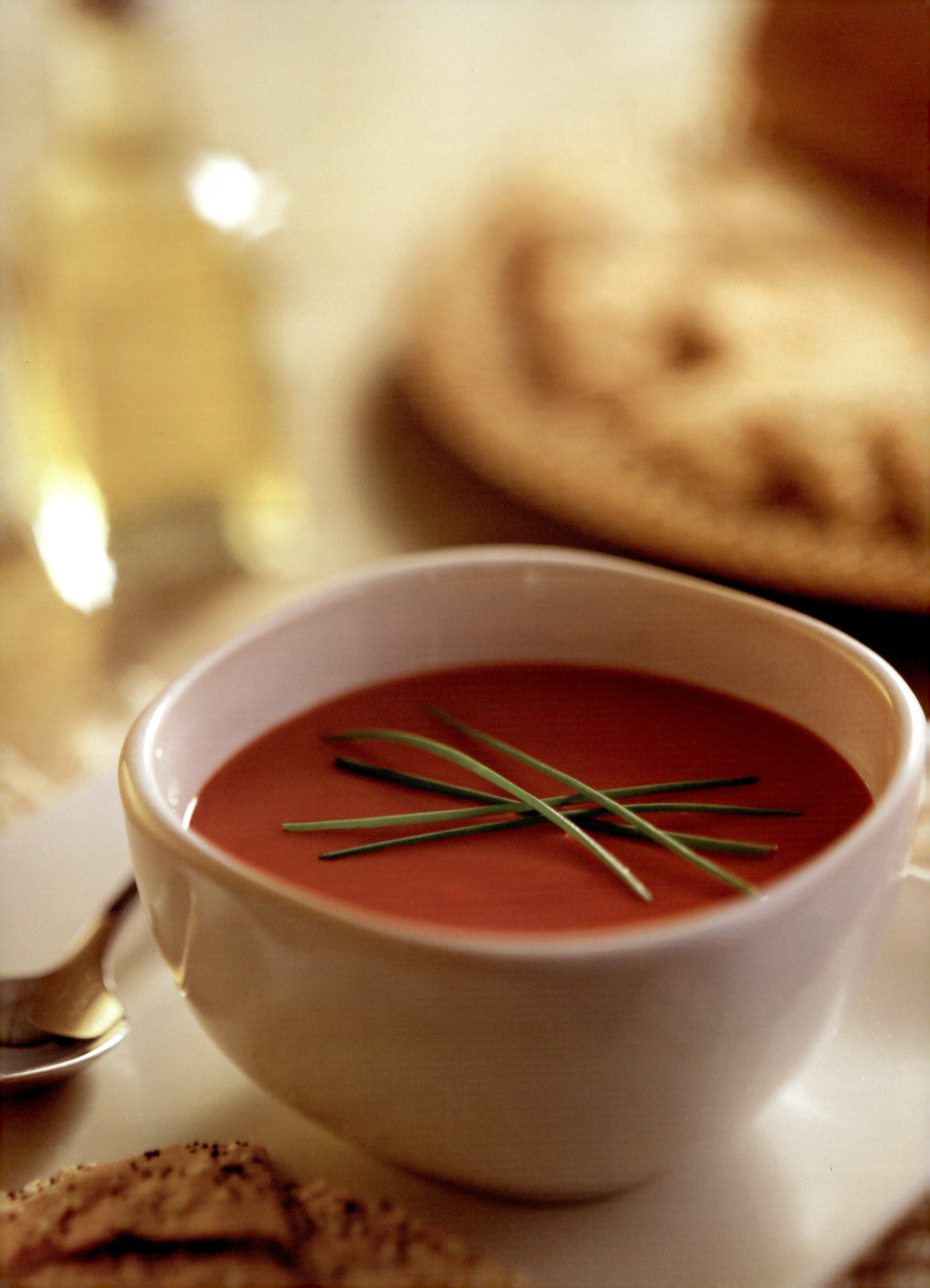

This shot uses both hard light and soft light to good effect. I really like the texture and the sparkle in the image. I used a grid spot to create the hard light. You can see the reflections in the water droplets. The soft light created the nice gradation on the surface of the violin. Hard and soft light work together to make great shots!

LIGHTING LARGE PRODUCTS

There is more to shooting large products than just backing off your lights. Large products are often not just big; they're also heavy. I had a machine that I had to get into the studio that was so heavy the wheels sunk into the asphalt in the parking lot.

IF YOU WANT TO SHOOT A LOT OF BIG PRODUCTS, YOU WILL WANT A BIG STUDIO.

If you want to shoot a lot of big products, you will want a big studio. You can also shoot big products on location, but you will need to see the space before the shoot. It can be a big problem if you show up to shoot a product but can't do it well in the space available. Remember that a large light source for a large product needs to be, well, large.

The image below is a heat-sealing machine. It is about 6 feet long and 4 feet high. The important characteristics of the machine are the orange logo color, the client name, the sliding shelf that serves the oven, and the dials. The most difficult thing is the stainless steel, because it reflects the details of the lighting. Remember that the client is coming to us to help him communicate information about the product, so you want to find out what is important. For me, the first step in setting up a product shot is to establish the location of the camera and its orientation to the product.

This product was very difficult to move because it was heavy and marked up the seamless backdrop. I used the gauges and the printing on the side of

Facing page—I used simple lighting for this shot. The warm filtration and a hard light in the background created the reflections in the background. **Right**—Stainless steel is hard to light. It reflects everything in the room, so large light sources are essential.

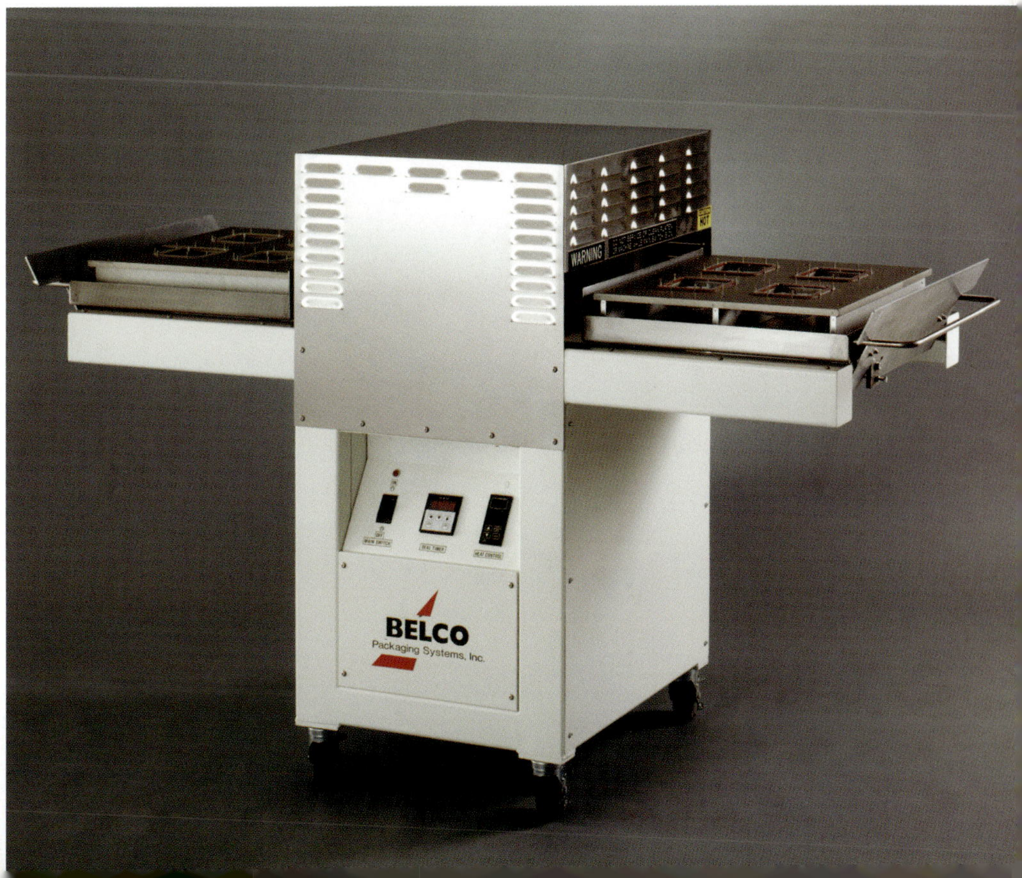

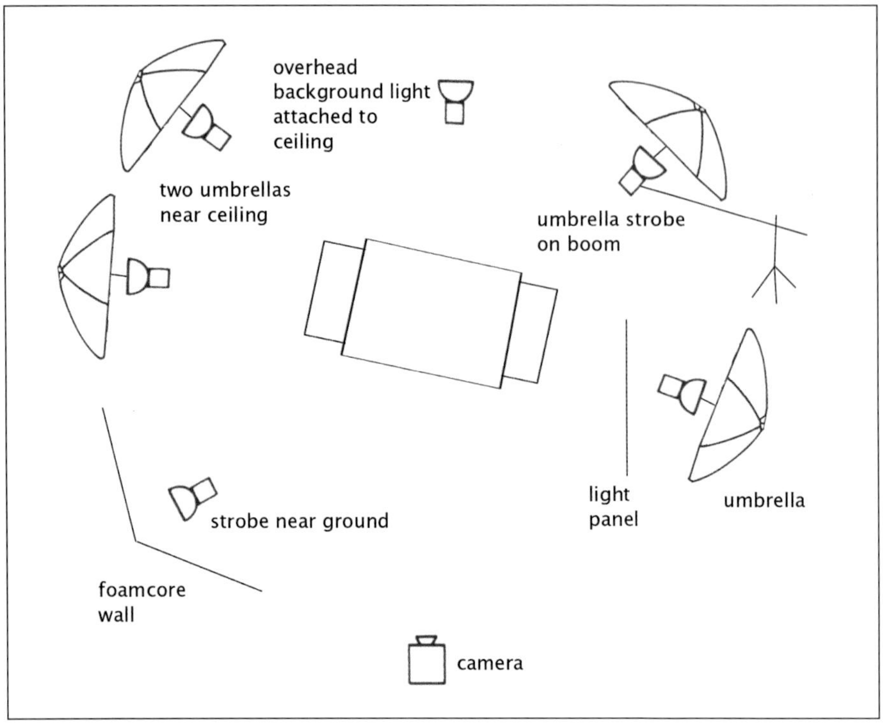

Here is the lighting diagram for the heat-sealing machine.

the orange oven to find the right position. Remember, it is important to think your shot through. This saves a lot of time and trouble.

In order to create a shot that will show this product in a good light, I needed a large, soft light source. In this case, I made a large wall from foam core. I bounced the light off the wall to create a gradation on the stainless steel. The reflection off the foam core is very smooth. In this case, I used two light panels, with umbrellas, to light the long side of the product. This ensured that this side was very evenly lit and had minimal shadows. A very large light source can practically eliminate shadows, but only when it is very close to the subject or very large. In this case, the light source was about 7 feet wide and was placed just a few feet from the product.

A VERY LARGE LIGHT SOURCE CAN PRACTICALLY ELIMINATE SHADOWS WHEN IT IS VERY CLOSE TO THE SUBJECT OR VERY LARGE.

I also used an umbrella and light panel at camera right. This made the right side lighter than the front of the machine and helped define the shape of the product. Finally, I had light coming in on one side of the background. This created a little gradation on the background. I should mention that I used a 12-foot wide gray seamless background for this shot. It works well when I am photographing large products.

Now, let's move onto another large-product shot. This was the last bike that Steve McQueen (born 1930, died 1980) owned. It was restored for the new owner. The motorcycle is in fantastic shape and was a real joy to photograph.

I thought this shot through before starting. I decided to use a black plastic drop cloth on the floor. I knew that, after moving the bike around, the plastic would look better than seamless paper. I used a 12-foot gray seamless on the back wall. We needed a big background and shoot area for such a large bike.

Before I began shooting, I established the camera-to-subject relationship. I needed to make sure that the background would surround the bike. A slight angle was chosen to highlight the front fender, as the fender design is a distinctive feature of all Indian motorcycles.

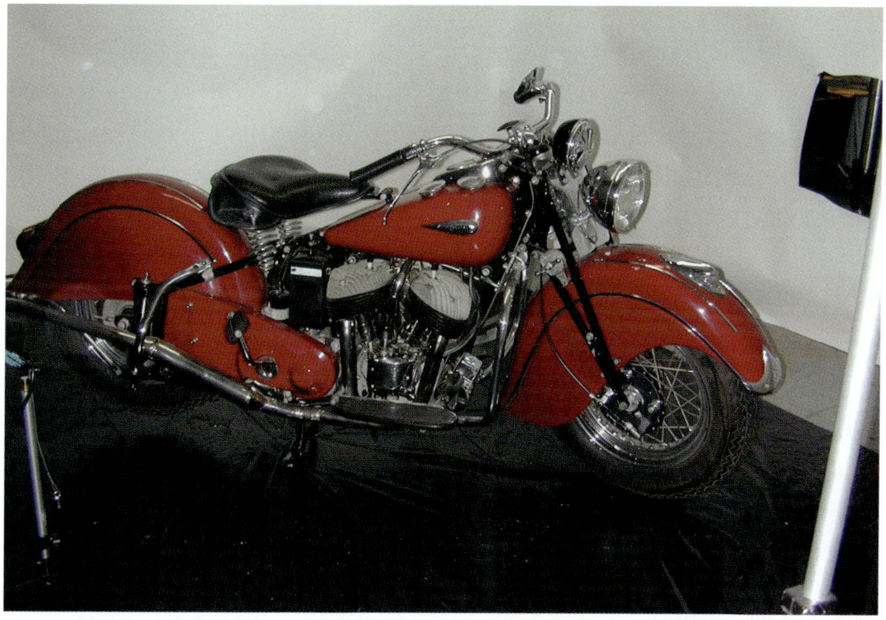

Top—A paper wall was set up behind the bike. Setting up a tent like this is difficult. **Bottom**—This is a 1947 Indian motorcycle. Motorcycles have many shiny, spherical parts, which makes them hard to light.

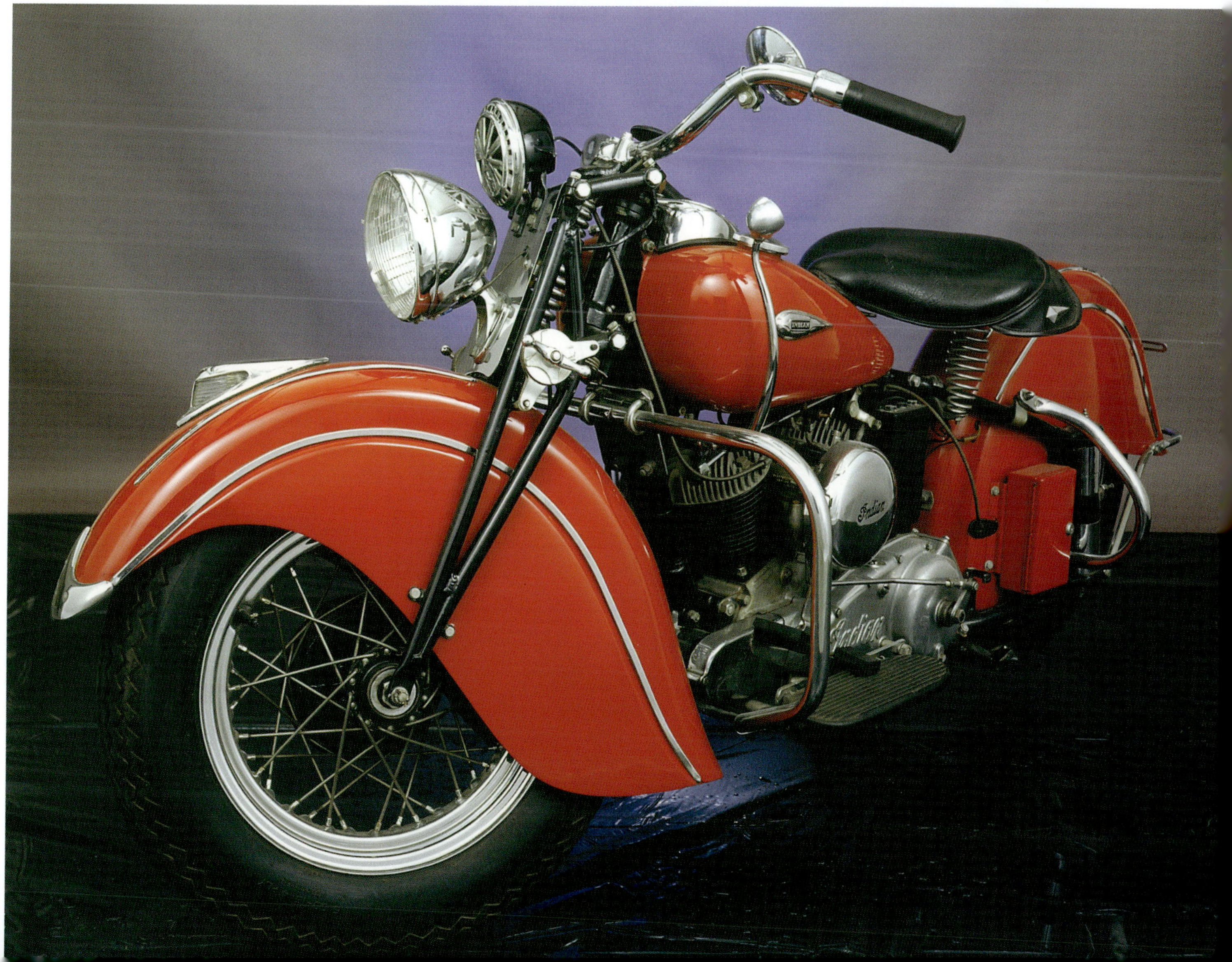

Shooting any motorcycle is difficult because of the shiny spherical surfaces made up of both glossy paint and chrome. These surfaces reflect light directly into the lens. If we were to light the bike with hard direct lights, it would be covered with hard, specular highlights and very dark areas. Obviously, very large, smooth light sources were needed to make this image work.

I used a 9x30-foot piece of white seamless paper to create a wall between the camera and the bike, determined where to cut a hole in it, and then had an assistant cut the hole, keeping the "window" for the camera as small as possible. Next, I spread the light on the new wall. Although seamless paper is usually used as a background, it did the job.

ANY TIME YOU CAN SET UP A TENT, OR EVEN A PARTIAL TENT, YOU WILL BE ABLE TO USE IT TO SHOOT A LOT OF PRODUCTS VERY QUICKLY.

I have several moveable, wooden poles mounted on the ceiling of my studio. I mounted some lights with Manfrotto Super Clamps and compendium arms. The lights were pointed at the white seamless wall, away from the bike. This instantly gave me a very smooth light on the motorcycle! I had essentially made a tent around the bike.

Next, I placed another light behind the bike to create a gradation across the background. This light had a blue filter on it. This light produced a pastel blue light behind the subject, with a circular falloff. The light is pastel because the blue is mixed with the white light reflected from the gray seamless, and the falloff is created by the spot pattern of the light.

I added one more light on the left of the bike to illuminate the ceiling and the left side of the white seamless. This was a case where barn doors were very important. This placement put additional light on the seat and the back fender, both of which needed the help.

The Indian shot is an example of photographing a large reflective object in a large tent. A tent is basically a white container that surrounds the subject. There are numerous ways you can build one yourself, and they are also commercially available. Don't be afraid to get creative: when I am photographing small objects, my tent is actually a laundry hamper from Ikea.

The basic principles behind shooting very reflective subjects, from motorcycles to jewelry, are the same. You need to light what the subject reflects

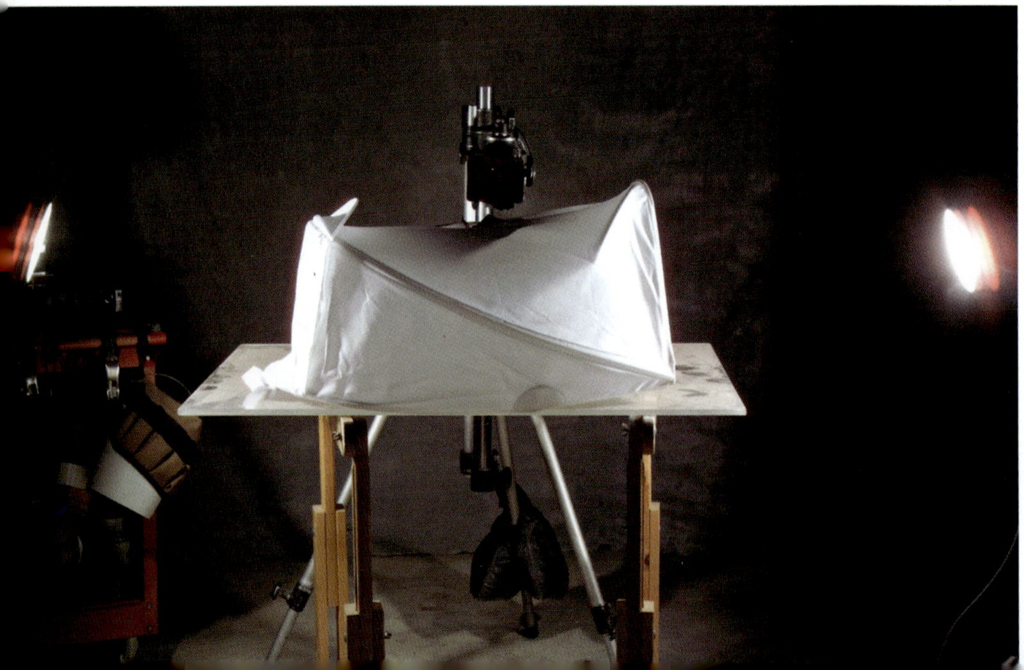

I used this setup to photograph the watches shown on the facing page.

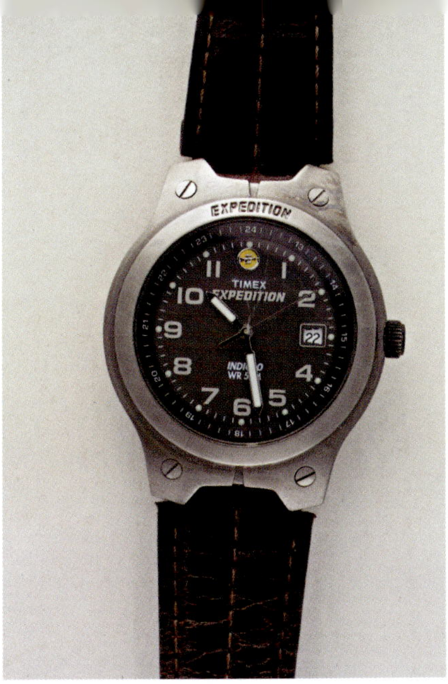

I was able to shoot these and several other watches very quickly using the same setup.

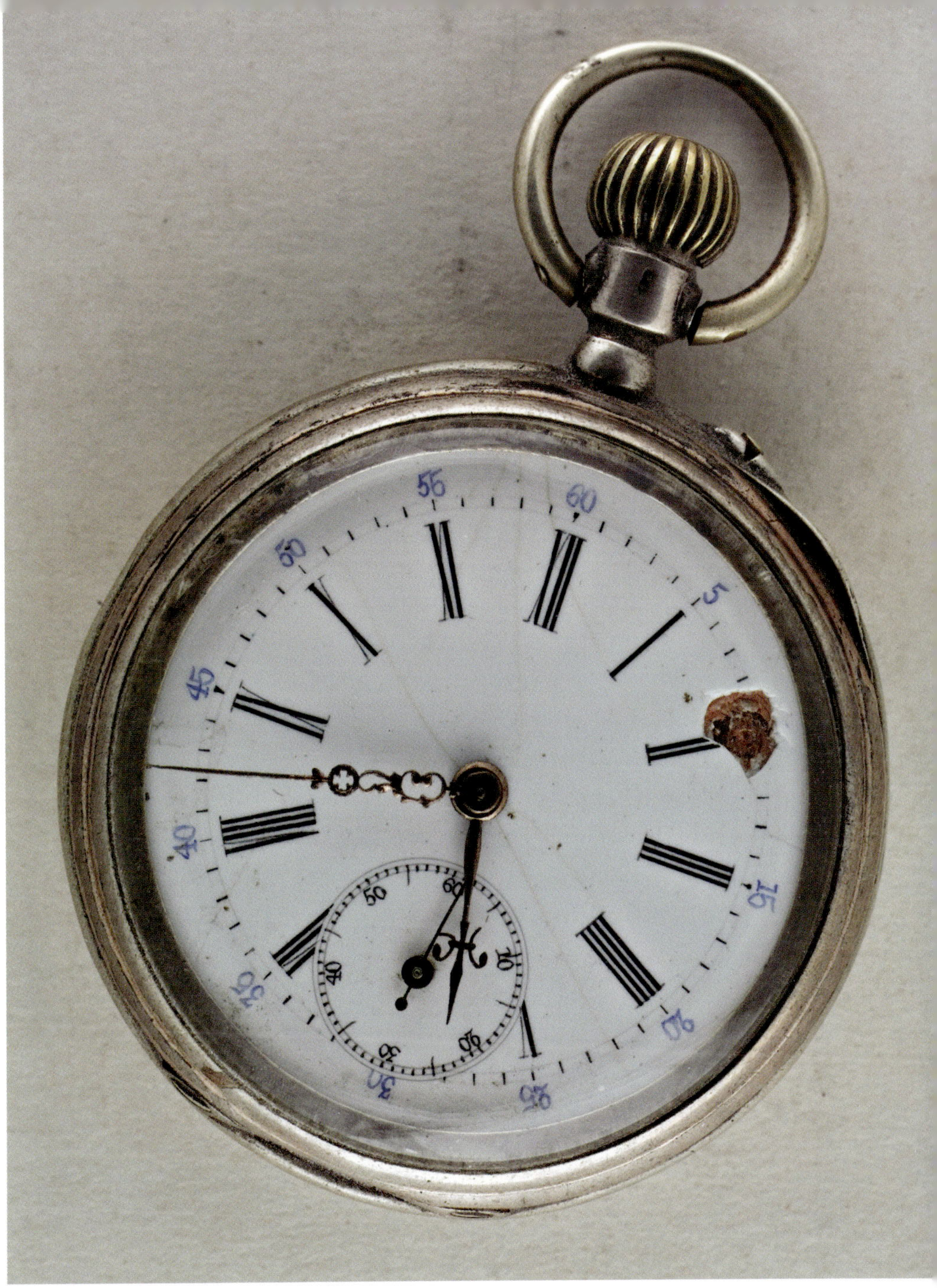

more carefully than you light the subject. If you think about the subject as a mirror, you'll understand why this is the case.

There are a variety of ways to light a tent. If you have a small tent, you will light it from the outside. If you are shooting with a large tent, you may actually have the lights inside the tent. If you light from inside the tent, its material doesn't need to be transparent, as you will be bouncing the light off the inside of the tent. You do not have to light a tent evenly; you can light it from one side to create a gradation in your light. Any time you can set up a tent, or even a partial tent, you will be able to use it to shoot a lot of products very quickly.

11. LIGHTING INTERIORS

When you encounter an interior you want to light, the first thing you should do is take stock of the existing light sources, everything from lamps to windows, and classify them as friend or foe. A window that throws diffused light into a room is a friend; fluorescent lamps, mercury vapor lamps, sodium vapor lights, and so on are generally foes but can be used under some circumstances, especially with digital. Tungsten lights can be friends, or at least brought onto your team.

Studying the room light will give you the information you need to choose the dominant color spectrum you will use in your shot. Color spectrum is somewhat similar to the key of a piece of music: it tells you what will fit easily and what will be dissonant. Really, you have three choices: daylight, tungsten, and fluorescent. Fluorescent is the most difficult spectrum to work in because the temperature of fluorescent tubes can be wildly different.

If you have a lot of daylight, you will want to light with your strobes. If your light is mostly from tungsten sources, you will want to use CTO filters to

Below—The overhead skylights in this location were a little help, but the mercury vapor lamps had to be turned off. Ten strobes were used. **Facing page**—This shot was done with a single large monolight and a 60-inch umbrella. I used a daylight spectrum, largely because of the window. Although the lamps in the shot are not corrected to daylight, the color seems to work in this shot. This shot had to be made very quickly, but it works well.

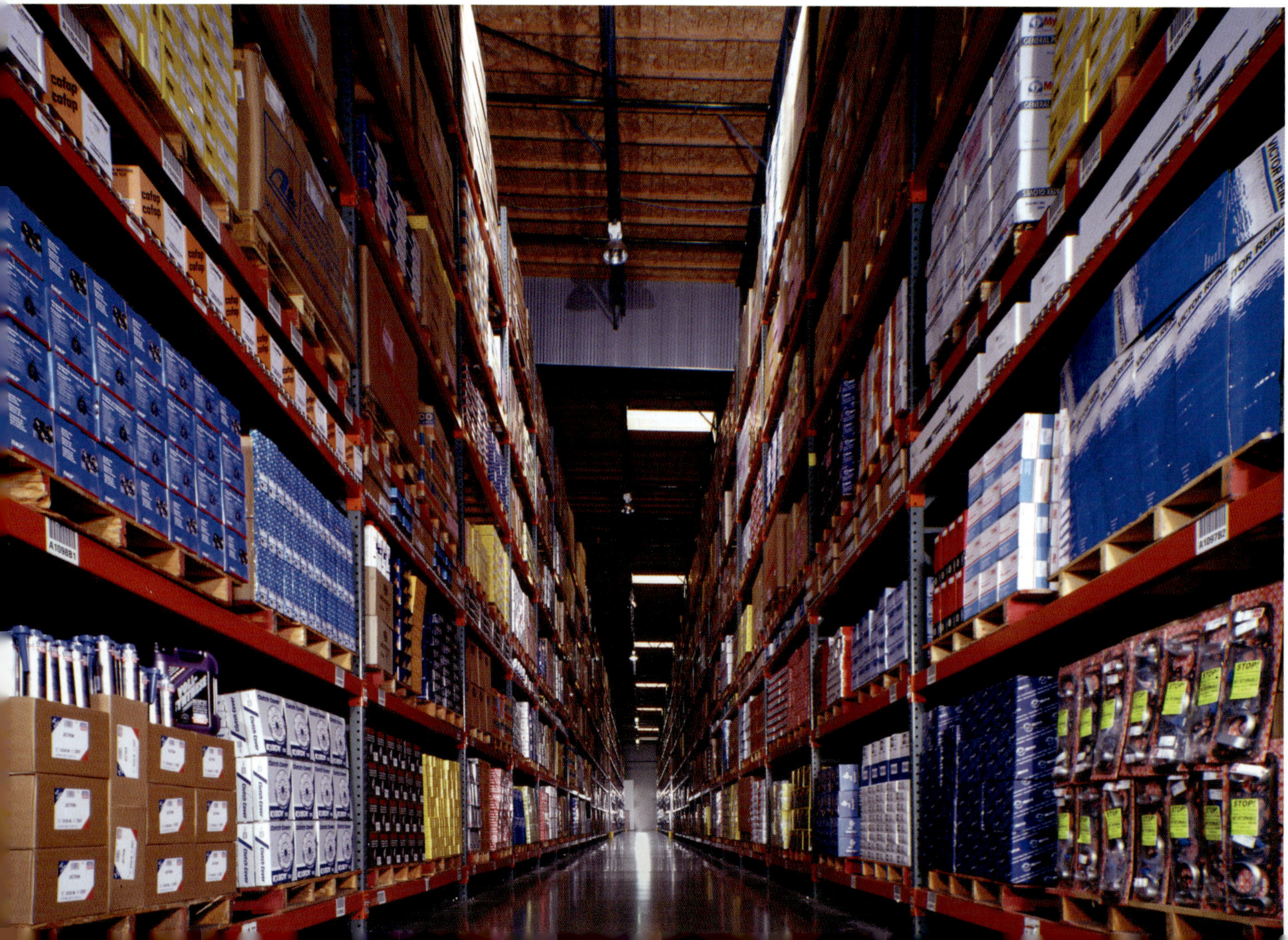

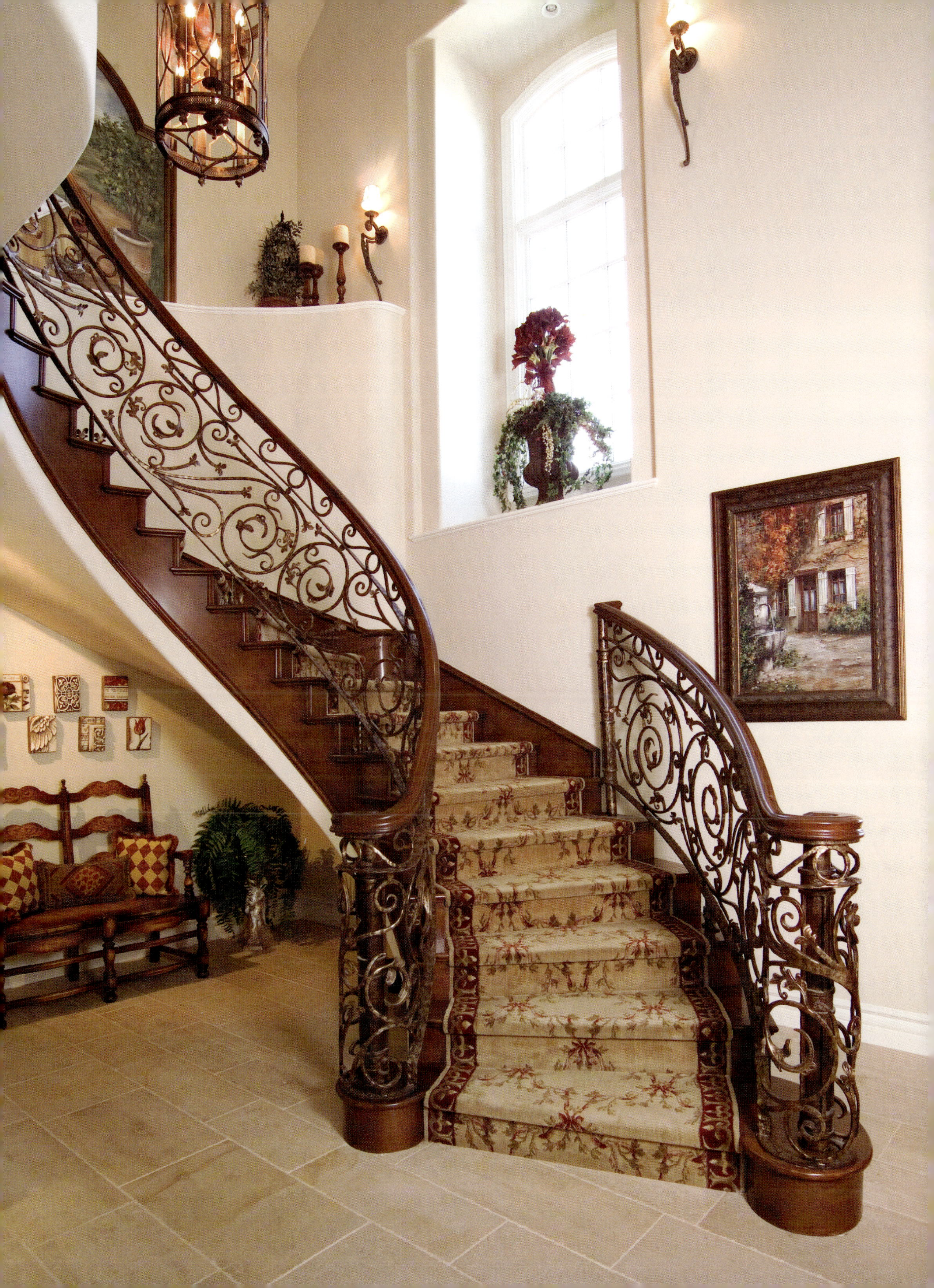

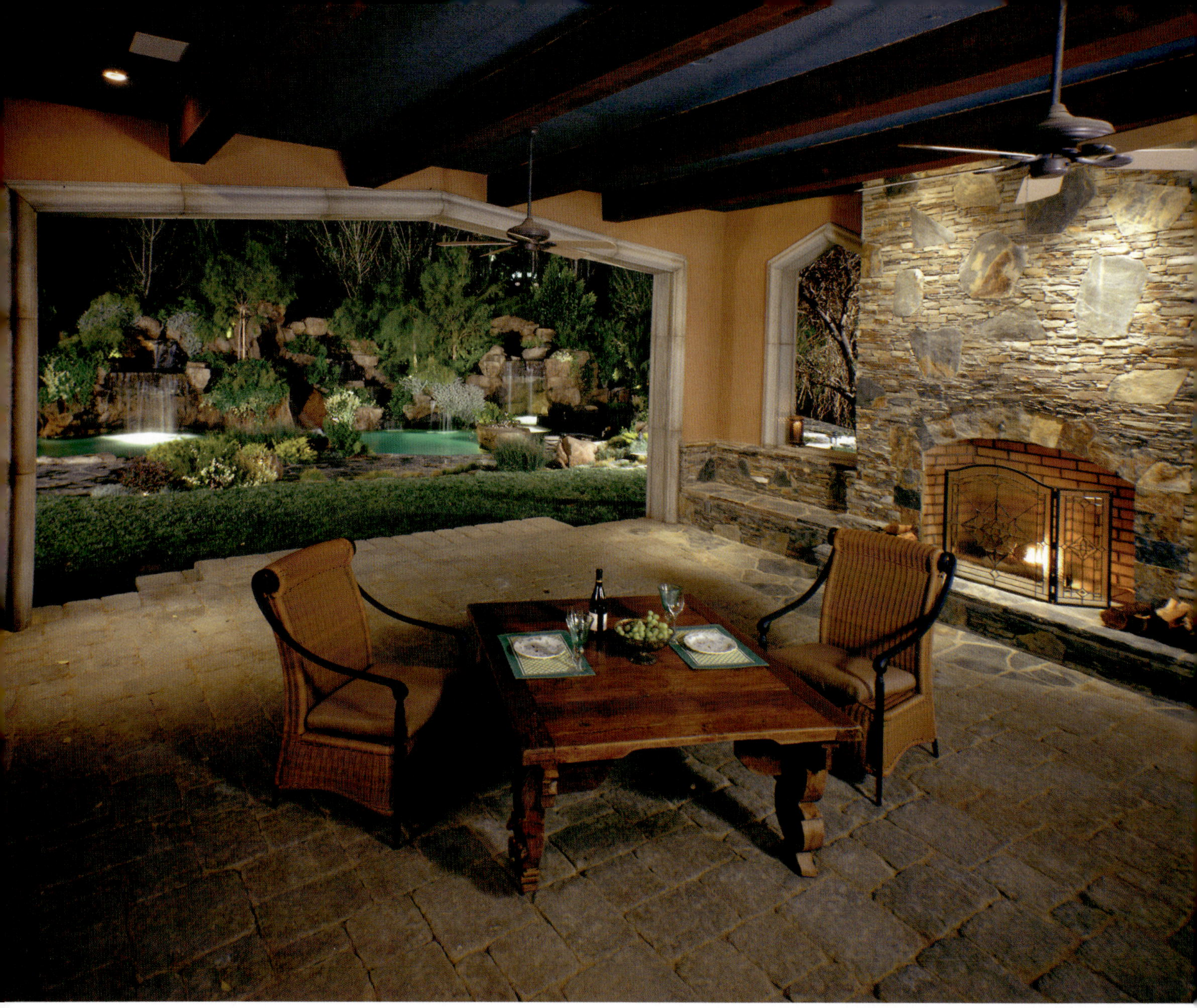

This shot required nine lights and took hours to do. I used a tungsten spectrum for the shot. The lights outside the room and the lights on the waterfall were all tungsten balance. I used strobes inside the room with full orange filters. This shot required several hours to get right.

convert your strobes to a tungsten balance. One of the advantages to filtering strobes is that these lights won't appear in the image frame, so the filters are hidden also. Room lights, of course, may appear in your shots, and then, so would the filters.

The next thing to do is consider where lights can be hidden. Generally there are only a few places you can put a light. Lights outside of the frame are easy to make look natural; a light from either side can look like window light. A light inside the frame will need to be much more subtle. You can put a light on the other side of a kitchen island to bring up the values on a stove, but if you add a lot of light in a place like that, it will look really weird. One important source to consider is bounce light off the ceiling. This can look very natural, but you want to keep the bright ceiling out of the frame, and if the ceiling isn't white, your color can be ruined.

Finally, I look at the room in terms of the best camera positions. The important characteristics of the room and the needs of the client will come into play here. I place the camera first, then work out the light placements. The camera is placed first because shadows and reflections are only important from the camera's point of view. Your camera placement must allow you to capture the key characteristics of a room, so if you are trying to show size, you don't want to back up and use a normal lens. Rather, you would use a wide-

There is a light hidden behind the wall at camera left and another in the doorway at the back of the shot.

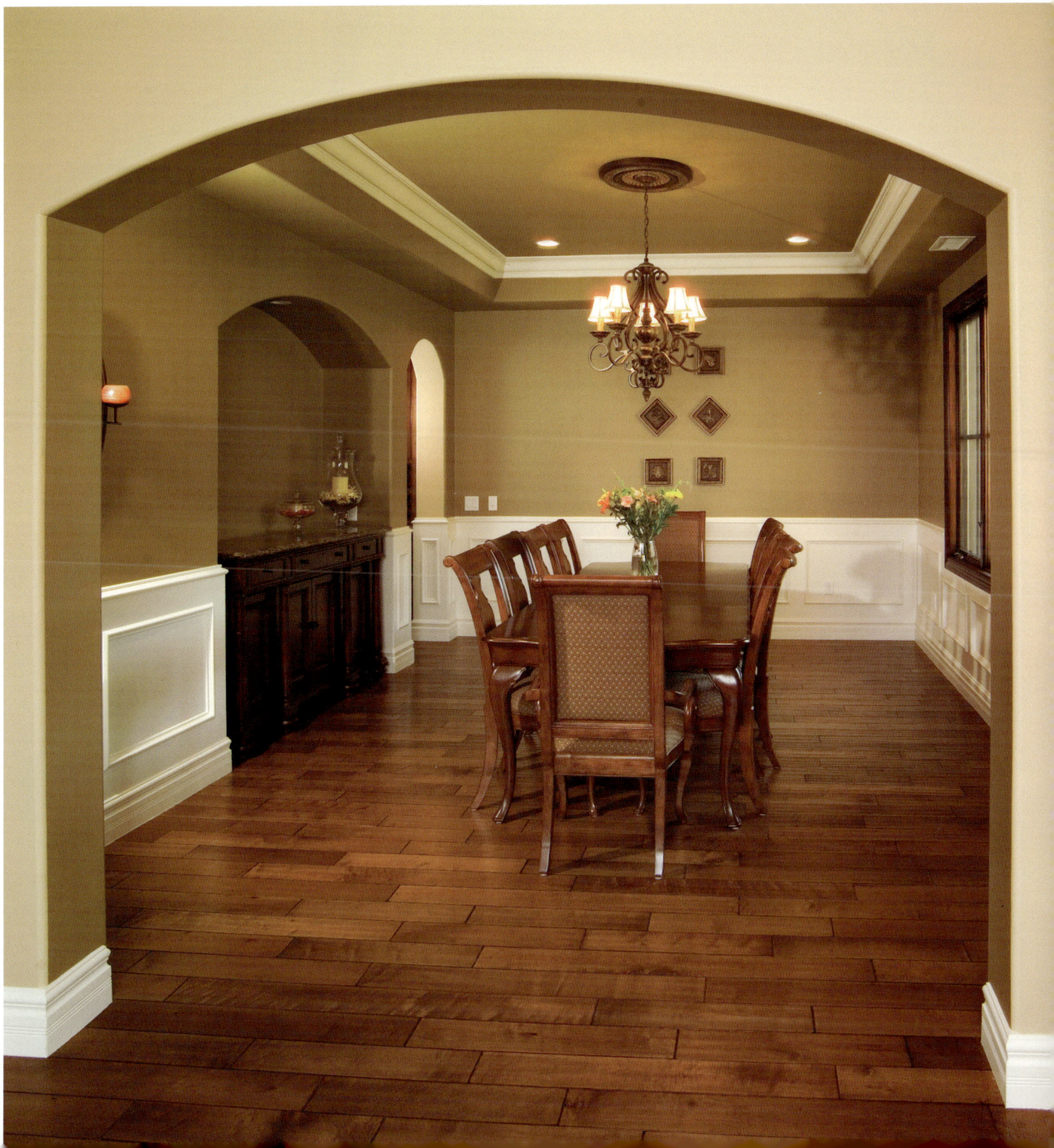

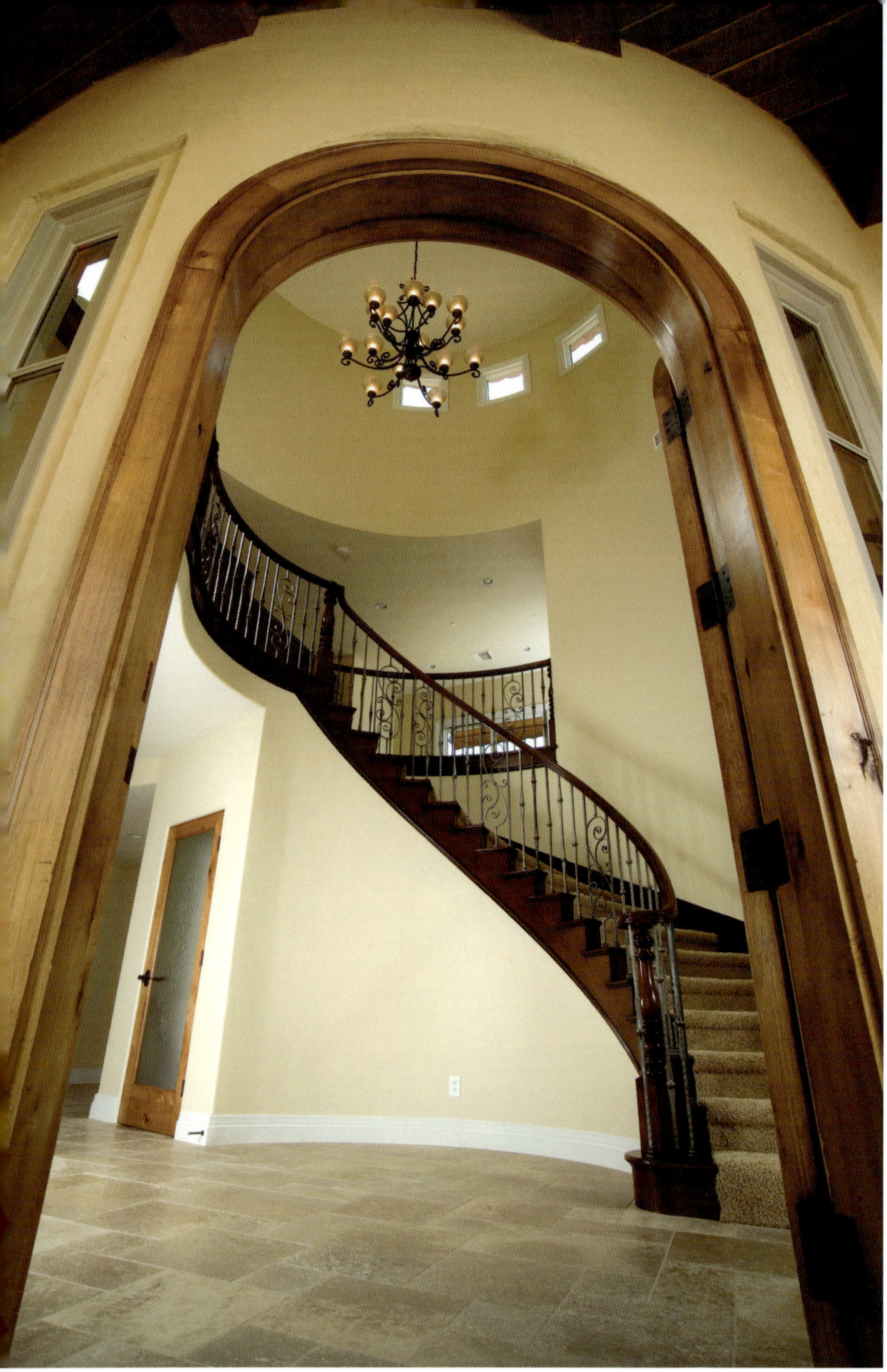

I used six strobes to create an even light throughout this shot. A large monolight was positioned just inside the door, and Norman 200B units were placed in the hallway to the left and right and at the top of the stairs.

angle lens to emphasize size. The height of the camera can also affect the feel of a room, so be aware that eye level is not always the best position.

Architectural photography is a very detail-oriented specialty, so I typically tether the camera to a laptop. Once you set this up, you might want to take a quick capture of the shot. This could be done on auto exposure, but it will be the last shot that you take on auto. Examine the shot to ensure you have a good angle and check for any problems.

Now, except in the unlikely event that the shot you just made was perfect, it is time to set up the first light. Lighting is always the great trick. In almost all circumstances, I will set up my first light as near to the camera as practical and as high as possible. I use a large monolight for this. My first choice for a light modifier is a 60-inch umbrella. The purpose of this light is to open up any shadows from the existing light sources. This brings down the contrast, which is an important aspect of lighting any interior. Also a large light source creates more spill light to fill in all the shadows. Since the light is above the camera, shadows will fall behind the objects and, hopefully, reflections will not go toward the lens.

Next, we will try to bring the lights into the same spectrum. If you are shooting daylight spectrum with strobes, you don't need to do anything, but if you are shooting in tungsten, you will want to put a Rosco 3407 CTO or equivalent filter over your strobe. This will make the light about 3000°K, which is a movie light spectrum. You may need additional filtration, but you

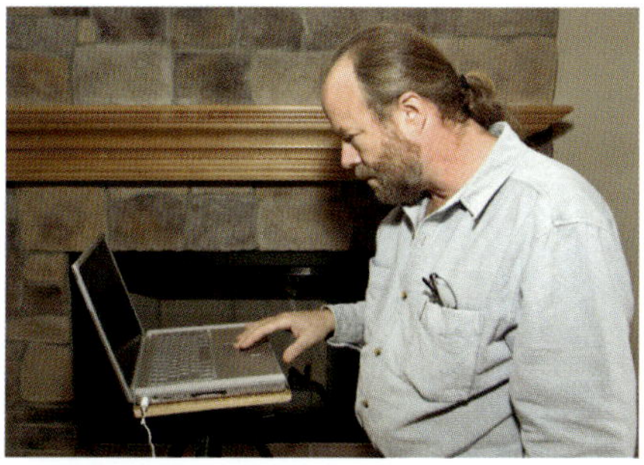

Above—Examining the image from the camera on location. **Right**—This is the first shot of this image. It shows the way the camera saw the light. I used this image to repair the reflections in the windows in postproduction. There are more versions of this image later in the chapter.

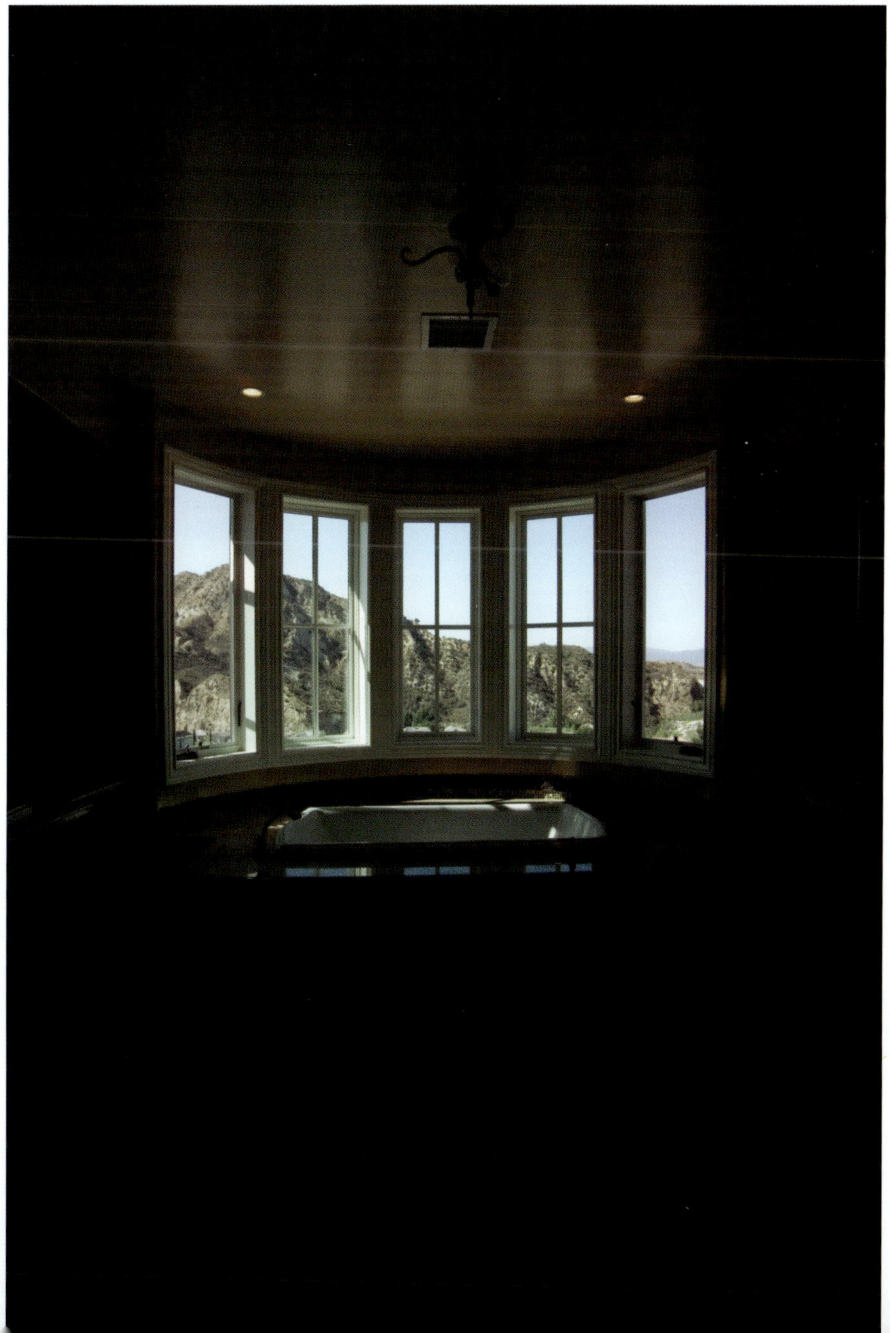

won't know until you shoot a test exposure. When I am trying to balance to fluorescent tubes, I usually use the Rosco 3315, which is the ½ plus green. It has worked better for me than the full green.

You can change the color of the light sources in your shot, but this is not always necessary. If you control the exposure so that the light source in the shot is bright but doesn't add much light to the surroundings, you may not need to adjust the color. Whites and blacks are self-cleaning; that is, a white or a black doesn't have a color cast. This means that a white bulb is white, regardless of the color balance. So if the lamp is bright but the light doesn't fall on anything, you are probably okay. If the lamps are critical, you can replace a tungsten bulb with a photoflood BCA bulb. This runs at almost 5000°K, similar to daylight. Doing this is dangerous, however: the bulb runs much hotter than a normal bulb, so only turn it on when you are actually exposing. You can also use a Britek or similar strobe with an Edison base, but these do not spread light like a bulb, so they don't always look natural. Additionally, you can put a Rosco 3202 CTB full blue over a lightbulb, but this will substantially reduce the output of the bulb. You can use a Rosco 3308 minus green filter over a fluorescent light source, but because the colors of the various tubes are very different, this doesn't always work.

Although I didn't correct the color from the existing light in this shot, the color works well. If the lights don't illuminate much of the subject, you can usually work with them.

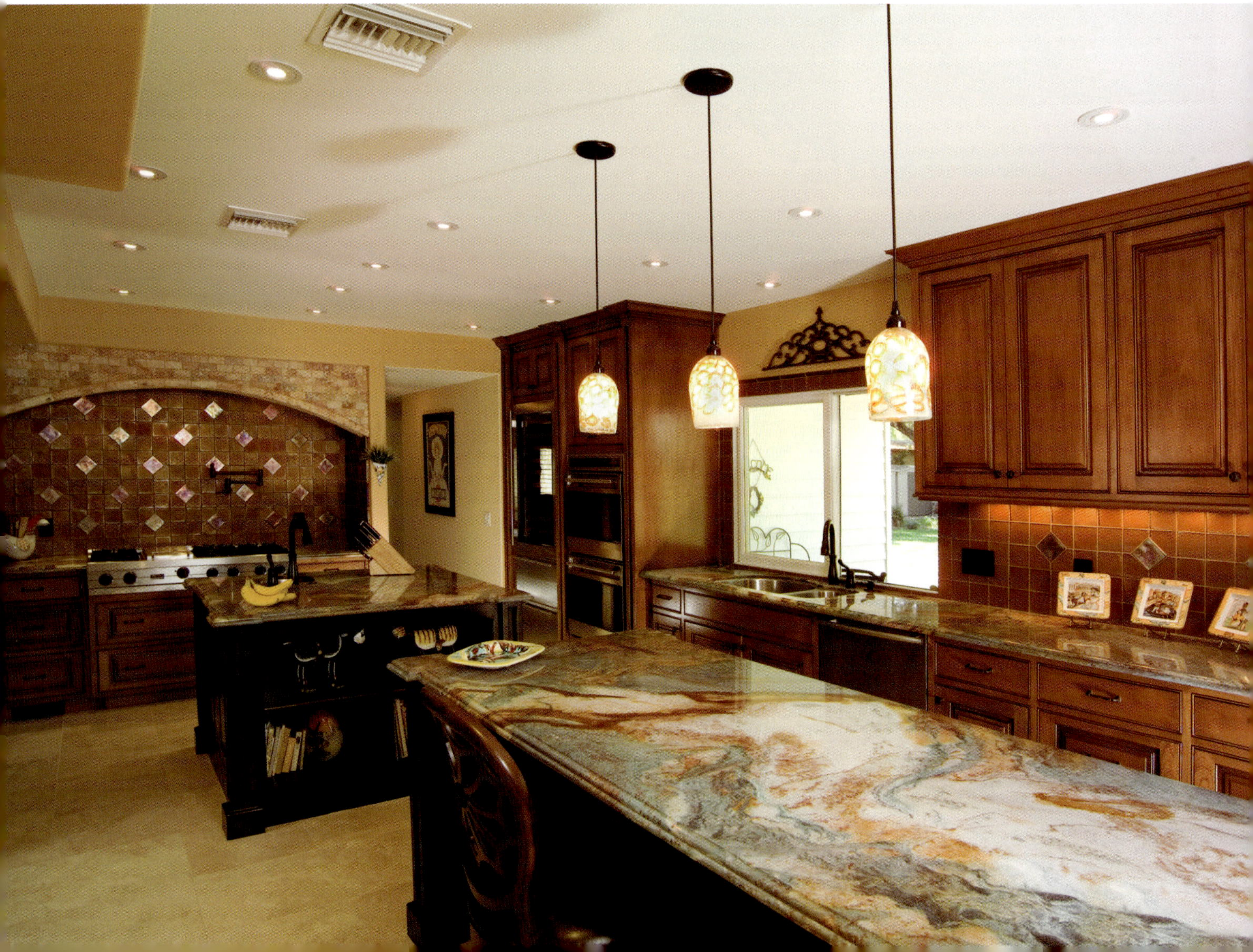

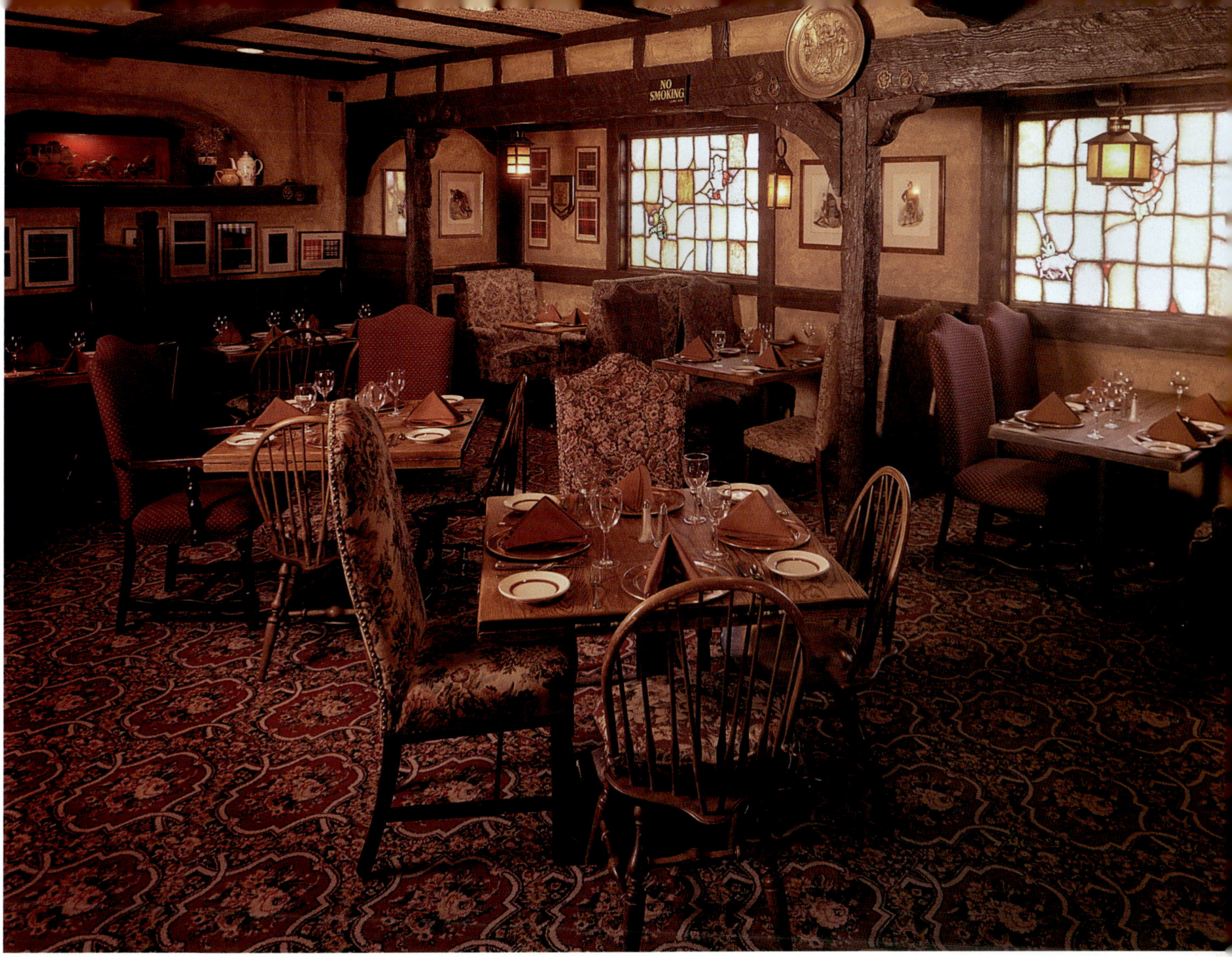

To create this shot, I used rolls of ½ orange outside the windows. The existing light was very warm. My lights were balanced to tungsten. If the windows had been bluer, the shot would not have worked well. I don't usually have to correct a window!

If you want to change a window to tungsten balance, you can do this too. The Rosco filters are available in rolls, so you can attach the filter to the outside of the window. I would recommend using the ½ CTO 3408, the half orange, rather than the full orange, as the additional blue will make the color feel a little more natural. The filter material can be reused, which is good because it is expensive.

You can certainly do much of this color control in Photoshop. There are good reasons for doing so, including the fact that you don't need to buy filters or bring them with you. If you shoot in RAW, you can convert the shot to several color balances and then use layers to make a final shot with adjusted color. But there are occasions when you should fix the color while you shoot (e.g., if there is a client watching, you would prefer not to tell him/her you'll fix the color later in Photoshop). Another consideration is, if you are shooting a large number of images that will require a similar fix, it may be better to avoid having to do a lot of fixing after the shoot. I think it is always advantageous to reduce postproduction work so you can deliver images to your client sooner.

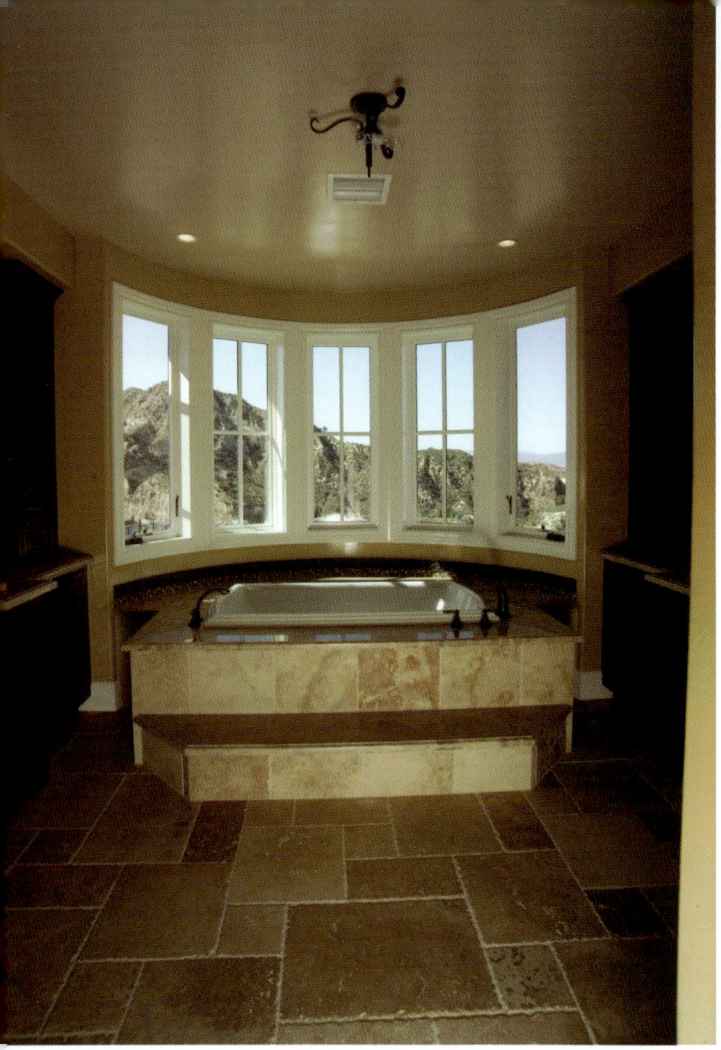

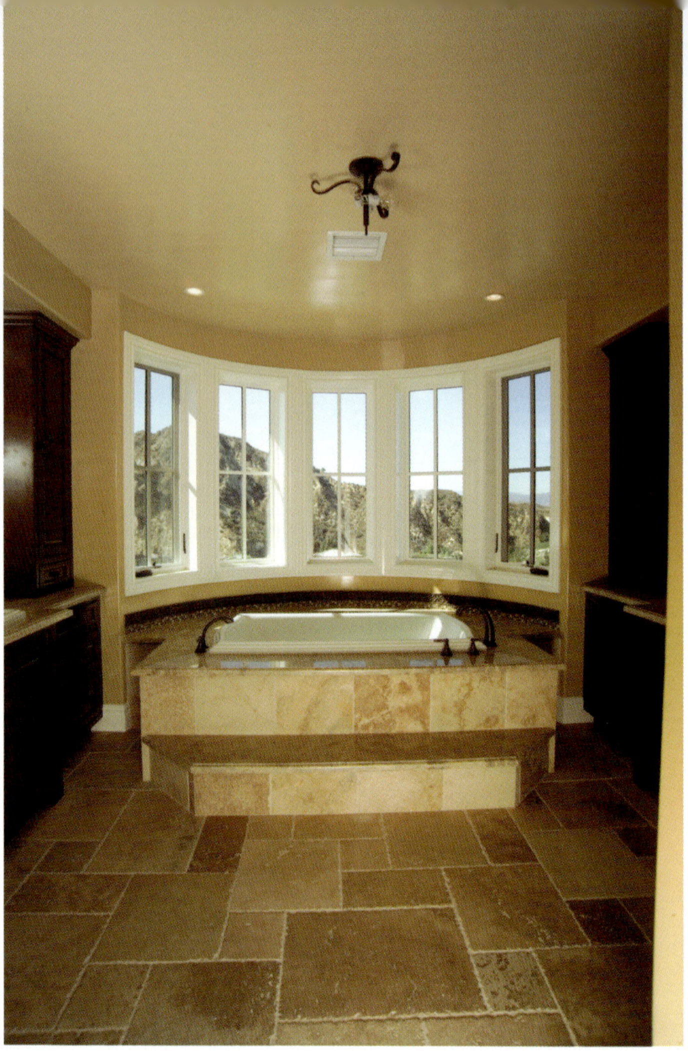

Left—This is the first shot with a single strobe. There is much more light inside the room. **Right**—There are now two strobes lighting the room. There are some reflections in the windows, but not too bad. There are a few perspective issues. So the shot is good, but not perfect.

When you shoot your next test shot, check the exposure and color right away. Don't forget to check for reflections and other problems as well. The strobes will allow you to balance the light by adjusting the shutter speed to control the ambient light. This is really helpful because you can effectively change the brightness of the continuous light sources in your shot without changing the light from the strobes.

You should pay close attention to the histogram and the image on your laptop at this time. Not only do you need to get the balance right, you must consider overall exposure. If there is too much contrast, try increasing the power of the strobe. If the windows are too dark, use a longer shutter speed. If a single lamp is too bright, you might want to put metal window screen over the bulb to reduce the light from that lamp or put a smaller bulb in the lamp. Metal window screen is really helpful at reducing the light from a bulb or strobe. You will also need to examine the color and look for problems with the strobe placement. Of course, this is also a good time to look for reflections or problem shadows.

For many small rooms, one light will work, and for other jobs it might be good enough. But, of course, we're shooting for something better than good enough, so let's look at the tools that will allow us to fix those remaining problems.

Since I use a wide-angle lens for architectural shooting, an aperture of f/8 usually provides enough depth of field. I can therefore use lower-powered lights for additional light sources in most situations. I use 200 watt-second battery-powered lights most of the time. The DC power makes it much easier for me to place the lights, as I don't need a wall socket. The small size of the strobe head also makes it easier to position these lights. While larger and more powerful lights would work as well, the chief goal is to have a large number of strobes. I usually take seven battery-powered lights in addition to the monolight. The idea is that control over light placement is more important than power.

Umbrellas are the best tools for interior work because they spread light evenly over a large area and create soft light. As I mentioned, I start with

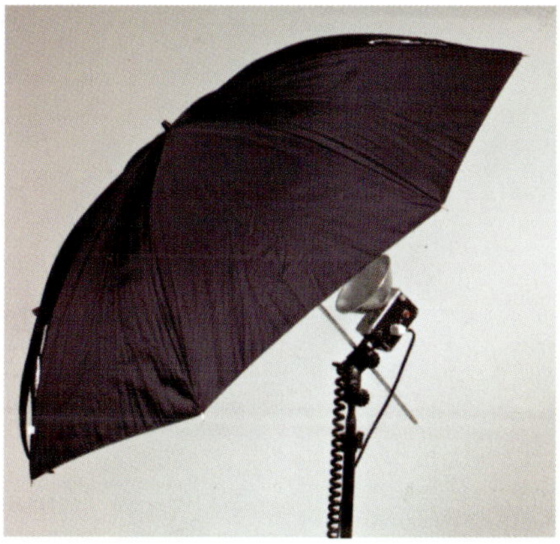

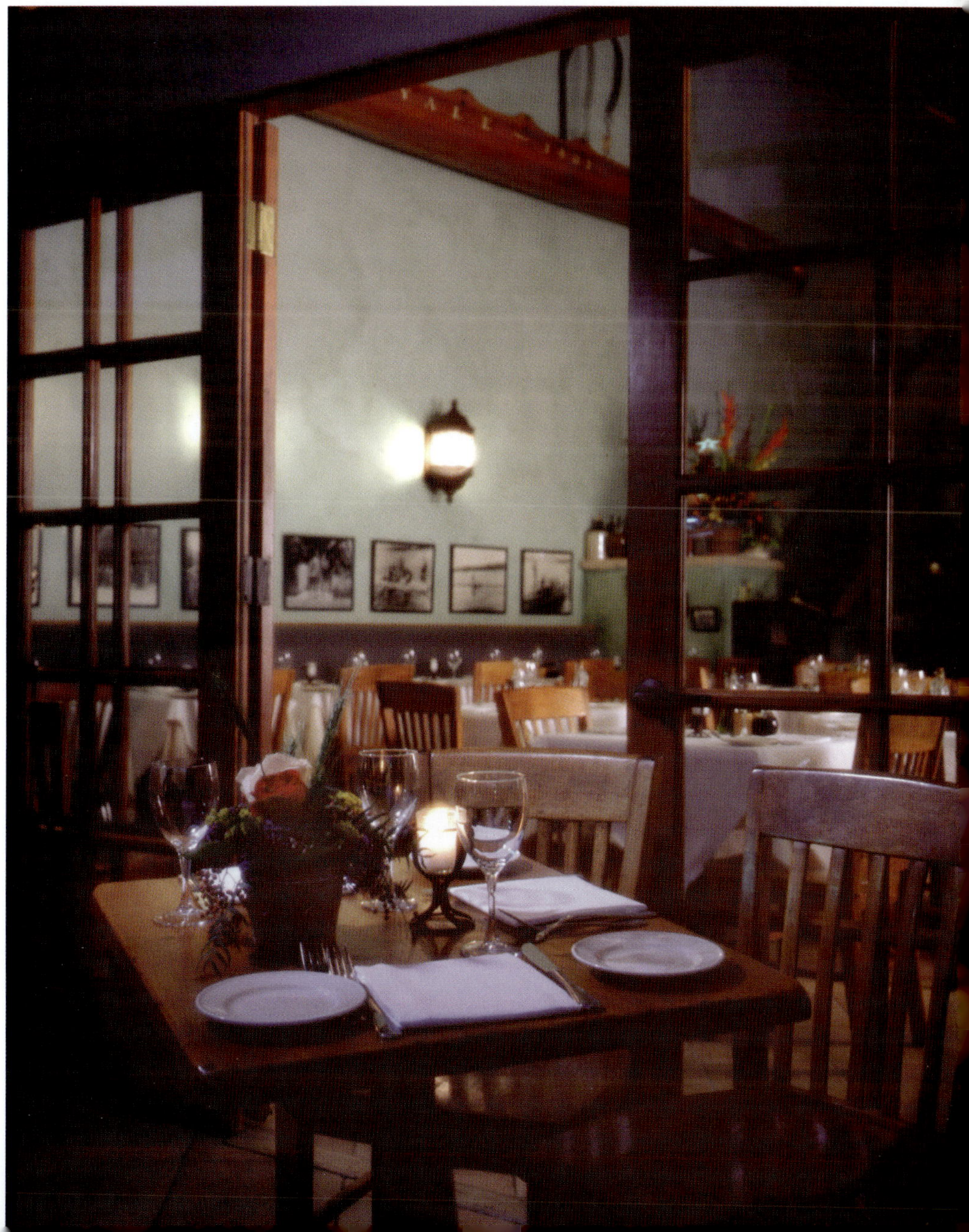

Above—A Norman 200B strobe with an umbrella. This shot doesn't show the battery pack. These strobes are helpful because they are small and don't need to be plugged in. **Right**—I used hard light on the front of this shot to create sparkle and help separate it from the rest of the shot. I used a soft focus filter to create a more magical effect. I used four lights.

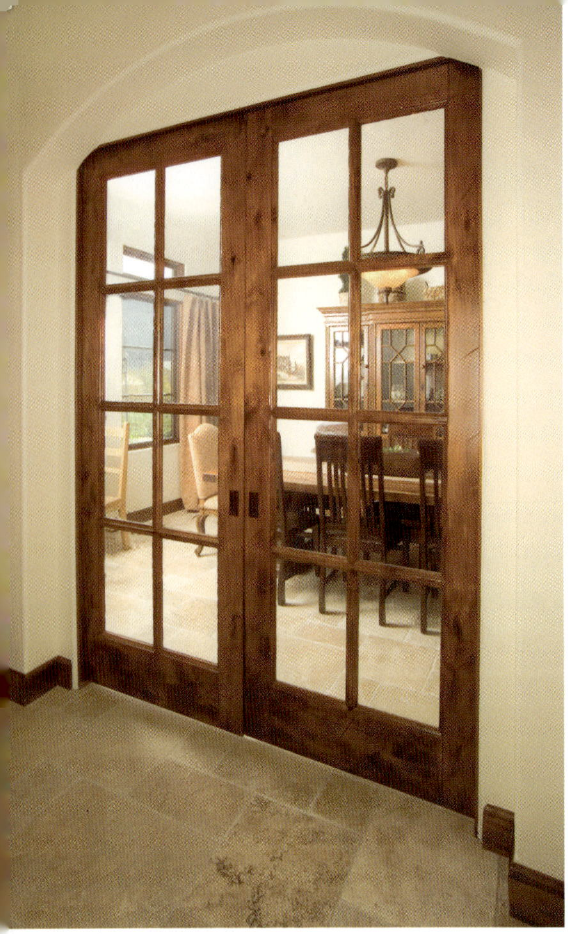

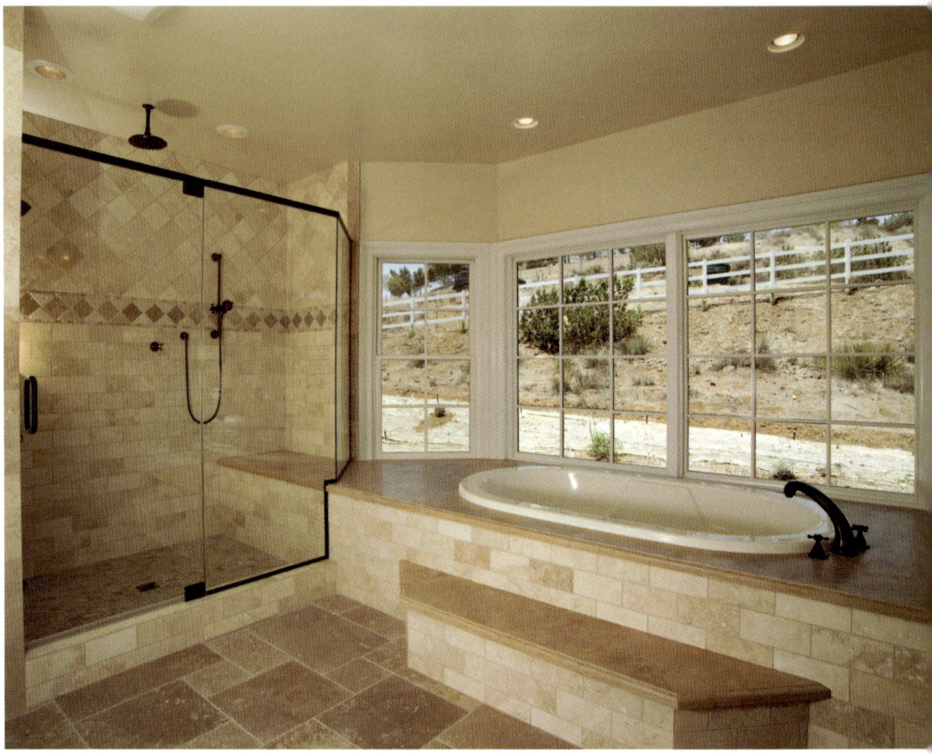

Left—I used just the shoe cover on a 200B in the hall. I used a second strobe, with an umbrella, inside the room. The shoe cover on the light gave good separation to the doorway. **Right**—I used the shoe cover in the shower. You can see the light it created.

a large umbrella. I tend to use umbrellas to bounce light rather than as a shoot-through light source, since the spill that can result from a shoot-through umbrella can hamper my control over the light. However, when I am pressed for space, I will use a shoot-through umbrella. This is especially good in a bathroom because the light that bounces back off the umbrella will bounce again into the shot and soften the overall light. I sometimes use silver umbrellas when I want a harder light or need extra light.

There are a couple of light sources I use to get myself out of a tight space, literally. The first is a bare strobe tube, appropriately called a bare bulb. This is not usually my first choice, but it fits into a small space and illuminates 360 degrees, which can be incredibly helpful. There are a couple of variations on this tool that I use: one is a shoe cover. This is just a white cover that fits over the bare bulb. It makes the light source a little bigger, softening it just a bit. It spills the light and reduces the output, which makes it useful for a light hidden inside a shot. This is a pretty useful accessory for a shoe cover. You can get these at home improvement stores. I use it behind short walls; it gives good light out the side and a ceiling bounce that is easy to hide.

Photoshop also allows you to fix a number of problems with an architectural image, especially reflections. If there is a reflection of one of my lights in a window, I will make a second capture of the shot with my lights turned off and

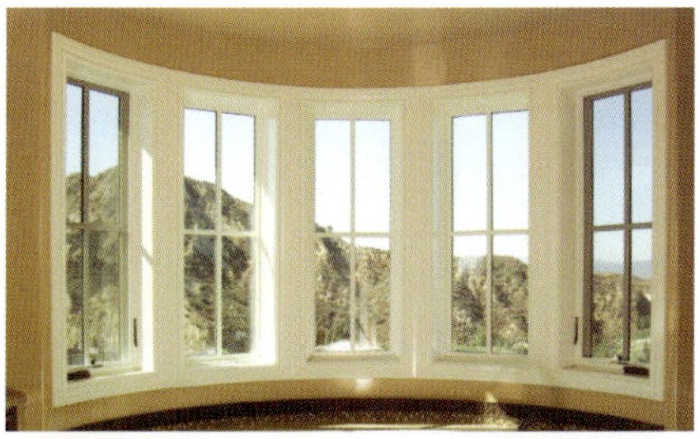

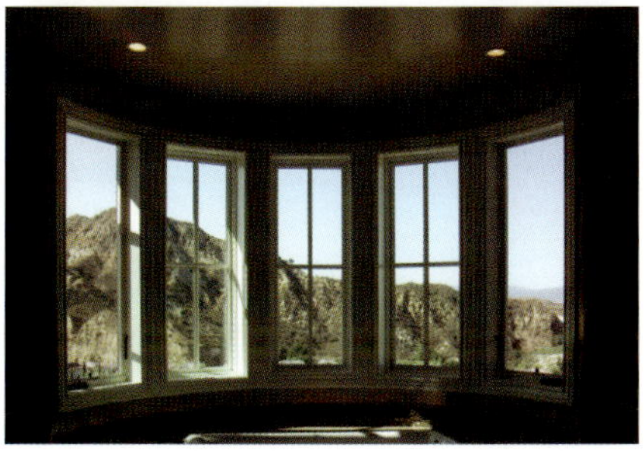

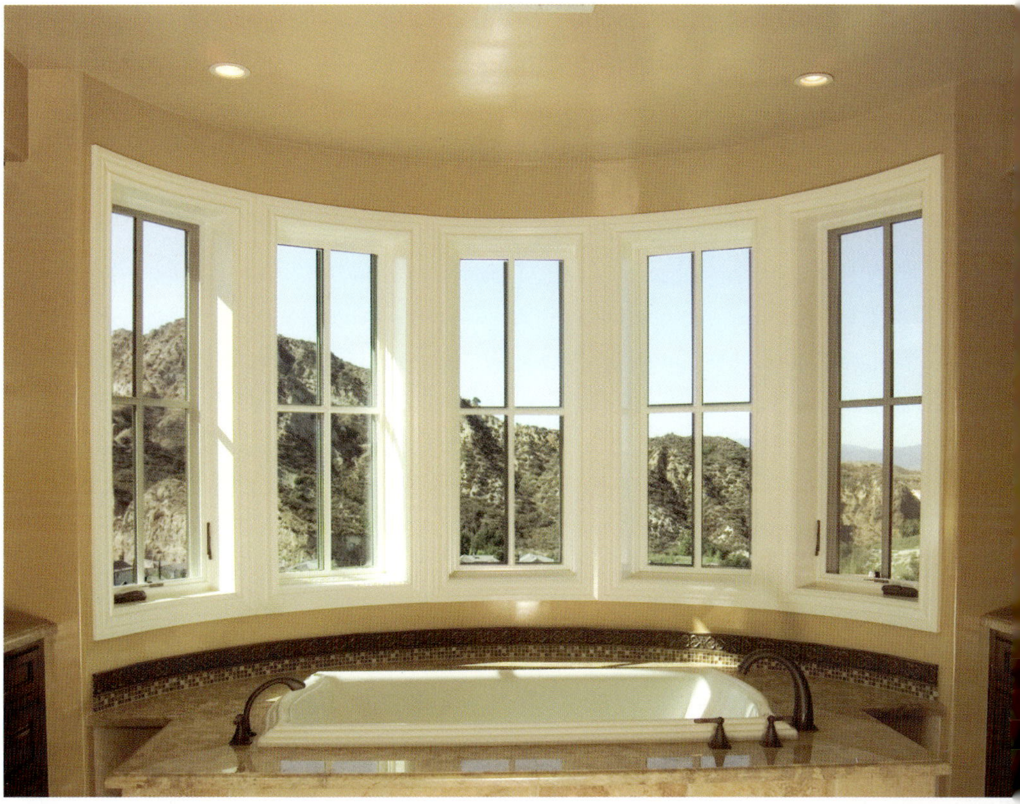

Top left—Here you can see some of the reflections from my lights. **Bottom left**—This is the original shot. The windows look much better. **Right**—Here's the fixed version of the shot. This was done with layers in Photoshop. Some things are best done after you take the shot.

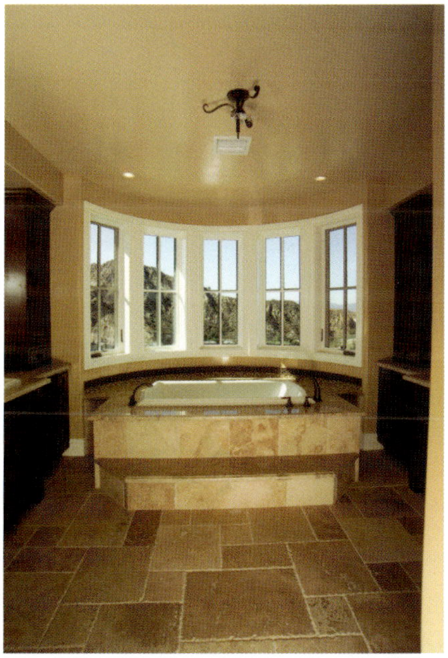

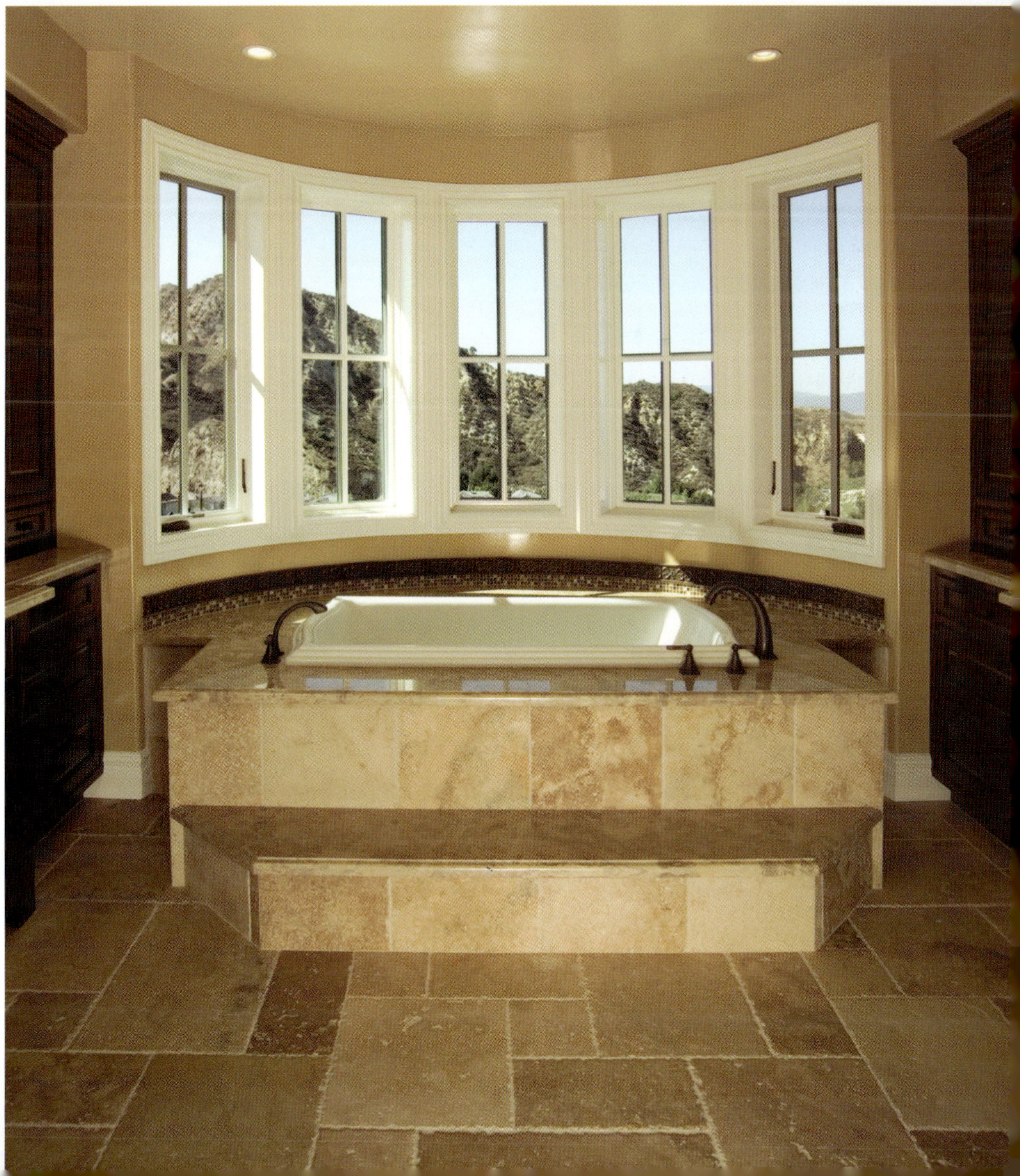

Above—The shot has some convergence and a little barrel distortion. Plus it needs to be cropped. **Right**—The final version.

use it to make an enhanced image in Photoshop. While I would like to be able to fix everything when shooting, I can't always get my lights to cooperate. I like to do all of the work, blending layers to control color or reflections, before I manipulate the perspective. If you're going to use multiple versions as layers, you won't be able to add a new layer after you manipulate the perspective, as the shape will change.

In addition to using layers, I use perspective control and lens correction. I usually use perspective control with the cropping tool, which makes my workflow a little bit faster. While I have a perspective control lens, I prefer the perspective of a lens wider than 28mm, so I need Photoshop for this. I have noticed that my lens has some barrel distortion (the straight lines tend to bow outward a little), so I really like lens correction. You'll find this tool under Filter>Distort.

Of course, it requires some patience when you try to make everything work together. I often find that I am working with half a dozen lights, so sometimes I don't know where the problem is. One important technique is to turn off each light individually. This will let you know where the problem is. I would also emphasize the importance of working tethered to the laptop. This will save you hours of grief.

Below—This image uses the large monolight near the camera, as well as smaller lights to camera left and in the room to the right, the hallway, and at the top of the stairs. All the lights have umbrellas. The light at the top of the stairs has a small shoot-through umbrella. **Facing page, top**—A hotel shot. I used four lights, all with umbrellas. I would have used a larger umbrella on camera right, but there wasn't room. **Facing page, bottom**—In this shot, the point of view was the most important thing. Two lights were used: one at ground level and one near the camera.

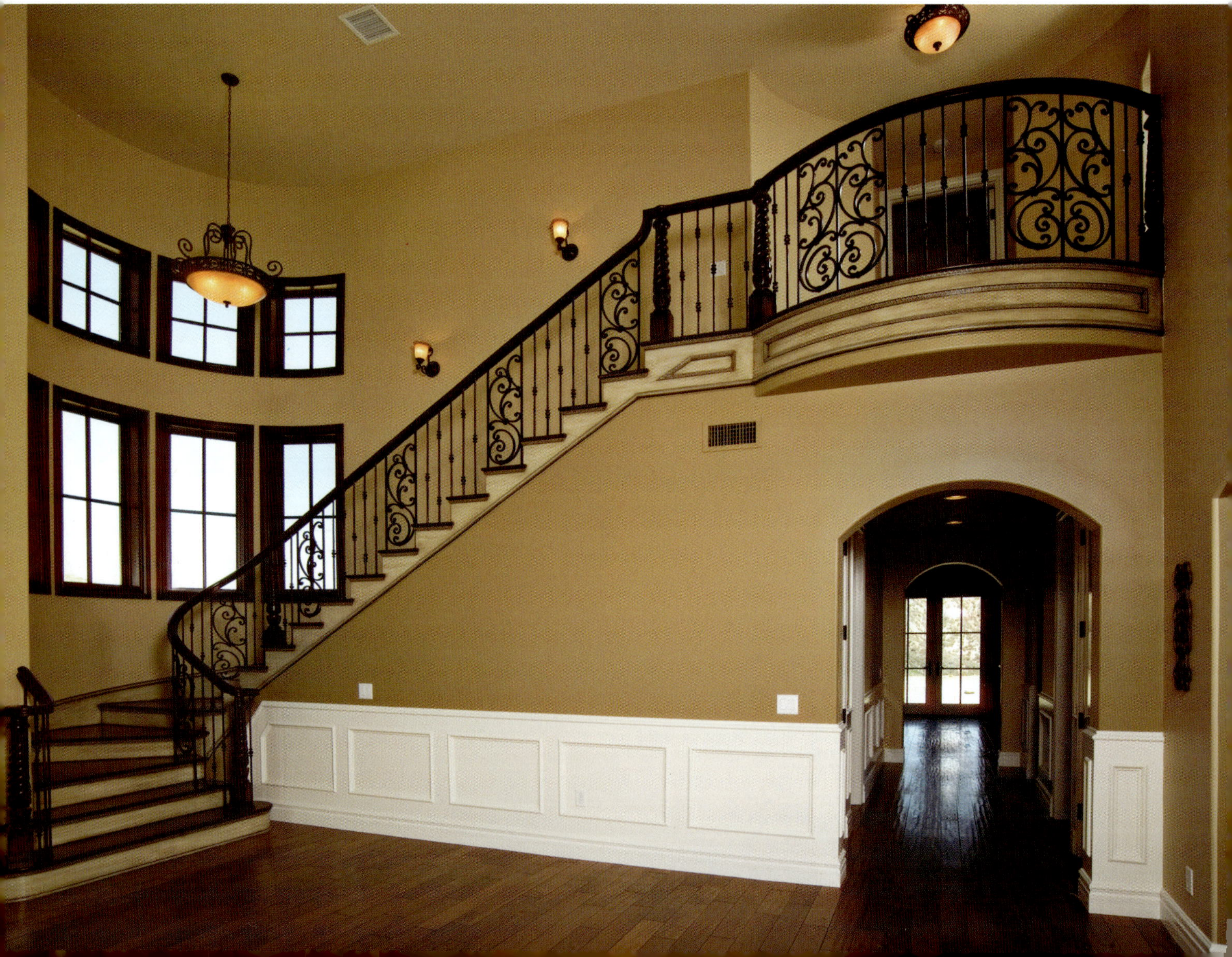

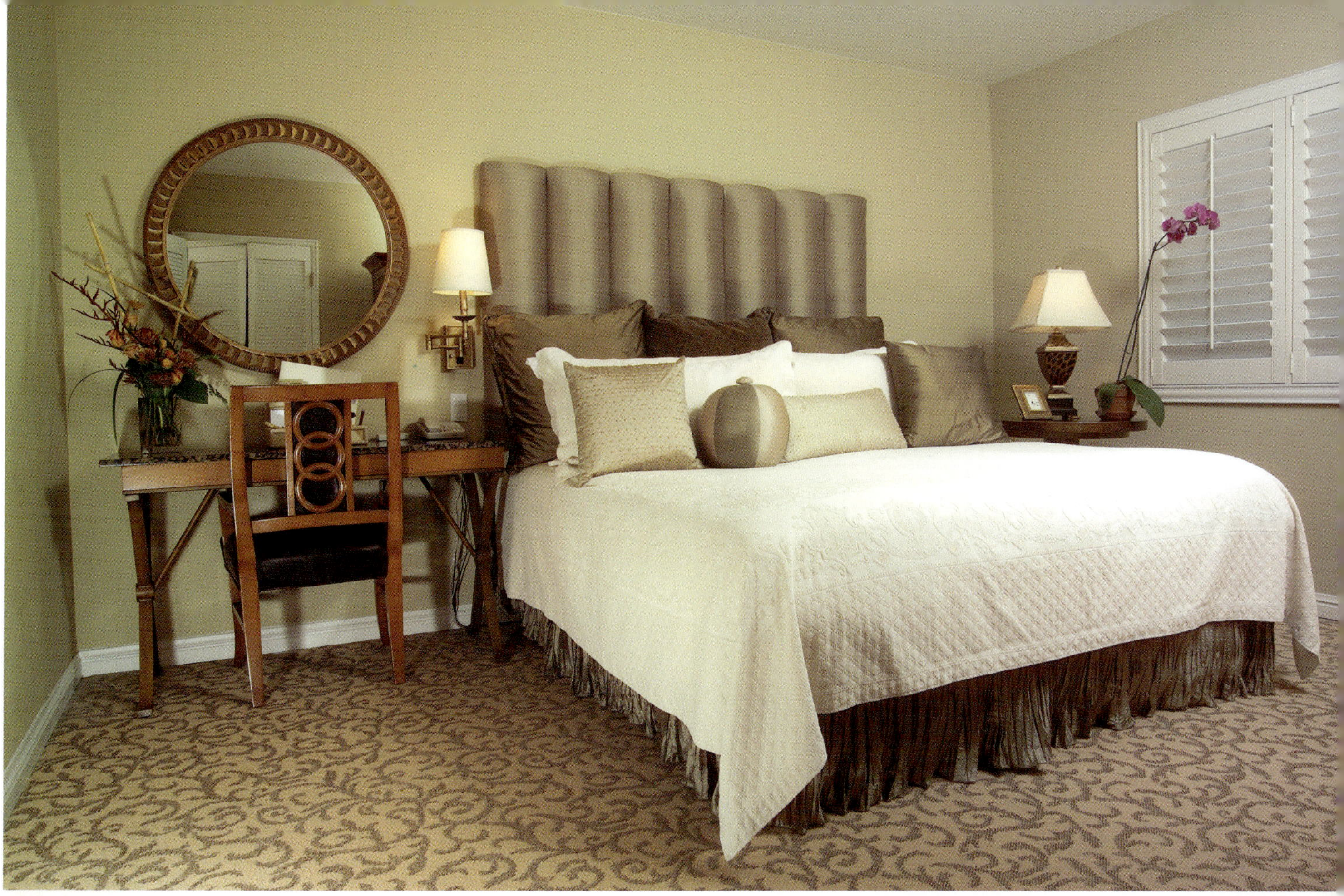

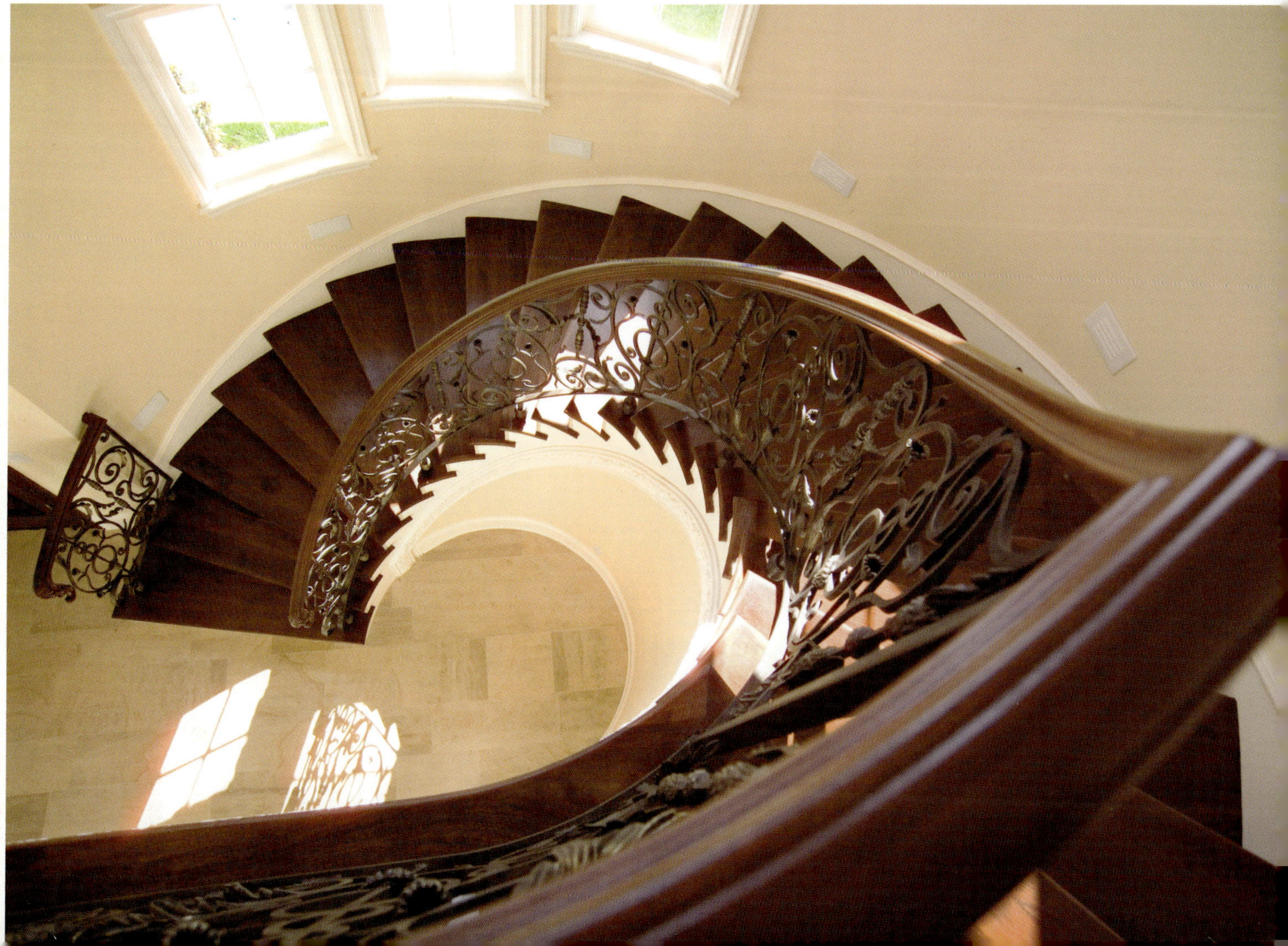

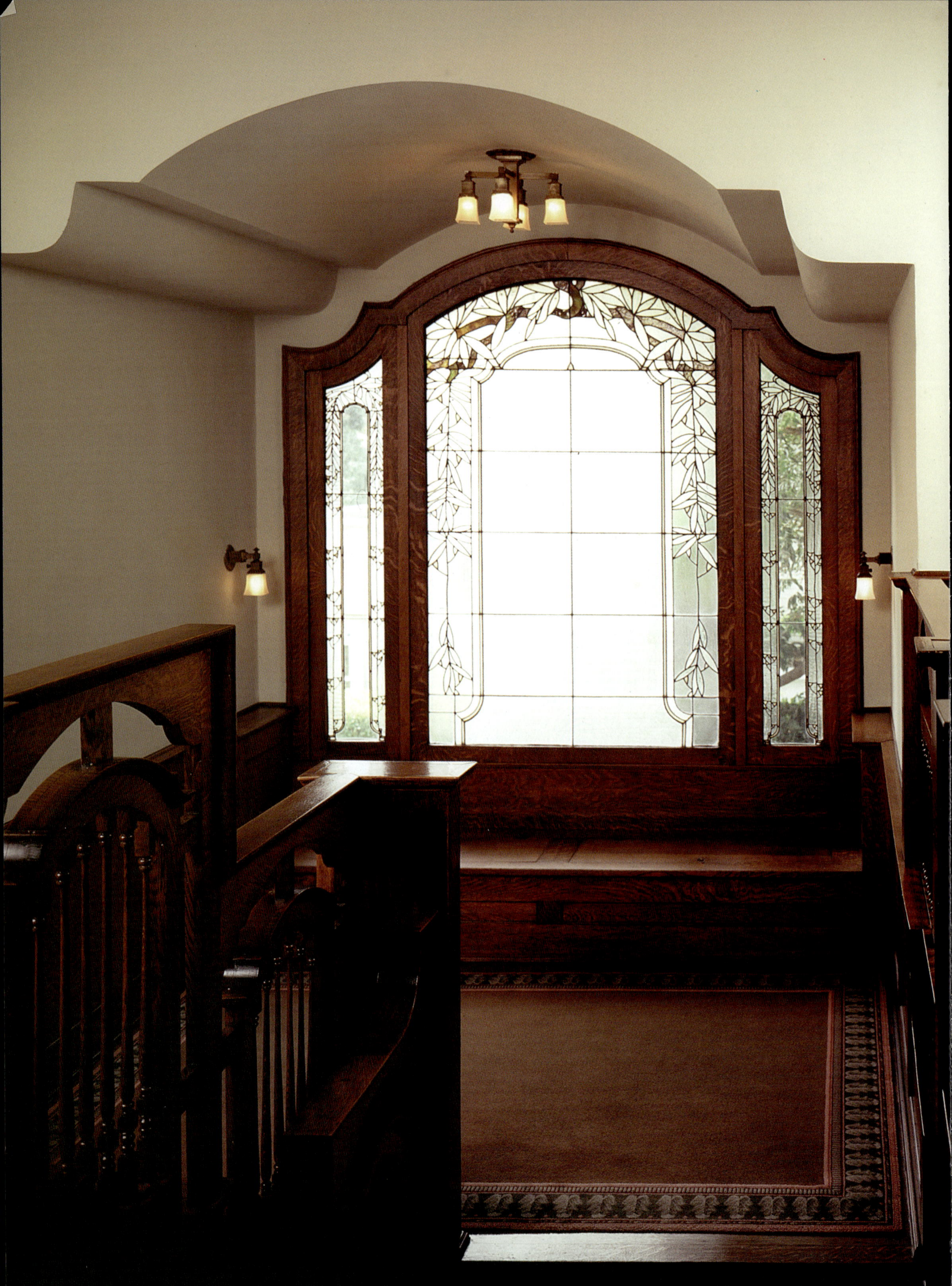

CONCLUSION

I have often heard lighting described as an art. Surely this is true, but it is also true that before it can be an art it must be a skill. Photography is a language, and light is one way we write in that language. Just as in learning a language, we begin with simple drills. In these pages, I have tried to give you an understanding of how the tools work. I hope that you will use them to write the images that you want to make, be they technical or poetic. I hope you will practice with these tools because practice is critical. Remember musicians practice so that they can play. We should practice with light so that we can shoot lyrical images.

Thanks for your time!
John Siskin

Facing page—There is a light near the camera. The key here is to watch for reflection and to get the correct balance between existing light from the window and the strobe. This house had beautiful windows. **Right**—All the light came from behind the glass. I used one grid spot on either side of the glass and used a Hoya Softener filter to make the highlights spread.

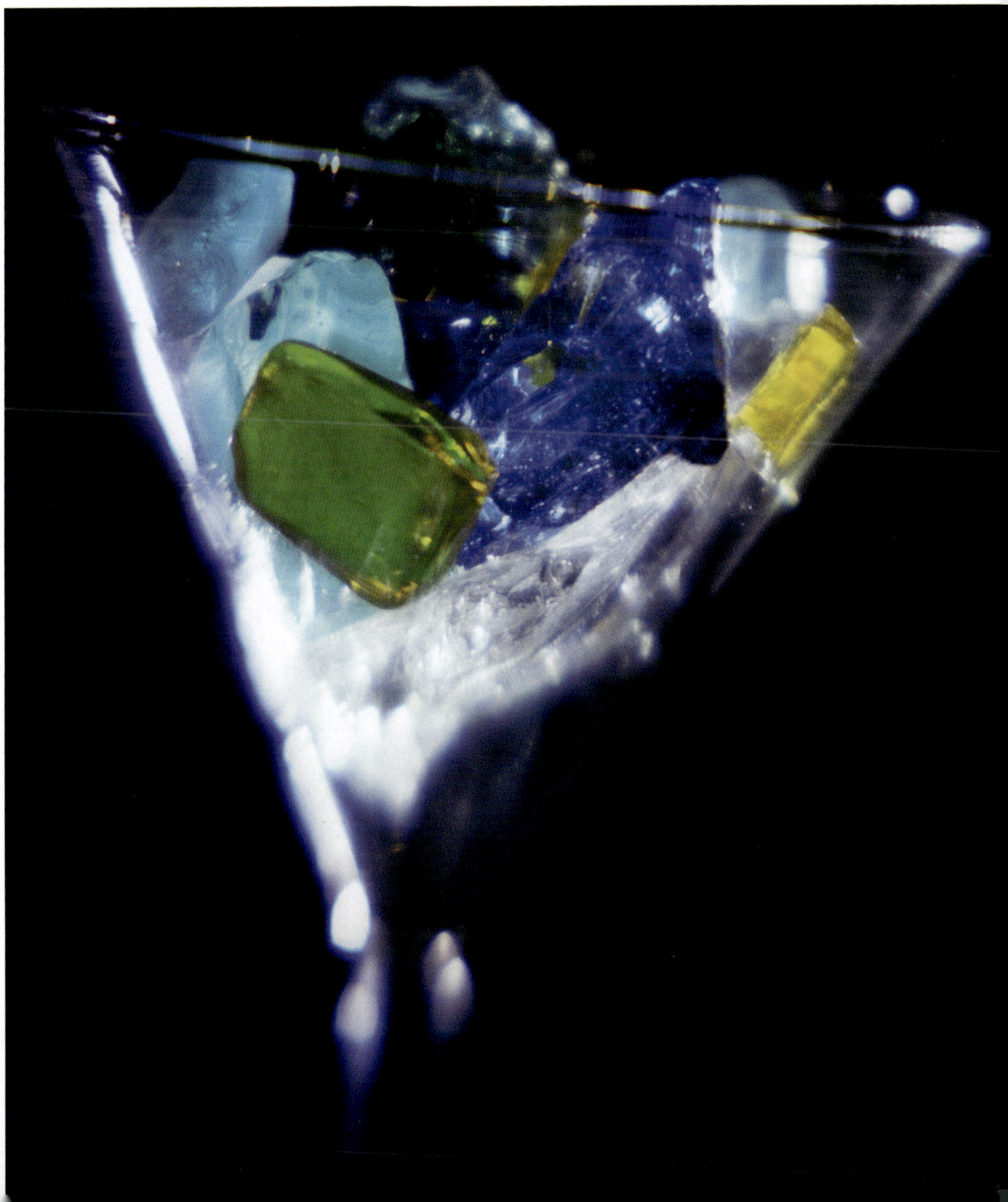

INDEX

OTHER BOOKS FROM

Amherst Media®

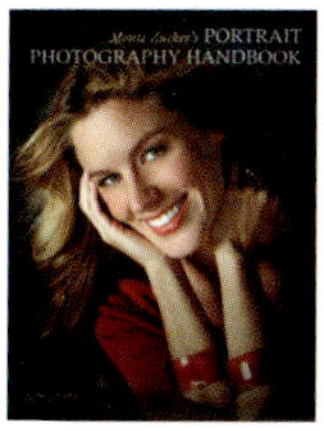

MONTE ZUCKER'S

Portrait Photography Handbook

Acclaimed portrait photographer Monte Zucker takes you behind the scenes and shows you how to create a "Monte Portrait." Covers techniques for both studio and location shoots. *$34.95 list, 8.5x11, 128p, 200 color photos, index, order no. 1846.*

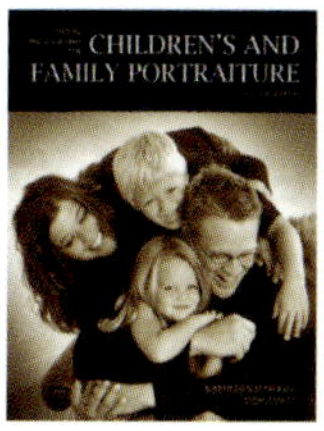

DIGITAL PHOTOGRAPHY FOR

Children's and Family Portraiture, 2nd Ed.

Kathleen Hawkins

Learn how staying on top of advances in digital photography can boost your sales and improve your artistry and workflow. *$34.95 list, 8.5x11, 128p, 195 color images, index, order no. 1847.*

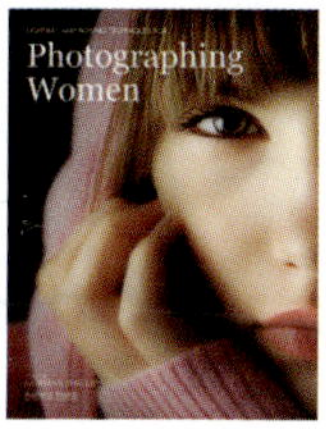

Lighting and Posing Techniques for Photographing Women

Norman Phillips

Make every female client look her very best. This book features tips from top pros and diagrams that will facilitate learning. *$34.95 list, 8.5x11, 128p, 200 color images, index, order no. 1848.*

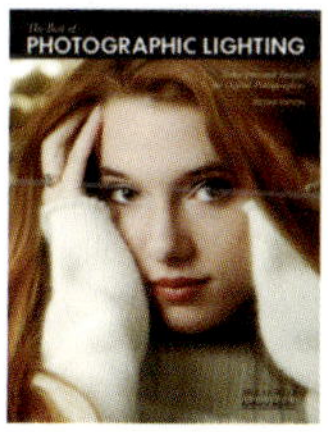

The Best of Photographic Lighting, 2nd Ed.

Bill Hurter

Top pros reveal the secrets behind their studio, location, and outdoor lighting. Packed with practical tips. *$34.95 list, 8.5x11, 128p, 200 color photos, index, order no. 1849.*

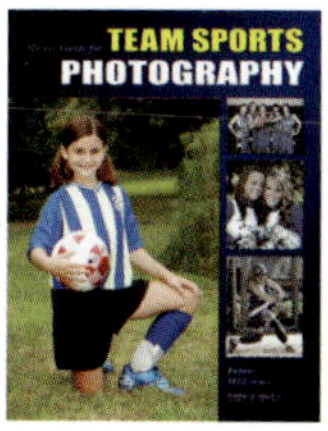

Master Guide for Team Sports Photography

James Williams

Learn how adding team sports photography to your repertoire can help you meet your financial goals. Includes technical, artistic, organizational, and business strategies. *$34.95 list, 8.5x11, 128p, 120 color photos, index, order no. 1850.*

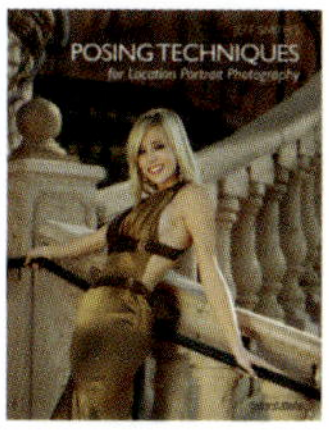

JEFF SMITH'S

Posing Techniques for Location Portrait Photography

Use architectural and natural elements to support the pose, maximize the flow of the session, and create refined, artful poses for individual subjects and groups—indoors or out. *$34.95 list, 8.5x11, 128p, 150 color photos, index, order no. 1851.*

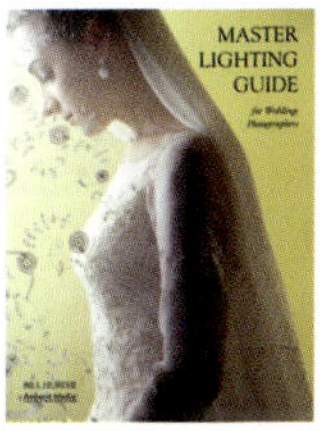

Master Lighting Guide

FOR WEDDING PHOTOGRAPHERS

Bill Hurter

Capture perfect lighting quickly and easily at the ceremony and reception. Includes tips from the pros for lighting individuals, couples, and groups. *$34.95 list, 8.5x11, 128p, 200 color photos, index, order no. 1852.*

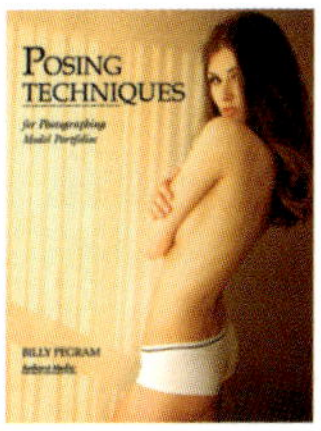

Posing Techniques for Photographing Model Portfolios

Billy Pegram

Learn to evaluate your model and create flattering poses for fashion photos, catalog and editorial images, and more. *$34.95 list, 8.5x11, 128p, 200 color images, index, order no. 1848.*

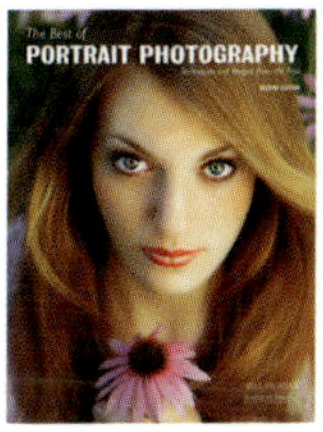

The Best of Portrait Photography, 2nd Ed.

Bill Hurter

View outstanding images from top pros and learn how they create their masterful classic and contemporary portraits. *$34.95 list, 8.5x11, 128p, 180 color photos, index, order no. 1854.*

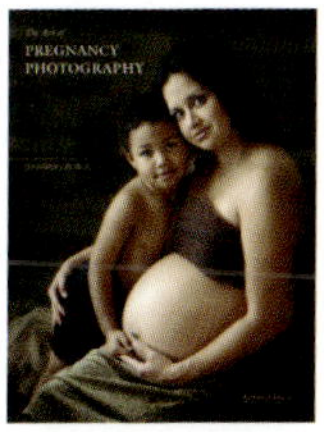

The Art of Pregnancy Photography

Jennifer George

Learn the essential posing, lighting, composition, business, and marketing skills you need to create stunning pregnancy portraits your clientele can't do without! *$34.95 list, 8.5x11, 128p, 150 color photos, index, order no. 1855.*

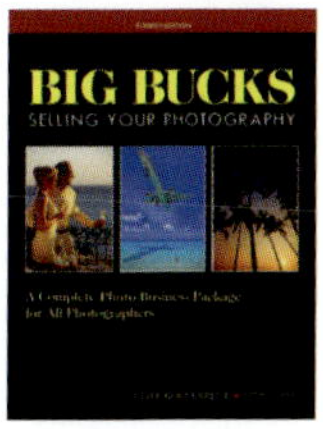

Big Bucks Selling Your Photography, 4th Ed.

Cliff Hollenbeck

Build a new business or revitalize an existing one with the comprehensive tips in this popular book. Includes twenty sample forms. *$34.95 list, 8.5x11, 144p, resources, business forms, order no. 1856.*

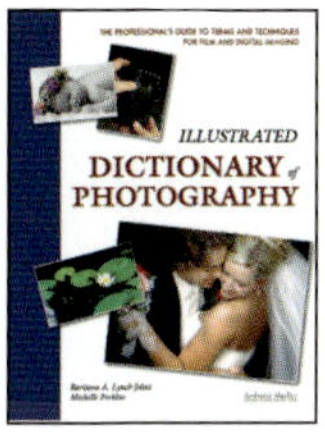

Illustrated Dictionary of Photography

Barbara A. Lynch-Johnt & Michelle Perkins

Gain insight into camera and lighting equipment, accessories, technological advances, film and historic processes, famous photographers, artistic movements, and more with the concise descriptions in this illustrated book. *$39.95 list, 8.5x11, 144p, 150 color images, order no. 1857.*

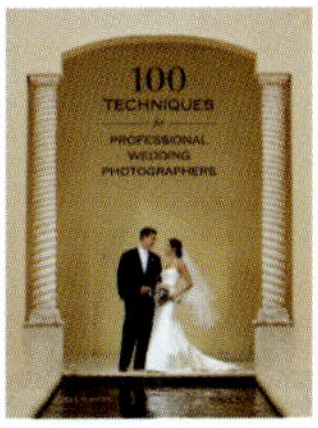

100 Techniques for Professional Wedding Photographers

Bill Hurter

Top photographers provide tips for becoming a better shooter. *$34.95 list, 8.5x11, 128p, 180 color images and diagrams, index, order no. 1875.*

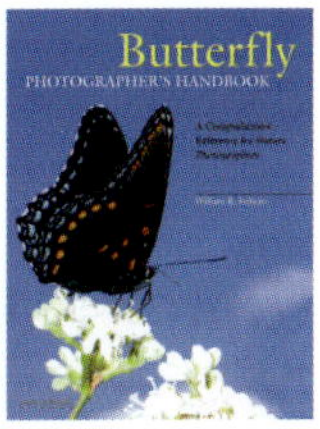

Butterfly Photographer's Handbook

William B. Folsom

Learn how to locate butterflies, approach without disturbing them, and capture spectacular, detailed images. *$34.95 list, 8.5x11, 128p, 175 color images, index, order no. 1877.*

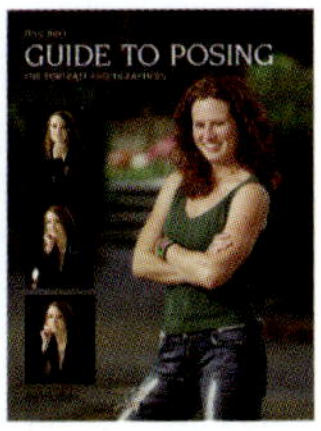

DOUG BOX'S GUIDE TO

Posing for Portrait Photographers

Based on Doug Box's popular workshops for professional photographers, this visually intensive book allows you to quickly master the skills needed to pose men, women, children, and groups. *$34.95 list, 8.5x11, 128p, 200 color images, index, order no. 1878.*

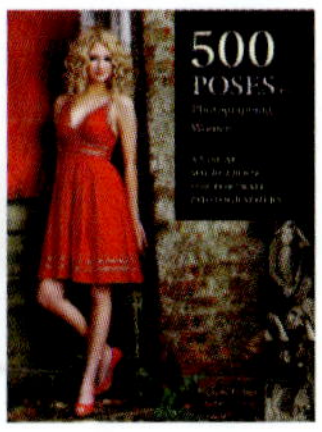

500 Poses for Photographing Women

Michelle Perkins

A vast assortment of inspiring images, from head-and-shoulders to full-length portraits, and classic to contemporary styles—perfect for when you need a little shot of inspiration to create a new pose. *$34.95 list, 8.5x11, 128p, 500 color images, order no. 1879.*

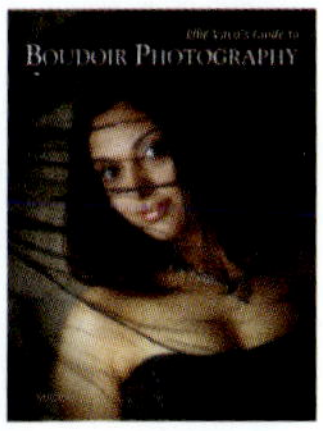

ELLIE VAYO'S GUIDE TO

Boudoir Photography

Learn how to create flattering, sensual images that women will love as gifts or keepsakes. Covers everything you need to know—from getting clients in the door, to running a succesful session, to making a big sale. *$34.95 list, 8.5x11, 128p, 180 color images, index, order no. 1882.*

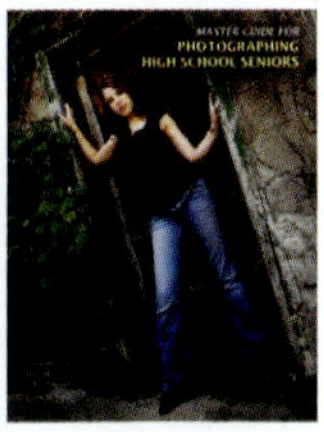

MASTER GUIDE FOR

Photographing High School Seniors

Dave, Jean, and J. D. Wacker

Learn how to stay at the top of the ever-changing senior portrait market with these techniques for success. *$34.95 list, 8.5x11, 128p, 270 color images, index, order no. 1883.*

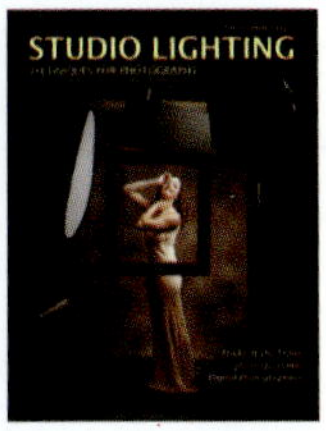

CHRISTOPHER GREY'S

Studio Lighting Techniques for Photography

With these strategies—and some practice—you'll approach your sessions with confidence! *$34.95 list, 8.5x11, 128p, 320 color images, index, order no. 1892.*

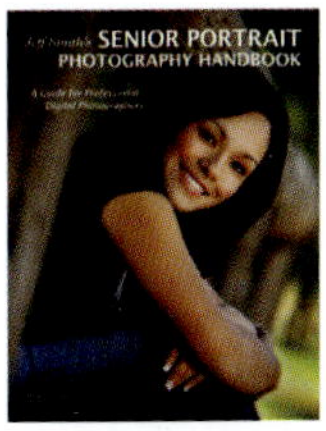

JEFF SMITH'S

Senior Portrait Photography Handbook

Improve your images and profitability through better design, market analysis, and business practices.*$34.95 list, 8.5x11, 128p, 170 color images, index, order no. 1896.*

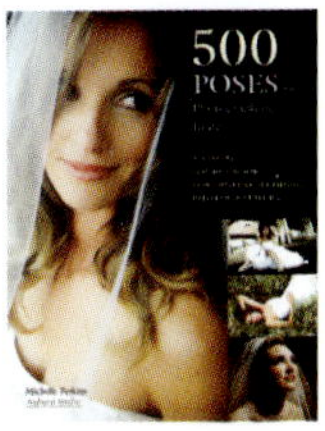

500 Poses for Photographing Brides

Michelle Perkins

Filled with images by some of the world's best wedding photographers, this book can provide the inspiration you need to spice up your posing or refine your techniques. *$34.95 list, 8.5x11, 128p, 500 color images, index, order no. 1909.*

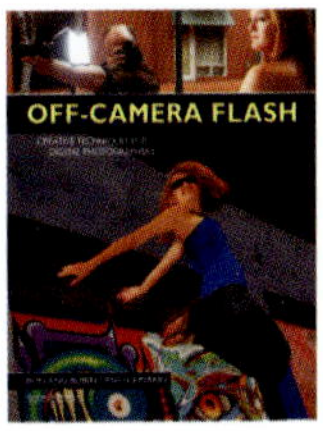

Off-Camera Flash

CREATIVE TECHNIQUES FOR DIGITAL PHOTOGRAPHY

Rod and Robin Deutschmann

Break free from the shackles of natural light and push the limits of design with these off-camera flash techniques. Covers portraits, nature photography, and more. *$34.95 list, 8.5x11, 128p, 269 color images, 41 diagrams, index, order no. 1913.*

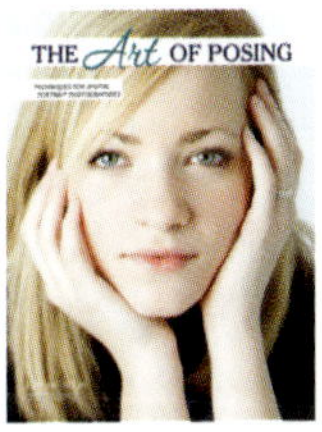

The Art of Posing

TECHNIQUES FOR DIGITAL PORTRAIT PHOTOGRAPHERS

Lou Jacobs Jr.

Create compelling poses for individuals, couples, and families. Jacobs culls strategies and insights from ten photographers whose styles range from traditional to modern. *$34.95 list, 8.5x11, 128p, 180 color images, index, order no. 2007.*

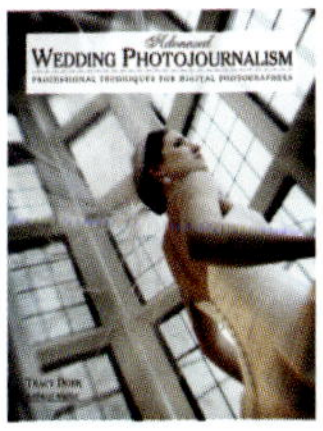

Advanced Wedding Photojournalism

Tracy Dorr

Tracy Dorr charts a path to a new creative mind-set, showing you how to get better tuned in to a wedding's events and participants so you're poised to capture outstanding, emotional images. *$34.95 list, 8.5x11, 128p, 200 color images, index, order no. 1915.*

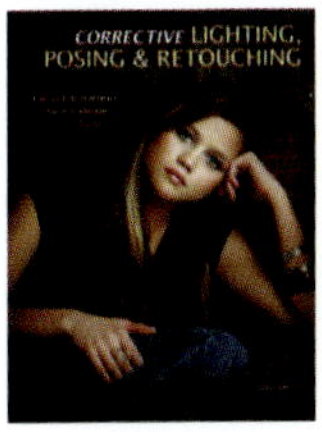

Corrective Lighting, Posing & Retouching

FOR DIGITAL PORTRAIT PHOTOGRAPHERS, 3RD ED.

Jeff Smith

Address your subject's perceived physical flaws in the camera room and in postproduction to boost client confidence and sales. *$34.95 list, 8.5x11, 128p, 180 color images, index, order no. 1916.*

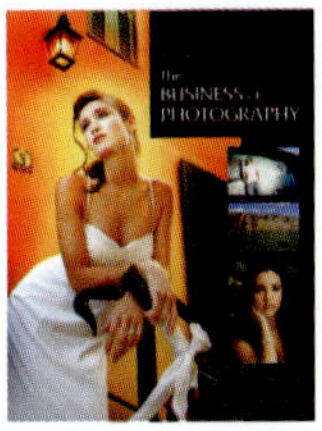

TUCCI AND USMANI'S

The Business of Photography

Damon Tucci and Rosena Usmani

Take your business from flat to fantastic using the foundational business and marketing strategies detailed in this book. *$34.95 list, 8.5x11, 128p, 180 color images, index, order no. 1919.*